DAN TOOMBS

THE CURRY GUY

ONE POT

**Over 150 Curries and Other Deliciously
Spiced Dishes from Around the World**

Photography by Kris Kirkham

Hardie Grant

QUADRILLE

For Caroline

CONTENTS

PREFACE

I've spent the past two years travelling and researching recipes for this cookbook of over 150 brand new recipes. It's been an eye-opening journey that took my wife, Caroline, and me through India, Sri Lanka, South East Asia, Europe and the United States. Thinking about it, this book simply wouldn't have been possible a few years back, when our kids were still at home. As one by one they all moved out to start their own adult lives, we decided it was time to hit the road.

We dusted off our old backpacks and travelled like students, in search of perfect meals, and I'm happy to say we found them. Lots of them! Perhaps equally as fun as experiencing many of these dishes in their countries of origin was getting back home to have a go at cooking them. I had already talked my way into numerous kitchens and got excellent advice and recipes from the chefs we met. But the ultimate test was whether we could recreate them at home and still be just as excited about the flavours and textures as when we experienced them on our travels.

Over the past year this book has evolved from a collection of deliciously spiced dishes from around the world to what you have in your hands. I looked through my recipe notes and realized so many of the dishes I'd seen being prepared were cooked in one pan, wok or baking tray.

Admittedly, this is not the typical 'one-pot' cookbook. There are few curries and stews that can truly be made in one pot if you want to achieve optimum flavour. Marinades need to be prepared, pastes and spice blends are ground to perfection, stocks are simmered and some sauces are blended until smooth. Authenticity was very important to me while developing the following recipes so you will often need extra bowls and other kitchen gadgets to prepare many of the dishes. However once the preparation is complete, you'll be able to cook each of these recipes in just one pan or wok. And if you wish to make things even easier on yourself, I have thrown in a few good cheats to make things even simpler.

People tend to purchase one-pot cookbooks for one of two reasons: either they want an easy cook or they want fewer dishes to wash at the end of it all. The latter applies to me, but either way, you'll find loads of recipes that will entice you to pick up that pan and get cooking. Although some of the recipes require more planning and work if you want to get the authentic results, much of the preparation can be done well in advance of cooking so you won't need to spend a lot of time in the kitchen in one go. And despite any extra preparation work, I hope you agree that the recipes are a lot of fun to prepare and serve.

To help you find the recipes you want to try, and to see how much work will be needed, I have included badges above each recipe. The explanation of these can be found on page 6.

This brings me to how important it is to cook these dishes in one pan. The answer is that it is as important as you want to make it. You might find that it is more convenient, for example, to fry chicken or fish in an air fryer or deep-fat fryer rather than in the pan. You'll be adding another cooking device, but if it works for you, then do it!

Likewise, the spicing of the dishes is also in your hands. Some of the dishes might be too spicy for your taste preferences or you might prefer even more heat. You can simply add more or less chilli to each dish you're making so that it is the perfect heat for you. So please don't flip past the chicken vindaloo because you think it's too spicy. Just tone the chillies down some. Likewise, don't avoid making Japanese chicken curry because you think it's too mild. A spoonful or two of chilli powder will remedy that.

I hope this will be a cookbook you turn to often regardless of which cuisine you're in the mood for. If you have any questions about any of the recipes, please get in touch. I manage all of my own social media accounts so if you ask a question, it will be me who answers. I'm @TheCurryGuy on Twitter, Facebook and Instagram and would love to hear from you.

Happy Cooking!

LET'S GET STARTED...

To help you find the recipes you want to try, I have labelled them with these badges.

 Gluten-free: So many of the recipes in this book are traditionally made gluten-free. This badge will help you find those that are gluten-free or can easily be made so by using gluten-free options. If you are on a gluten-free diet, then you probably already know to look for hidden gluten in common ingredients such as soy sauce, fish sauce and oyster sauce.

 Vegetarian: If you're looking for vegetarian recipes, you'll find quite a few in this book. I have labelled each with this badge. I recommend reading a bit deeper, though, as many of the non-vegetarian recipes can easily be adjusted to suit your diet. In a lot of recipes, it's all about the sauce! If the chicken tikka masala isn't your thing but you love a good paneer tikka masala, just substitute cubed paneer at the end of cooking. If you like the look of the curry ramen, the freshly made green sauce will still be delicious without the chicken. Try adding firm tofu and/or more vegetables of choice.

 Quick and easy: Look for this badge if you just want to whip up a meal in little time with minimum fuss.

 Weekend Wonders: These are recipes that take longer than usual to prepare and/or cook so they might be best left for the weekend or for when you have time to really get into the recipe. Don't pass them by though! I have offered shortcuts where possible should you wish to make the recipe but don't have the time or energy for a long cook.

 Marinating and soaking: I have included this badge so that you know you will need to do a little advance preparation. Just follow the preparation instructions and let nature take its course. I have provided 'make it easier' options for some of these recipes, so don't pass them by if you are looking for a quick meal.

CUISINE RECIPE INDEX

There are so many different cuisines from around the world featured in this book. On pages 264–5 I have listed the recipes by the cuisine type or region. Each recipe can, of course, be served on its own, but if you would like to serve several dishes from one cuisine or region, check out this recipe index for ideas.

SOURCING INGREDIENTS

All of the ingredients in the following recipes can be sourced either online or at specialist grocers. I know because I did exactly that. I live in rural Yorkshire, so obviously I'm not going to be able to source many of the ingredients at my corner shop. If you happen to live in a large city, your ingredient sourcing will be much easier.

Before doing a shop for ingredients, I recommend thumbing through this book and choosing some of the recipes you want to try. Note the ingredients down and go and get them. Long lists of ingredients are part of the game with these kind of recipes, so try to make sourcing ingredients part of the fun of getting the recipes right rather than a chore. Who knows, you might just find an ingredient you've never heard of before that you can no longer do without. I have listed some of my online ingredient sources on page 263 but there are, of course, many more. I have also given ingredient substitute ideas when applicable.

Following is a list of ingredients used in the book that I usually have at hand in my kitchen. With these in stock, I rarely need to do a last-minute shop. However, I cook these kind of recipes all the time for my blog, www.greatcurryrecipes.net. Your best bet would be to note the recipes you want to make and then source the required ingredients or their substitutes. I purchase my fresh ingredients on the day I cook, so that they are really fresh. Those listed below, however, I always have ready.

WET INGREDIENTS

- Light soy sauce
- Dark soy sauce
- Kecap manis (sweet syrupy soy sauce)
- Oyster sauce
- Thai fish sauce
- Distilled white vinegar
- Light and black rice vinegar
- Chinese cooking wine or dry sherry

DRY INGREDIENTS

- Rice noodles (check the recipe to see which type you need)
- Rice paper
- Ramen noodles
- Dried Chinese egg noodles
- Palm sugar
- Rice flour
- Tapioca starch/flour
- Cornflour (cornstarch)
- Plain (all-purpose) flour
- Dried red finger chillies
- Peanuts
- Cashews
- Candlenuts

WHOLE SPICES AND SPICE BLENDS

You will get a better flavour if you prepare your own spice blends using whole spices, but you can absolutely purchase them ready-ground if you prefer. The following whole spices and spice blends are ones I always have on hand for quick cooking. When time permits, I roast and grind all my spices from whole just as I do in the garam masala recipe on page 259. So if you like, you could toast cumin seeds in the same way and grind your own homemade cumin powder, for example. Of course, that isn't necessary as

you can purchase good-quality ground spices. I recommend purchasing spices from an Asian grocer as you will get a lot more for your money.

- Mixed powder (see page 258)
- Garam masala (see page 259)
- Tandoori masala (see page 260)
- Chilli powder
- Black peppercorns
- Ground cumin and/or cumin seeds
- Ground coriander and/or coriander seeds
- Ground fennel and/or fennel seeds
- Cloves
- Real cinnamon sticks
- Ground turmeric
- Dried fenugreek leaves (kasoori methi)

CANNED (TINNED) AND PACKAGED INGREDIENTS

- Shrimp paste
- Thick coconut milk
- Condensed milk
- Salted turnip
- Chipotle chillies in adobo sauce
- Chinese sesame paste
- Chickpeas
- Kidney beans
- Pinto beans

FRESH AND FROZEN INGREDIENTS

Garlic, galangal, ginger, chillies and tofu can all be frozen. Herbs can also be frozen to use in curries and stocks but will not make an attractive garnish if frozen first.

- Garlic
- Galangal
- Ginger
- Red and green finger chillies
- Red spur chillies
- Coriander (cilantro)
- Mint leaves
- Wonton wrappers
- Firm tofu

SPECIAL EQUIPMENT

You probably already have everything you need to cook the recipes in this book. A good pan and large saucepan are really all you need. That said, I wanted to share with you some of the equipment I have that always comes in useful.

- Large non-stick wok (for electric or gas hobs)
- Large carbon steel wok (for gas burners only)
- Large stockpot
- Deep-fat fryer
- Sharp chef's knife
- Mandoline (for presentation purposes only)
- Cheese grater
- Granite pestle and mortar
- Spice grinder
- Blender
- Food processor

INGREDIENTS AND SUBSTITUTES

Depending on where you live and shop, you might find some of these ingredients difficult to source on the high street. I'd like to stress here that all of these ingredients are available online and at specialist grocers if they aren't at your local supermarket.

AROMATICS AND VEGGIES

Ginger: This is a popular ingredient in cuisines all over the world. Ginger is a rhizome that offers a mildly sweet and spicy flavour to dishes. It can be easily grated, chopped or blended depending on the recipe. When you purchase ginger, look for large, hard pieces with a tight skin. As it ages, it will become softer and smaller and will no longer be at its best. Instead of allowing this to happen, go ahead and freeze any fresh ginger you are not using as it freezes really well. You can also finely chop, blend or grate the ginger and freeze that way too. Contrary to popular belief, you do not need to peel ginger. As long as it is washed, you can use it all or peel it if you wish.

Galangal: Although galangal looks similar to ginger and is also a rhizome, it is not the same. Galangal has a more citrusy and piney flavour. It is also a lot woodier than ginger so is more difficult to finely chop. Galangal is popular all over South East Asia and is often used instead of or with ginger, blended into a spice paste. Many chefs will tell you that you cannot substitute ginger or galangal for each other. This makes sense because they do taste different. That said, when I can't get my hands on galangal, I do use ginger and the dish is still delicious. Like ginger, galangal freezes well but will discolour slightly.

Lemongrass: Fresh lemongrass stalks are a lot easier to find these days. I purchase mine from Asian shops and at supermarkets. The white end of the stalk has the most flavour but the green, woodier ends are excellent for flavouring soups and stocks or using as skewers. When preparing lemongrass, you need to remove the tough outer layer as it is too difficult to use and can be woody and chewy. To release the citrus flavour, lightly bruise the stalks before using. If using in a curry paste, thinly slice the white part of the stalk and pound in a pestle and mortar or blend with other ingredients into a paste. The stalk can also be thinly sliced and served over different dishes.

Lemongrass freezes well. I often freeze the parts of the stalk I don't use, to flavour soups and stocks or to use as skewers. Although there is no real substitute for lemongrass, you could add lemon juice to your recipes until you achieve the citrus flavour you are looking for. Stay away from the pickled, jarred stuff or pastes in a tube.

Makrut lime leaves: The leaves of makrut limes are one of the most delicious ingredients in South East Asian food. They have a strong fragrance and a mild but lasting flavour of lime. The stalks of the leaves are tough so are best removed if used in a paste or garnish. Then you can pound or blend the leaves into a paste or thinly slice them. They are sometimes sold as 'kaffir lime leaves'.

Chillies (fresh, dried and powder): The recipes call for different types of chillies depending on the cuisine. You'll find that most, if not all, can be sourced at your local supermarket. Most of the recipes from the Indian subcontinent and South

East Asia call for green and red finger chillies, dried and fresh. They also call for dried finger chillies and Kashmiri chilli powder. If these are not available where you live, just substitute what you can get easily and like. Serrano chillies and jalapeños will work. You could also use cayenne chilli powder – though it is a bit spicier than Kashmiri, so you should add that (or another chilli powder you like using) to taste.

The dishes of the Caribbean and the southern US call for chillies that are popular there such as habanero and jalapeños, as well as cayenne chilli powder and paprika. Hugely popular in Mexican cuisine are the large dried guajillo and ancho chillies, which are available in specialist grocers and online as well as some supermarkets. Again, use what you can get, as experimenting with chillies is part of the fun. With some recipes, such as the Korean ones, it's best to source the chilli pastes and flakes that the recipe calls for. They are available almost everywhere online.

Real cinnamon sticks: Real cinnamon is only grown commercially in Sri Lanka and the Maldives. The tightly rolled bark can be torn apart into paper-thin pieces. You can get it online and at some supermarkets and specialist shops. Cassia is a good substitute as it tastes the same, but it is woodier and therefore not the best option for a curry paste as it is difficult to blend. You could substitute ground cinnamon, which is available pretty much everywhere. Although it states 'cinnamon' on the label, it's made from the cheaper cassia and you'll see 'cinnamon cassia' on the packaging in small text, too. Finely ground cassia like this is a good substitute for real cinnamon in pastes, but add it to taste so that you don't overpower the paste with the flavour of cinnamon.

Shallots: The majority of South East Asian spice pastes call for shallots. I watched many of these pastes being prepared in South East Asia, where their shallots are small and round. They throw in a lot of them. At home, I use the longer and larger banana shallots. Keep this in mind if you are using smaller, round shallots as you might want to use a few more. You really can't spoil a spice paste by adding a few more or less than suggested, so don't worry too much.

Fresh herbs: You will most likely be familiar with all of the herbs required in these recipes. Herbs such as coriander (cilantro), mint leaves, parsley and thyme are all popular additions. They don't stay fresh for long, but you can freeze many herbs to add later to stocks, soups and curries. Coriander, parsley and mint leaves all freeze well, although frozen herbs won't make a good garnish. I often blend my herbs with a little water then freeze them in ice-cube trays to use as little herb stock cubes. Thyme dries well on its own and can also be used in the same way. Just remove the dried leaves from the stocks, store in an air-tight container and use as needed.

Curry leaves: These offer an amazing flavour and aroma to a dish. They are used a lot in Indian, Sri Lankan and some South East Asian cuisines. They are best purchased fresh and can be frozen. If freezing, wash them first, as putting them in the freezer wet helps maintain their colour. Curry leaves can also be refrigerated in a tightly sealed container. It is best not to wash them before storing in this way. Shaking the container every day will help them stay fresh for up to three weeks. Stay away from dried curry leaves as they don't have the same intense flavour.

Pandan leaves: These long, green leaves are a popular ingredient in Sri Lankan, Thai and other South East Asian cooking. They offer a floral flavour to curries and soups and there isn't a good substitute. They can also be used to wrap and flavour meats. Pandan leaves can usually be found in the freezer section of Asian shops, though from time to time you might find them fresh, too. If you can't source them for these recipes, you can simply leave them out.

Banana leaves: These offer a very mild flavour of banana when wrapped around meat and seafood. They are used not only for their flavour, but also to protect their contents as they fry. They are available at Asian markets and online. If you have trouble sourcing them, leave them out.

Candlenuts: These are used in many South East Asian spice pastes. You can substitute macadamia nuts. Unlike macadamia nuts, candlenuts are quite hard and are not eaten whole.

In my opinion, the best recipes are those that use salty, sweet, sour and spicy flavours to perfection. That's why it is so important that you taste as you cook. Getting to know the following ingredients will help you taste and adjust the recipes in this book to your own preferences.

Soy sauce: I'm sure this needs little explanation. Often referred to as 'light soy sauce', it is used to add saltiness to dishes. If you are gluten-free, please note that most soy sauces contain gluten but gluten-free versions are available such as tamari. Coconut amino is also a good substitute.

Dark soy sauce: This is not used as much as light soy sauce. It is added not only for its salty flavour but also to add a deeper, darker colour. It is thicker than light soy sauce and less salty. Gluten-free brands are available.

Kecap manis: This sweet, salty and syrupy sauce plays an important role in many Indonesian and Malaysian recipes. It is available at Asian shops and online, and I've given a recipe on page 258.

Fish sauce: This adds a salty flavour to many South East Asian dishes. It is made from fermented anchovies, salt, sugar and water. I like to use the fish sauce produced in the country a dish is from, but you don't need to source lots of bottles! Just find a brand you like and use that whenever fish sauce is called for. I often use the Thai brand 'Squid'. As a general rule, look for fish sauce that is clear and brown in colour. Gluten-free, vegan and vegetarian versions are available.

Oyster sauce: Although oyster sauce contains oysters or oyster extract, it is not at all fishy; instead it is a delicious mixture of salty and sweet. Always look for one that has oysters as the first ingredient. Gluten-free brands are available.

Vinegar: Unless otherwise stated, use distilled vinegar or rice vinegar to add a nice sour flavour.

Garlic and ginger paste: This can be purchased either in jars or frozen at Asian grocers and many supermarkets. You can also make it yourself quite easily; I have provided a recipe on page 257.

Passata: Unseasoned passata is called for in many of the recipes in this book. It is added to dishes not only for flavour but for colour as well. It might be Italian in origin but unseasoned passata is simply stewed, blended tomatoes. The seasoned version contains Italian herbs so isn't best for these recipes. If you don't want to open up a whole container for a recipe, see my passata alternatives on page 257.

Tamarind paste: You can purchase tamarind paste or concentrate to add a delicious sour flavour. I usually make my own from block tamarind because I find the flavour nicer; I've included my recipe for this on page 256, as well as a recipe for tamarind sauce.

Gochujang: This Korean hot pepper paste is savoury, mildly sweet and spicy. It is available online and at Asian supermarkets. There are gluten-free brands available.

Shrimp paste: This pungently strong, fishy ingredient doesn't smell very nice when raw, but when used in cooking and when pounded or blended into a curry paste, it's delicious. The salty paste is used sparingly as it can quickly overpower a dish, so use as directed in my recipes. Although flavours and texture vary depending on where it is produced, I recommend using a Chinese fermented shrimp paste for these recipes unless you really want to go all out and source shrimp pastes by cuisine.

Asian sesame paste: Asian sesame paste is not the same as tahini, which is popular in Mediterranean cooking. Tahini is made with blended, raw sesame seeds. With Asian sesame paste, the seeds are toasted to a chocolate brown before blending. There is a big difference in flavour – like the difference between white bread and toast.

A NOTE ON MSG

MSG (monosodium glutamate) is a flavour enhancer used a lot in Asian cuisine. It has about a third of the sodium of salt and tastes great. I use it, but I know some people are concerned about its health effects so I have indicated if MSG is included in certain ingredients in recipes. Feel free to leave it out if you are at all concerned.

COCONUT PRODUCTS

These need a special mention, as they come in so many different forms. The idea behind using coconut products is to give the dish a mild or intense flavour of coconut. Coconut oil, coconut milk powder, block coconut and coconut milk are all used in many of the following recipes. A question I get asked often is whether you can substitute one coconut product for another, and the answer is often yes.

Block coconut is coconut milk in block form. If you look at a block, you will notice that one end is bright white and the other is a dirty, more solid white. The bright white end is coconut oil. If you were to chop it off and throw it in a hot pan, it would melt and become clear, as it is oil. The dirty, more solid end is solidified coconut cream or milk. That is what you want to add to your curries for a creamier sauce. Substitute coconut milk if you like. If you live somewhere where you can't get block coconut, you can add thick coconut milk to taste and vice versa. Many of the curry house-style curries call for coconut milk powder. This is a powder made from dehydrated coconut milk. I prefer it to coconut flour, which is made from the dried and ground meat of the coconut, because it has a creamier consistency. You can use either. These powders and flours are used at curry houses because they are less expensive than coconut milk. So again, you could substitute coconut milk or block coconut to taste.

Dried coconut flakes and desiccated coconut are pretty much the same thing, but processed differently. The flakes are great toasted and used as a garnish for curries such as korma and pasanda. I do not recommend using desiccated coconut in sauces, as they are nowhere near as nice to eat as sauces prepared with the finer coconut milk powder, flour or another of the coconut milk products mentioned above. Both coconut flakes and desiccated coconut are made with dehydrated coconut meat and both are often used ground into curry powders.

Avoid buying tinned (canned) light coconut milk. It costs the same as thick coconut milk but is just a watered-down version. Going into how light and thick coconut milks are prepared is a bit too much information for this book, but you could just purchase thick coconut milk and water it down a little to make a lighter version.

DRIED VERSUS TINNED (CANNED) CHICKPEAS, KIDNEY BEANS AND BLACK BEANS

To make things quick and easy, I suggest using tinned (canned) beans instead of dried in the recipes that call for them. Dried beans that you cook yourself are a better product, though. So although the recipes call for tinned beans, which work perfectly well, I normally cook dried beans at home. The cooked beans have a better texture, and if using in a sauce, you can also add the cooking liquid instead of plain water. Cooked beans can be frozen along with the cooking liquid for later use. You also get a lot more for your money.

OILS

Rapeseed (canola), sesame and olive oils are used in this book, depending on the cooking method and cuisine. For most of the recipes, you will need an oil that has a high smoking point such as rapeseed oil, but you could also use oils such as sunflower and peanut oil that have high smoking points.

REUSING COOKING OILS

Some of the dishes are shallow- or deep-fried, and these need to be fried in oils with a high smoking point. Oil used for frying can be saved and used again, but you do need to consider the following:

- If you intend to reuse cooking oil, be sure to filter it to remove any bits that are left floating in it after cooking. You could do this simply by running it through a sieve, but placing something like a thin cloth or muslin in your sieve will help filter and preserve your oil even better.

- Each time you reuse an oil that has a high smoking point, the smoking point for that oil will reduce a little. I usually use oil for deep-frying at least three times before discarding it. If you find that the smoking point of your oil has reduced substantially over time or it has a foul aroma, don't use it. For your information, the natural smoking point of refined rapeseed (canola) oil is 230°C (446°F), refined sunflower oil is 232°C (450°F) and refined peanut oil is 232°C (450°F).

SOUPS

In the West, many people think of soups as cold weather
food. Let's debunk that myth. Although a good bowl of
soup is very nice when it's cold outside, they are also
enjoyed for breakfast, lunch and dinner in places like
Vietnam in scorching hot heat. The truth is, the following
soups can be devoured whenever you feel like taking a bit
of time to prepare these one-pot wonders. Some do take
some time to cook, but the actual work is minimal and
you might just find one of your favourite meals of all time.
I know I did… homemade bun bo hue (see page 26)!

A GOOD STOCK IS THE BACKBONE OF SO MANY RECIPES

Are you looking for authenticity or a quick and easy recipe? That's something I had to consider when I put this collection together. There is no doubt in my mind that you will get better results if you prepare your own homemade stocks for these soup recipes, as well as the other recipes where stock is called for. If you don't want to make your own stocks, however, this should not stop you from making these recipes as you can still achieve fantastic results using ready-made stocks or stock cubes.

I wanted to show you how to cook these recipes in a similar way to how they are prepared in their counties of origin, and in most cases I did this. However, some of the recipes were very long and laborious so I developed methods using shop-bought stocks or stock cubes. These changes, however, have been highlighted so that you can make homemade alternatives should you wish to do so. In recipes where there are possible shortcuts, you will find these too. Look for 'make it easier' under these recipes. Using this advice, you will often shorten the cooking time substantially and be left with less mess to clear up too. Bonus!

HOMEMADE STOCKS... ONE POT OR TWO?

All of these recipes have been written so that they can be prepared in just one pot. I always find this really useful when I'm camping or cooking outdoors, but when I'm in my kitchen, I often find two pots works best – that way I can cook a stock and fry vegetables, spice blends and/or meat at the same time. It's a time saver if nothing else.

I love a good beef pho so I often cook up a batch of Asian-style meat (beef) stock (page 251), use what's needed and then freeze the bulk of it for later. Little things like this mean you can prepare an authentic beef pho in minutes rather than hours whenever you want to, but you'll technically be using two pots to do so. For that matter, using a homemade stock instead of shop-bought will usually mean using two pots, but as mentioned, that's up to you.

Meat and vegetable stocks freeze really well, so this idea can be applied to many of the recipes for quick and easy meals during the week. Fish stock takes a fraction of the time to make and doesn't freeze as well, so that should be made on the day of cooking or perhaps one day before if more convenient.

SUBSTITUTING HOMEMADE STOCK WITH SHOP-BOUGHT

Most readily available commercial stocks contain herbs and other ingredients that aren't used in Asian dishes. Shop-bought stocks are also usually darker, as the bones to produce a Western-style stock are first roasted, whereas in most Asian cuisines they are boiled for about 10 minutes, washed thoroughly and then added to the pot again to simmer gently for a few hours.

The good news is that, although not authentic in flavour or colour, shop-bought stocks still taste great in these recipes. Looking at the beef pho recipe on page 25, you'll see that ginger and onions are used to flavour an authentic pho stock. You could do the same by using shop-bought stock or stock made from stock cubes and adding these ingredients.

I can assure you that you can still prepare delicious-tasting recipes using these shortcuts, but be sure to taste the stock first before adding the salt or other salty ingredients, such as fish sauce, as most commercially available stocks already have salt added.

CHICKEN PHO
SERVES 4–6

This authentic chicken pho can be made from scratch any day of the week. A whole chicken is stewed in water with spices, ginger and onion until you have a delicious pho broth. You might like to consider preparing the Asian-style chicken stock on page 250 to have on hand (it also freezes well). Do that and you can make this chicken pho in half the time, as described in the 'make it easier' instructions below.

PREP TIME: 10 MINS
COOKING TIME: 90 MINS

7 star anise
2 green cardamom pods, seeds only
3 cloves
2 x 5cm (2in) cinnamon sticks
1 tsp rapeseed (canola) oil
1 large onion, quartered
5cm (2in) piece of ginger, sliced
  thinly down the centre and lightly
  smashed
1 x 1.5–2kg (3lb 5oz–4½lb) whole
  chicken, quartered with skin on
  or off
1.5 litres (6 cups) water
1 small handful each of fresh basil
  and coriander (cilantro) leaves
  (optional)
1–2 Asian (preferred) or Western
  chicken stock cubes (optional)
1 tsp palm sugar or light brown sugar
  (more or less to taste)
1–2 tbsp fish sauce (gluten-free
  brands are available)

TO SERVE
200g (7oz) dried rice pho noodles
Generous portions of Thai sweet
  basil, coriander (cilantro), bean
  sprouts, green and red chillies, cut
  into rings, and lime wedges.
Vietnamese sate, Chinese chilli oil
  with chillies and/or sriracha sauce
  (optional)

Heat a saucepan that is large enough to hold all the chicken and water over a medium–high heat. Add the star anise, cardamom seeds, cloves and cinnamon sticks and dry-fry them, stirring often, until warm to the touch and fragrant but not yet smoking. Pour into a bowl and set aside.

Add about a teaspoon of rapeseed (canola) oil to the saucepan and rub it over the surface of the pan with a piece of the quartered onion. Add the rest of the onion and sliced ginger to the pan and fry for about 5 minutes, or until the onion and ginger is browning and charring in a few places.

Add the chicken quarters, skin-side down (if keeping the skin on), and fry to brown for about 5 minutes, turning once. Now carefully pour in the water and add the roasted spices along with the basil and coriander (cilantro), if using. Push the chicken pieces down so they are completely submerged in the water. You can add a little more water if needed. Bring to a simmer and be sure to skim any foam and fat that rise to the top. This will result in a clearer stock.

Once you have skimmed as many impurities from the top as possible, allow to simmer gently over a medium heat for 60 minutes. Avoid letting it simmer too rapidly as it will become cloudy.

While the stock is simmering, place the dried pho noodles in a bowl and cover with boiling water. Hot water from a kettle is fine. Allow to soak for 10–15 minutes, or until cooked to your liking. Strain and set aside.

After the chicken has simmered for 60 minutes, remove it from the pan. Allow to cool a little and thinly slice or shred it.

Try the stock. You have three options: leave it as it is; return the chicken bones and simmer them longer; or add a stock cube or two for a richer stock. Once you have your stock as you want it, add sugar and fish sauce to taste. If using shop-bought stock cubes, they could be salty already so consider this when adding the fish sauce. Strain the stock into a bowl, then return it to the pan and bring to a rolling boil.

To finish, divide the soaked noodles between four to six large bowls. Cover with some of the shredded chicken and the hot pho broth. Then serve at the table with your garnishes of choice.

★ MAKE IT EASIER ★
You can reduce your cooking time by using about 350ml (1½ cups) of shop-bought chicken stock or homemade chicken stock (page 250) per serving. To do so, follow the recipe until the end of the second paragraph. Then add the stock and simmer for 20 minutes if using homemade stock or 30 minutes if using shop-bought. Towards the end of simmering, add a couple of chicken breasts to cook through for about 10 minutes. Remove the breasts and slice thinly. Season the stock with sugar and fish sauce to taste and serve as above with your garnishes of choice.

MEXICAN STREET CORN SOUP
SERVES 4–6

This popular Mexican street-food soup can be made chunky or smooth. I prefer it chunky, which is less fussy to make. Making this quick and easy soup brings back great memories of trips to Mexico with friends in my late teens. It was always just a snack which we slurped back with lots of ice-cold beers: a luxury we weren't legally allowed north of the border. Nowadays I think it makes an excellent meal in its own right. The soup can easily be made vegetarian by leaving out the chicken and using a vegetable stock.

PREP TIME: 10 MINS
COOKING TIME: 20 MINS

2 tbsp unsalted butter
1 tbsp light olive oil
700g (1lb 9oz) boneless chicken
    thighs, cut into small bite-sized
    pieces
1 onion, finely chopped
1–2 jalapeño chillies, finely chopped
½ green (bell) pepper, finely chopped
4 garlic cloves, finely chopped
1 tsp ground cumin
500ml (2 cups) chicken stock,
    homemade (see page 250) or shop-
    bought
500ml (2 cups) single (light) cream
225g (8oz) medium cheddar or jack
    cheese, grated
400g (14oz) fresh, frozen or tinned
    (canned) sweetcorn
400g (14oz) tinned (canned) black
    beans, drained and rinsed
Salt and pepper, to taste
Juice of 1 lime

TO SERVE
4 tbsp coriander (cilantro), finely
    chopped
2 medium tomatoes, diced
Fried corn tortillas
Hot sauce of your choice and to taste

Heat the butter and olive oil in a saucepan over a medium–high heat. When visibly hot, stir in the chicken and fry until brown and about 80% cooked. If cooking the smooth version of this soup, transfer the chicken to a plate and set aside. For the chunky version, you can leave it in the pan.

Stir in the chopped onion, chillies and green (bell) pepper and fry to soften for about 5 minutes. Add the garlic and fry for a further minute, while stirring to combine. Then add the cumin followed by the stock and bring to a boil. Reduce the heat to medium and simmer for 5 minutes.

Stir in the cream, grated cheese, corn and black beans. Continue simmering over a low heat until the cheese has melted into the stock. Season with salt and pepper to taste and squeeze in the lime juice.

The soup is now ready to serve, but if you prefer a smooth soup, blend it with a stick blender or transfer it all to a countertop blender and blend to your liking. Return the smooth soup to the pan and add the cooked chicken.

Serve topped with coriander (cilantro), the chopped tomatoes, fried, sliced corn tortillas and hot sauce, if wanted.

SPICY WONTON SOUP

SERVES 6—8

Homemade spicy wonton soup is a real treat. For this recipe, you use the carcasses of three chickens or one whole chicken to make the stock. If you use a whole chicken, the chicken meat isn't used in this recipe but I'm sure you can find another use for it. Use it as a filling for a sandwich or stir it into some pasta, for example.

PREP TIME: 45 MINS
COOKING TIME: 70 MINS

FOR THE SOUP

10 dried shiitake mushrooms
  (optional)
2 tbsp Chinese chilli garlic oil plus
  more to garnish (see page 246 or
  shop-bought)
4 garlic cloves, finely chopped
5cm (2in) piece of ginger, cut into
  thick coins and lightly smashed
4 spring onions (scallions), roughly
  chopped
1 onion, roughly chopped
1 tbsp Szechuan peppercorns, lightly
  crushed
1 x 1.5kg (3lb 5oz) chicken or the
  carcasses of 3 chickens
1 tsp dark brown sugar (or to taste)
4 tbsp black rice vinegar
Salt, to taste

FOR THE WONTONS

3 garlic cloves, finely chopped
1 tbsp finely chopped ginger
2 spring onions (scallions), finely
  chopped
2 tsp sesame oil
1 tbsp soy sauce
½ tsp sugar
300g (10½oz) minced (ground) pork
150g (5½oz) raw prawns (shrimp),
  peeled and cleaned
30 (approx.) square wonton skins

TO SERVE

4 spring onions (scallions), thinly
  sliced
Chilli oil (preferably homemade, see
  page 246) and some of the goop at
  the bottom, to taste

Cover the dried mushrooms with boiling water, if using. Set aside for later. Heat the chilli garlic oil (see page 246) over a medium heat in a saucepan that is large enough to contain the chicken or chicken carcasses. Add the garlic, ginger, spring onions (scallions) and onion and fry for about a minute to soften.

Add the Szechuan peppercorns, stir for a few seconds and then add the chicken or chicken carcasses and just enough water to cover. Simmer for 1 hour. If using a whole chicken, be sure to remove it after an hour so that you don't overcook the meat. The chicken meat isn't used in this recipe, but is delicious served hot or cold and dipped into soy sauce with chopped chillies mixed in, or in warmed sesame oil with chopped spring onions and salt to taste. If using just bones, you could simmer the stock much longer for a richer flavour.

While the stock is simmering, you can prepare the wontons. Place all of the wonton ingredients up to and including the sugar into a food processor and blend to a paste. Add the pork and prawns (shrimp) and process a little longer until you have a coarse paste. Take a wonton skin and put about a tablespoon of the filling in the centre. Wet the sides with a little water and fold it over to form a triangle shape and then bring two of the corners together around the filling. Press the seams tightly so that there is no way the filling can escape. Repeat with the remaining filling and wonton skins.

Once the stock is finished, strain it, discarding the solids, and return the stock to the pan. Add the soaked mushrooms, if using, along with the brown sugar and black rice vinegar. Taste it and adjust to your liking, adding more sugar, vinegar or salt to your preference.

Add the prepared wontons and simmer for about 5 minutes, or until the filling is cooked through. To serve, divide the soup and wontons into serving bowls and top with more chilli oil and the solids from the oil to your preference, along with finely chopped spring onions to garnish. You could also do the same with shop-bought Chinese chilli garlic oil if you don't want to make your own.

★ MAKE IT EASIER ★

Prepared wontons with a variety of fillings can be found in the frozen section at many Asian shops. They are usually quite good and will save you having to make your own, though I really hope you give it a go.

BO KHO
SERVES 4–6

'Bo' means beef and 'kho' is a cooking method in Vietnam. Kho on its own is a dish where meat is cooked until tender, braising it until most of the liquid has evaporated and you are left with a thick sauce. Bo kho, however, is nothing like that. This is much more like a hearty stew. Like in many Vietnamese recipes, achiote oil is added to give this dish a deep red colour and earthy flavour. It's really easy to prepare and highly recommended, but totally optional. To make it, lightly simmer 3 tablespoons of achiote seeds in 250ml (1 cup) of rapeseed (canola) oil for about 20 minutes. The oil will turn a bright orange and take on the flavour of the achiote seeds. Strain the oil into a jar or bowl. Any leftover oil will keep for months in an air-tight container in the fridge.

PREP TIME: 10 MINS, PLUS
  OPTIONAL MARINATING TIME
COOKING TIME: 40 MINS

1.25kg (2¾lb) stewing steak, cut into
  large bite-sized pieces

FOR THE MARINADE
6 garlic cloves, finely chopped
5cm (2in) piece of ginger, finely
  chopped
70ml (¼ cup) fish sauce (gluten-free
  brands are available)
1 tsp five spice powder
2 tsp light brown sugar

FOR THE STEW
2 tbsp rapeseed (canola) oil
4 star anise
1 large onion, finely chopped
2 lemongrass stalks, woody outer
  layer removed and then finely
  chopped
10 garlic cloves, finely chopped
2 tsp red chilli powder
1 tbsp paprika
2 x 400g (14oz) tins (cans) chopped
  tomatoes
750ml (3 cups) coconut water
4 tbsp light soy sauce (gluten-free
  brands are available)
4 carrots cut into 5mm (¼in) coins
Additional fish sauce, to taste

TO SERVE
150–200g (5½–7oz) rice noodles
2–4 tbsp chilli oil or achiote oil
  (optional)
Sliced red onion
Chopped herbs such as basil, mint
  and/or coriander (cilantro)
Lime wedges

Start by marinating the beef. Place the chopped garlic and ginger, fish sauce, five spice powder and brown sugar in a bowl and whisk until you have a smooth marinade. Add the beef and stir it in until nicely coated with the marinade mixture. Allow to marinate while you prepare the stew ingredients or overnight – the longer, the better.

When you're ready to prepare the stew, heat the oil in a large saucepan over a medium–high heat and add the star anise to infuse into the oil for about 30 seconds. Add the chopped onion and fry for about 5 minutes, or until soft and translucent. Then stir in the lemongrass and chopped garlic and fry for a further 30 seconds. Add the marinated beef with any remaining marinade and brown on all sides for about 5 minutes.

Stir in the chilli powder and paprika and then add the chopped tomatoes and coconut water. Bring this to a simmer and cook until the beef is almost tender enough to eat. This should take about 1 hour and 20 minutes. Add the soy sauce and carrots and cook until the beef is tender and the carrots are cooked through. Add more fish sauce to taste.

To serve, place the rice noodles in a bowl and pour boiling water over them. Allow them to cook in the boiling water for about 10 minutes, or until cooked to your liking. The noodles will continue to soften in the stew. Divide the noodles between four to six bowls and spoon the hot stew over them. Top each with a little chilli or achiote oil (optional), sliced red onion, herbs and lime wedges.

INDONESIAN BEEF SHORT RIB SOUP
SERVES 4

After eating nothing but grilled fish for about a week in Jimbaran, Bali, I was ready for meat. Although I could easily have killed a couple of cheeseburgers, Caroline and I had set ourselves a strict rule that Western food was off limits during our stay. After trying this amazing beef short rib soup we were glad we stuck to our guns! We happened upon a restaurant called Bendito and the owner shared his mum's recipe for pindang palembang, from Sumatra where he grew up. Although this is a soup, it is often served like a curry, ladled over rice at the table. If you like spicy food, be sure to serve this with sambal oelek (see page 252); just some of his helpful advice which we accepted gratefully.

PREP TIME: 15 MINS
COOKING TIME: 60 MINS

1 tsp shrimp paste
3 tbsp rapeseed (canola) oil
8 red finger chillies, roughly chopped, seeds and membranes removed if you don't want it too spicy
6 banana shallots, thinly sliced
6 garlic cloves, peeled and thinly sliced
5cm (2in) piece of ginger, thinly sliced
5cm (2in) piece of galangal, thinly sliced
1 tsp ground turmeric
1kg (2lb 2oz) meaty beef short ribs
1.5 litres (6 cups) water
2 lemongrass stalks, pounded lightly and each cut into 3 pieces
3 makrut lime leaves
3 medium tomatoes, quartered
2 spring onions (scallions), thinly sliced
Salt and pepper, to taste

Add the shrimp paste to a large saucepan over a medium heat and toast it for about 2 minutes, stirring regularly. Then pour in half the oil and add the chillies, shallots, garlic, ginger and galangal and sauté for about 5 minutes, or until the shallots are turning soft. Stir in the turmeric and then transfer it all to a bowl. Set aside.

Pour the remaining oil into the same pan and add the short ribs. Fry the meat for about 5 minutes to brown and then cover with water and bring to a boil. Simmer for 10 minutes, skimming off any foam and other impurities that float to the top. Then pour it all through a colander, discarding the cooking water. Wash the meat thoroughly under running water and then return to the pot and cover with 1.5 litres (6 cups) of water. Bring to a boil again and return the cooked vegetables to the pan along with the lemongrass and lime leaves and simmer over a medium heat, covered, for about 90 minutes, or until the beef is really tender. Remove the lid from the pan and continue simmering to reduce until you only have about 1 litre (4 cups) of stock in the pan. Add the quartered tomatoes and spring onions (scallions) and give it all a good stir. Season with salt and pepper to taste.

★ MAKE IT EASIER ★

Boiling the short ribs in water first and then washing them produces a clearer stock. You can skip this step though. Your stock won't be as clear but it will still taste good.

BEEF CONGEE
SERVES 6–8

Congee is similar to porridge but made with rice instead of oats. It's popular all over South East Asia and in East Asia as well, although its name, and what it's served with, varies from country to country. This is just like the congee served in Vietnam. You could cook it without the beef or fish sauce for a vegetarian version. The congee itself is quite bland, so you spice it up to taste at the table adding coriander (cilantro), salt and pepper, finely chopped chillies and/or soy sauce. You can really use any white rice for this recipe, but I use broken basmati as it's cheaper and gets the same flavour and results as normal basmati.

PREP TIME: 10 MINS
COOKING TIME: 2 HOURS

FOR THE BEEF
500g (1lb 2oz) minced (ground) beef
1 tsp sesame oil
2 tbsp fish sauce (gluten-free brands are available)
500ml (2 cups) water

FOR THE RICE
210g (1 cup) broken basmati, basmati or jasmine rice
2.5 litres (10 cups) water, plus more if needed
3 garlic cloves, smashed (optional)
2.5cm (1in) piece of ginger, sliced into 3 and smashed (optional)
2 tbsp fish sauce (more or less to taste; gluten-free brands are available)

TO SERVE
3 tbsp coriander (cilantro), finely chopped
Salt and pepper, to taste
4 green chillies, thinly sliced
Chopped spring onions (scallions)
Soy sauce (gluten-free brands are available)
Chilli oil (see page 246 or shop-bought), to taste

Rinse the rice in several changes of water until the water runs almost clear. Cover with clean water to soak for at least 4 hours or overnight.

When ready to cook, place the minced (ground) beef in a mixing bowl and add the sesame oil, fish sauce and water. Mix it all up to combine – it will look quite soupy, like a meaty porridge. Place a 4–6-litre (4–6-quart) pot over a medium–high heat and pour in the minced beef. Fry, stirring continuously to break the beef down so that it is smooth with no lumps. Most, if not all, of the water will evaporate in this cooking process.

Once the beef is cooked, strain the rice and add it to the pot with 2.5 litres (10 cups) of water and the garlic and ginger, if using, and bring to a boil. Reduce the heat and simmer for about 90 minutes, stirring every 20 minutes, or so until the congee looks like a creamy porridge. Be sure to top up with water if the congee is getting too thick but is not yet creamy-smooth. Taste it, and if you want a more savoury flavour, add fish sauce to taste.

Serve hot at the table sprinkled with coriander (cilantro) and add salt and pepper, chillies, spring onions (scallions), soy sauce and chilli oil to taste.

EASY BEEF PHO

SERVES 4–6

An authentic beef pho takes over 5 hours to make, and you probably wouldn't want to go to the trouble for just four people – I usually save that luxury for when we're having a lot of guests over for dinner. Instead, I came up with this easy weekday version that gets delicious results in a fraction of the time. For this recipe, you can use a good-quality shop-bought beef stock or even stock cubes. If you want to take it up a notch, you could make the Asian-style meat stock on page 251 and use that instead of the shop-bought stock. If you use beef brisket in your homemade stock, you could thinly slice it and add it to your pho instead of the skirt steak.

PREP TIME: 10 MINS
COOKING TIME: 30 MINS

7 star anise
2 green cardamom pods, seeds only
3 cloves
2 x 5cm (2in) cinnamon sticks
1 tsp rapeseed (canola) oil
1 large onion, quartered
5cm (2in) piece of ginger, sliced thinly down the centre and lightly smashed
400g (14oz) skirt steak or sirloin, cut thinly against the grain
2.5 litres (10 cups) low-sodium shop-bought or homemade (preferred) beef stock (see page 251)
200g (7oz) dried rice pho noodles
1 tsp palm sugar or light brown sugar (more or less to taste)
1–2 tbsp fish sauce (gluten-free brands are available)
1 x 120g (4oz) piece of beef fillet, brought to room temperature, thinly sliced, to garnish
Generous portions of Thai sweet basil, coriander (cilantro), bean sprouts, green chillies cut into rings and lime wedges, to serve
Vietnamese sate (see page 253) or Sriracha sauce (optional), to serve

Place a 3-litre (3-quart) saucepan over a medium–high heat and stir in the star anise, cardamom seeds, cloves and cinnamon sticks and dry-fry them, stirring often until warm to the touch and fragrant but not yet smoking. Pour the roasted whole spices into a bowl and set aside.

Now add the oil to the pan over a medium–high heat. Add the quartered onion and move them around in the pan to spread the oil in a thin layer. Add the sliced ginger and fry for about 5 minutes, turning the onion and ginger often until browned and charred in places. Then add the thinly sliced beef and move it around in the pan for a few minutes until browned all over.

Pour in the beef stock and roasted spices and bring to a simmer over a high heat. Lower the heat to medium and simmer for 30 minutes.

While the stock is simmering, place the pho noodles in a bowl and pour boiling water over them. Water from a kettle is fine. Allow to soak for 10–15 minutes, until softened to your liking, and then strain and set aside.

Once the stock has been simmering for 30 minutes, try it and add the sugar and savoury fish sauce to taste. If using shop-bought stock, it could be salty already so consider this when adding the fish sauce. Fish out the thin slices of cooked beef and then strain the stock into a bowl. Discard the aromatic ingredients. Pour the strained stock back into the saucepan and ensure it is boiling hot.

To serve, place four large bowls on the table and fill each with a good mound of the soaked noodles. Top with the thinly sliced beef and pour the hot beef stock over them to fill the bowls. The raw fillet will cook in the hot broth. Everyone can then top their bowls of pho with the suggested garnishes as they wish.

BUN BO HUE

SERVES 4–6

I'm a big fan of the late Anthony Bourdain, so when Caroline and I arrived in Ho Chi Minh City, a visit to The Lunch Lady, which he made famous, was a must. Nguyen Thi Thành prepares a different dish every day and when it's gone, it's gone. Our first attempt to eat there was unsuccessful, but we returned the next morning and were treated to the best bun bo hue we had for the whole month we were in Vietnam. Bun bo hue is like a spicier version of beef pho, with added pork. Traditionally, congealed pigs' blood cubes are added to the broth but it's near impossible to get in the West, so I left it out. There really isn't a big flavour loss. Other popular additions are Vietnamese meatballs and sausage, which can be found in the freezer section of Vietnamese grocers, but I usually leave them out. Although I enjoy making bun bo hue just as I saw it prepared, it is a bit much for a one-pot weekday meal so I developed this recipe. It is a lot easier but still very tasty.

PREP TIME: 15 MINS
COOKING TIME: 2½ HOURS

FOR THE ANNATTO (ACHIOTE)
    OIL (OPTIONAL)*
125ml (½ cup) rapeseed (canola) oil
2½ tbsp annatto (achiote) seeds

FOR THE STOCK
1 large onion, quartered
5cm (2in) piece of ginger, sliced thinly
    down the centre and lightly smashed
3 garlic cloves, peeled and lightly
    smashed
450g (1lb) skirt steak or sirloin, cut
    thinly against the grain
225g (8oz) pork loin
2 tsp Kashmiri chilli powder (more or
    less to taste)
½ tsp ground cumin
2.5 litres (10 cups) low-sodium shop-
    bought beef stock or homemade
    (preferred) Asian-style meat stock
    (see page 251 and note below)
4 lemongrass stalks, lightly smashed
100g (3½oz) pineapple, tinned
    (canned) or fresh, diced
Sugar, to taste (optional)
Salt, to taste

TO SERVE
200g (7oz) dried rice noodles, soaked
    in hot water for 10 minutes
Bean sprouts
Spring onions (scallions), roughly
    chopped
Green chillies, thinly sliced
Herbs such as coriander (cilantro)
    and basil
Banana flower (optional), finely
    chopped
Chilli sauce such as Vietnamese sate
    (see page 253 or shop-bought) and/
    or the annatto (achiote) oil above
4 limes, quartered

To make the optional annatto (achiote) oil, pour the oil and annatto (achiote) seeds into a large saucepan that is big enough to cook the whole dish. Place over a medium–high heat and when bubbles start to form around the seeds, turn off the heat and allow them to sit for about 5 minutes. Remove the seeds using a slotted spoon and discard them. Then pour/scrape the oil out into a bowl. There will be more than you require but it keeps for ages in a jar in the fridge.

Place the saucepan back on the heat and add the quartered onion, ginger and garlic cloves. Fry for about 5 minutes, or until these ingredients are lightly browned and charring in places. Add the beef and pork and stir it around in the pan to brown for a few more minutes. Stir in the chilli powder and ground cumin. If you are at all unsure about the spiciness of the chilli powder, only add about a teaspoon. The rest can be added at the end of cooking to taste.

Now carefully pour in the stock, lemongrass and pineapple and bring to a rolling simmer over a medium–high heat. Once simmering, reduce the heat to medium and continue simmering with the lid on the pan for 30 minutes. While the stock is simmering, place the dried rice noodles in a bowl and cover with boiling water. Hot water from the kettle is fine. Allow to soak for about 10–15 minutes, or until cooked to your liking. Set aside.

After 30 minutes, remove the beef and pork. Allow the pork loin to cool a little and then slice it into thin rounds. Strain the stock into a bowl and then return it to the pan. Bring to a boil and keep hot. Season with sugar and salt to taste. Drizzle some of the annatto (achiote) oil or chilli oil over the top so that it becomes a shiny red colour.

To finish, divide the cooked noodles between four to six bowls. Add some of the beef and pork to each, then pour the hot stock over them and top with the garnishes of your choice.

NOTES

*The optional annatto (achiote) oil is used to give the bun bo hue its characteristic red glow. You could just add some Chinese chilli oil or Vietnamese sate to do that. Or add a bit of each.

If you are making homemade Asian-style meat stock for this recipe, you might like to throw in a few pork bones with everything else, as bun bo hue stock does normally call for pork bones.

SINGAPORE-STYLE BAH KUT TEH
SERVES 4

Bah kut teh has Chinese origins and is very popular at the Hakken stalls in Singapore and Malaysia, where they both have their own distinct versions of this pork soup. The Malaysian version is darker and includes a lot of difficult-to-find Chinese herbs. This Singapore-style bah kut teh is much more peppery and also includes freshly chopped chillies. Serve this soup as is, or over white rice.

PREP TIME: 10 MINS
COOKING TIME: 90 MINS

3 tbsp white peppercorns
2 tsp black peppercorns
3 star anise
7.5cm (3in) cinnamon or cassia stick
750g (1lb 10oz) meaty pork spare ribs, cut into 5cm (2in) pieces
450g (1lb) pork belly, cut into bite-sized pieces, skin removed
15 garlic cloves, lightly crushed
5 dried shiitake mushrooms, quartered
225g (8oz) tofu puffs (optional), shop-bought or homemade*
1 tbsp light soy sauce (gluten-free brands are available)
1 tbsp fish sauce (or to taste; gluten-free brands are available)

FOR THE DIPPING SAUCE
(OPTIONAL)
Light soy sauce (gluten-free brands are available)
4 red finger chillies, finely chopped

Coarsely grind the black and white peppercorns in a pestle and mortar or spice grinder. Place the ground pepper on top of a clean muslin with the star anise and cinnamon and tie it really tightly so that the spices can't escape. Set aside.

Put the pork ribs and pork belly in a large saucepan, cover with water and bring to a boil over a high heat. After 10 minutes of boiling, strain the pork into a colander and wash off any blood or impurities. Wipe the pan clean and return the pork to it with 2 litres (8 cups) of water and place over a high heat. Bring to a simmer and reduce the heat a little to simmer lightly for 10 minutes. Scoop off any foam that rises to the top.

Place the prepared spices in the pot along with the garlic and simmer lightly, covered, for 30 minutes. Then stir in the shiitake mushrooms and tofu puffs, if using, and continue simmering for another 30–45 minutes, or until the pork is really tender. Add the soy sauce and fish sauce – I suggest adding these to taste. Divide between four soup bowls. If you want to eat this Hakken-style, you could serve it with lots of white rice (see page 248) and chilli soy sauce – simply pour some light soy sauce into four small dipping bowls and add finely chopped red chillies to each.

NOTE

*Tofu puffs are optional and available at many Asian grocers and online. They are also easy to make. To do so, pat a block of fresh, firm tofu dry and cut into bite-sized cubes. Heat about 10cm (4in) of vegetable oil in a wok over a medium–high heat. It is ready for cooking when thousands of little bubbles form when you place a wooden chopstick or spatula in it. Fry in small batches for about 10–15 minutes, or until the tofu is light brown, puffed and spongy. After about 5 minutes of frying, the tofu begins to float to the top, which is a good indication it is becoming light and airy.

★ MAKE IT EASIER ★

Boiling then washing the bones produces a clearer stock. You can skip this step, though. Your broth won't be as clear but it will still taste good.

TOM KHA GOONG
SERVES 4

Thai tom kha soups are hugely popular around the world. This is a creamy and spicy soup made with coconut milk and prawns (shrimp), but you could add other proteins, too. Use chicken stock and add pieces of chicken to make a tom kha gha, or try it with tofu and vegetable stock for a vegetarian version.

PREP TIME: 10 MINS
COOKING TIME: 20 MINS

500ml (2 cups) Asian-style chicken stock (see page 250), unsalted chicken stock, prawn (shrimp) stock* or water
1 lemongrass stalk (white part only with thick outer layer removed), bruised and cut into about 6 slices
3 makrut lime leaves, stalks removed and leaves thinly sliced
1 thumb-sized piece of galangal, bruised and sliced into 7 pieces
10 coriander (cilantro) stalks, finely chopped
250g (9oz) raw prawns (shrimp), peeled and cleaned
400ml (14oz) tinned (canned) thick coconut milk
2 tbsp palm sugar (or to taste)
8 mushrooms, quartered or halved
70ml (¼ cup) Thai fish sauce (gluten-free brands are available)
2 tbsp roasted Thai chilli oil with some of the goop at the bottom (see page 246 or shop-bought – preferably Thai but Chinese is fine), or Thai red curry paste (see page 153 or shop-bought) to taste
80ml (⅓ cup) lime juice
3 spring onions (scallions), roughly chopped

Pour the stock or water into a large saucepan and bring to a boil over a high heat. Add the lemongrass, lime leaves, galangal and coriander (cilantro) stalks. Let this simmer for about 10 minutes to allow the aromatic ingredients to flavour the stock. Add the prawns (shrimp) and simmer for about 3 minutes, or until the prawns are just cooked through.

Pour in the coconut milk and add sugar to taste. Then stir in the mushrooms, fish sauce and the chilli oil along with some of the goop at the bottom – this is usually made up of chilli flakes and perhaps garlic or shallots. My homemade version is on page 246 but you can also buy it at Asian shops. You could also just add Thai red curry paste if that is more convenient.

Finally, add the lime juice to taste and the chopped spring onions (scallions). Simmer for another minute or so and then taste it and adjust the sweet/spicy/sour flavouring to your preference. To serve, divide the soup between four bowls.

NOTE
*Making fresh prawn (shrimp) stock: You can whip up a delicious prawn stock quickly and easily. Purchase prawns that still have the shells and heads. Break off the heads and peel off the shells. Heat a tablespoon of oil in a small saucepan and fry the heads and shells until they turn pink. Add 500ml (2 cups) of water and simmer for 15 minutes. Done!

TOM YUM WITH RICE VERMICELLI

SERVES 4–6

Although this popular soup can be made on your stovetop, I often cook and serve it at the table. If you have a portable, electric burner or even a table hot pot, you can cook this at the table, snacking on prawn crackers and enjoying a drink while the soup cooks to perfection.

PREP TIME: 20 MINS
COOKING TIME: 20 MINS

180g (6oz) mee hoon (Thai rice vermicelli noodles)
2 tbsp rapeseed (canola) oil
2 shallots, finely chopped
1 litre (4 cups) Asian-style chicken stock (see page 250), unsalted chicken stock, prawn (shrimp) stock* or water
2 lemongrass stalks, smashed and cut into about 5 pieces
8 lime leaves, stalks removed and leaves thinly sliced
2.5cm (1in) piece of galangal, thinly sliced
3 garlic cloves, roughly chopped
1 tbsp tamarind paste (see page 256 or shop-bought)
8 mushrooms, quartered
1 tbsp chilli jam (nam prik pao), homemade (see page 253) or shop-bought (optional)
1 tbsp roasted chilli garlic oil with some of the goop at the bottom (see page 246 or shop-bought is fine)
3–4 tbsp Thai fish sauce (gluten-free brands are available)
3 green finger chillies, smashed and cut lengthwise
1 small handful of coriander (cilantro), roughly chopped
450g (1lb) prawns (shrimp), deveined
450g (1lb) mussels, debearded and cleaned
1 tbsp evaporated milk (optional)
2 tomatoes, quartered
2 tsp palm or white sugar (optional and to taste)
3 spring onions (scallions), roughly chopped
Handful of chopped or sliced vegetables, such as cabbage, bean sprouts, par-cooked carrots (optional)

Put the mee hoon (Thai vermicelli rice noodles) in a bowl and cover with boiling water. Allow to sit in the water for about a minute and then drain and set aside.

Heat the oil in a large saucepan over a medium–high heat until shimmering hot. Add the shallots and fry for about a minute. Add the stock or water, lemongrass, lime leaves, galangal and garlic and bring to a boil. Reduce the heat and simmer this aromatic liquid for about 10 minutes. Stir in the tamarind paste.

Add in the mushrooms, chilli jam, chilli oil, fish sauce, green finger chillies and coriander (cilantro). Continue simmering and stir in the prawns (shrimp) and mussels and continue cooking for 5–10 minutes, or until the prawns turn pink and the mussels have opened. Discard any mussels that don't open. Once all of these ingredients have been added and are cooked through, taste it and adjust the seasoning as desired.

To finish, add the evaporated milk, if using, and quartered tomatoes and let them cook through in the hot stock. At this stage you should try the soup and add sugar to taste if you prefer a sweeter flavour, and/or adjust the sour, spicy and savoury flavours to taste. Add the spring onions (scallions) and any other vegetables you would like to add. I often add bean sprouts, cabbage and carrots but this is totally optional – add whichever veggies you like. Just be sure to cook them through.

To serve, divide the noodles between four to six bowls and pour the hot broth and seafood over them.

NOTE

*Making fresh prawn (shrimp) stock: You can whip up a delicious prawn stock quickly and easily. Purchase prawns that still have the shells and heads on. Break off the heads and peel off the shells. Heat a tablespoon of oil in a small saucepan and fry the heads and shells until they turn pink. Add 500ml (2 cups) of water and simmer for 15 minutes. Done!

★ MAKE IT EASIER ★

Instead of using homemade stock, you could purchase tom yum paste and prepare a stock as per the instructions on the packaging. Some of these pastes include a lot of salt, so be sure to taste the stock before adding salt and fish sauce.

SEAFOOD LAKSA
SERVES 6

I love a good laksa, and there are so many amazing recipes for it. This is one of my favourites. Made from scratch with homemade prawn (shrimp) stock and then served with big chunks of meaty white fish and shellfish, what's not to like? You can have a good play with this recipe, adding other types of seafood as well.

PREP TIME: 10 MINS
COOKING TIME: 30 MINS

400g (14oz) dried pho noodles or
   other thick rice noodles
2 tbsp rapeseed (canola) oil
1 tbsp sugar or less, to taste
2 tbsp fish sauce (gluten-free brands
   are available)
400ml (1¾ cups) coconut milk
Raw prawns (shrimp) from the 500g
   (1lb 2oz) saved after removing the
   head and shells for the stock
200g (7oz) skinless halibut
200g (7oz) skinless cod

FOR THE PRAWN (SHRIMP)
   STOCK
2 tbsp rapeseed (canola) oil
500g (1lb 2oz) head-on large prawns
   (shrimp) – remove the heads and
   shells for the stock and put the
   prawns aside for use in the soup
Approx. 1.2 litres (5 cups) water

FOR THE LAKSA PASTE
15g (½oz) dried Kashmiri chillies
   soaked in water for 20 minutes
20g (1oz) dried shrimp soaked in just
   enough water to cover
20 plain cashews
2 green finger chillies
10 garlic cloves
3 small shallots
1 lemongrass stalk, peeled, white
   part only
10 slices galangal
½ tsp ground turmeric
1 tsp fermented shrimp paste

TO SERVE
Handful of raw bean sprouts per
   serving
Lime slices
Handful of basil and mint to garnish
Sliced chillies of choice or chilli flakes
   (optional)
Sambal oelek (optional; see page 252
   or shop-bought)

Soak the rice noodles in hot water for 10–15 minutes, or until you are happy with their doneness. Drain, rinse and set aside.

To make the prawn (shrimp) stock, heat 2 tablespoons of oil in a saucepan and add the prawn shells and heads. Fry for a couple of minutes, or until the shells turn red and then add 1.2 litres (5 cups) of water. Simmer for 20 minutes to 1 hour. A longer simmering time will achieve a stronger-flavoured stock.

Meanwhile, prepare the laksa paste. Place all of the ingredients in a food processor and blend until you have a paste. You can add a drop of water if necessary to help the paste blend. Set aside.

When your prawn stock is cooked to your preference, strain it into a bowl and wipe the pan clean. Place the pan back on the heat and add the other 2 tablespoons of oil. When hot, stir in the laksa paste and fry for about a minute to cook out the rawness.

Slowly add the prawn stock and bring to a simmer. Stir in the sugar, fish sauce and coconut milk and then add the prawns and fish to poach in the hot broth until just cooked through. Taste and adjust the flavours to your liking.

To serve, divide the soaked noodles between four to six bowls. Pour the hot seafood laksa over the noodles with a good selection of prawns and fish in each bowl. Top with bean sprouts, lime slices, basil and mint. I like to add a little black pepper and/or chilli flakes to mine but that is optional. If you like it spicy, be sure to top with some shop-bought or homemade sambal oelek (see page 252).

★ MAKE IT EASIER ★
Although I highly recommend making the prawn stock, you can reduce your cooking time by using shop-bought fish stock or fish stock made with stock cubes.

MEXICAN SEAFOOD SOUP

SERVES 4–6

Lupe's Cantina Mexicana in Leeds serves some of the best Mexican food on the planet. The Mexican co-owner and chef, Rudy Gonzalez, ensures that all of the dishes served are spot on and authentic. Whenever we dine there, we order pretty much everything on the menu as we don't want to miss a thing. This Mexican seafood soup recipe they sent me is out of this world! The more fresh seafood you add to this, the better, so go for it!

PREP TIME: 15 MINS
COOKING TIME: 45 MINS

1–3 guajillo chillies, seeds and
    membranes removed

FOR THE FISH STOCK
Bones and heads of 1–2 fish such as
    sea bass, bream or halibut
1 onion, roughly chopped
2 garlic cloves, smashed
1 bay leaf
5 black peppercorns
3 litres (12 cups) water

FOR THE SOUP
3 tbsp olive oil
1 onion, roughly chopped
3 garlic cloves, smashed
1 celery stick, thinly sliced
3 tomatoes, diced
2 bay leaves
2 tbsp coriander (cilantro), chopped
1 sprig fresh epazote or ½ tsp dried
    (optional)
1 large potato, diced
1 carrot, diced
2 tsp Mexican dried oregano or other
    dried oregano
A selection of seafood such as approx.
    30 mussels and/or clams, 2 sea
    bass, 300g (10½oz) halibut and
    10 prawns (shrimp)

Using the saucepan you intend to cook the soup in, toast the guajillo chillies over a medium–high heat for about a minute per side or until fragrant. Be careful not to blacken them or they will turn bitter. Transfer the chillies to a bowl and add just enough hot water to cover them. Soak for 20–30 minutes to rehydrate and soften and then blend the chillies with the soaking water until smooth. Set aside.

To make the fish stock, place the fish head/s and bones in the pan and add the remaining stock ingredients. Bring to a simmer over a medium–high heat and simmer for 15–20 minutes. Strain through a fine sieve into a bowl and set aside. Discard all the solid ingredients.

To make the soup, wipe the pan dry and heat the olive oil in it over a medium–high heat. Add the chopped onion, garlic and celery to the oil and fry for about 3 minutes to soften. Stir in the blended chillies and the diced tomatoes and cook, stirring constantly, for about 4–5 minutes. Pour in the fish stock, bay leaves, chopped coriander (cilantro) and epazote and bring to a boil.

Add the diced potato, carrot and oregano to the boiling stock. Reduce the heat, cover and simmer for about 10–15 minutes, or until the potatoes and carrots are tender. Add the suggested seafood or other seafood of choice and continue simmering until the mussels and clams have opened and the fish is just cooked through.

★ MAKE IT EASIER ★

If you want the real taste of Lupe's you'll need to prepare your own seafood stock, as explained above, but you could simply use some seafood stock cubes instead.

BRITISH CURRY-HOUSE CURRIES

In my previous books I showed how to make curry house-style curries just as they do at British Indian restaurants by first preparing a large batch of base sauce.

For this book I've made things simpler so you can cook everything in one pan. This chapter contains all of the most popular curry-house curry recipes, but without the need to make a base sauce. There is less work involved but you'll still get restaurant-quality results.

BRITISH CURRY-HOUSE CURRIES

Having written several books focusing on British curry house-style recipes, I learned that many of you want to be able to make them without the 'essential' base curry sauce: a slowly simmered and mildly spiced smooth onion stock with a few other veggies thrown in. So I went to work developing curry house-style curries that you can make in one pan without the need to first cook a batch of base sauce. The following recipes are therefore not cooked in the way they would be cooked at curry houses, but the results will still be delicious. However, there are a few things to consider before you start cooking.

- **Blending your sauces:** In these recipes, I suggest blending the sauces to give you a smoother sauce. This step is optional, but it takes less than three minutes to do and will get your curry sauces closer to those at curry houses. It will also break those ground spices down even more. I find it easier to blend the sauces in a countertop blender, but you could use a hand-held stick blender.

- **Adding stock or water:** Each of these recipes calls for water, chicken stock or beef stock. In the red meat recipes, the stock is made during the cooking process. Tandoori chicken or raw chicken is suggested in the chicken curry recipes, so use either water, homemade chicken stock or shop-bought chicken stock for these recipes. Remember that most stock cubes and prepared shop-bought stocks contain salt, so you should taste the sauces before adding additional salt.

- **The spice blends:** At curry houses around the UK, a special curry powder called 'mixed powder' is used. (See my recipe for this on page 258.) Using mixed powder will achieve a flavour closer to what you might expect at a curry house, but you could simply substitute a good-quality, shop-bought curry powder or my curry powder on page 259. Other popular shop-bought spice blends, such as tandoori masala and chaat masala, are fine to use in these recipes. You can purchase these online or at Asian grocers and supermarkets. I have also provided recipes for these on page 260.

- **Choosing proteins:** Although I have used specific meats or proteins in the following recipes, you are not limited to them. These curry-house recipes are all down to the sauce. Just like when you go to an Indian restaurant and choose which meat, seafood, paneer or veggies go into your tikka masala sauce, you can and should do this at home too.

- **Using pre-cooked or raw meat:** Pre-cooked meat such as tandoori or stewed chicken and lamb is often used at restaurants to speed up the cooking process and add another layer of flavour. I have featured two different tandoori chicken recipes in the book (on pages 158 and 203) that you could use in these curries. You could also just add raw or cooked chicken from the supermarket or prepared chicken tikka or lamb meat from the frozen section at many Asian shops. During the photoshoot for this book, we did exactly that! We added raw bite-sized chicken to some of the sauces and cooked tandoori chicken for others. Although adding prepared tandoori chicken adds another layer of flavour, raw chicken worked very well too. So it's really down to you and the amount of prep work you want to do.

  The stewing of the red meat is all part of the one-pan recipes – you stew the meat until tender, and then use the meat and cooking liquid in the curry. Chicken could also be cooked for about 20 minutes in the same way, with the same spices used in the red-meat curries. This will produce a good chicken stock that has more flavour than simply adding water to the curry sauces.

WHICH PAN?

At curry houses, the chefs usually use aluminium pans, though stainless steel pans are also used. The advantage of these pans is that they heat up really quickly and they are not non-stick, which means the sauce will caramelize to the side of the pan as it cooks over the high heat. Scraping that caramelized sauce back in adds another delicious layer of flavour. Of course, you don't need to purchase a new set of pans to cook these recipes, so use what you have. Non-stick pans are fine to use; you just won't get quite the same flavour.

CHICKEN BALTI
SERVES 1–2

I included this recipe not only because I love a good balti curry, but because I wanted to demonstrate the basics. In the other 'one-pan' curry house-style recipes in the book, ingredients such as garlic and ginger paste are used and the sauce is blended to give the curries that famous British Indian-restaurant, smooth-curry gravy. In this recipe you finely chop the garlic and ginger and no blending is required. Raw chicken is added to the pan, too. You get what you cook with very little fuss and it tastes great. You can apply the same, no-fuss cooking to the other curry house-style recipes. Likewise, you could have a bit of fun and use some of the ideas from those recipes in this balti.

PREP TIME: 10 MINS
COOKING TIME: 15 MINS

2 tbsp rapeseed (canola) oil or ghee
½ large onion, finely chopped
3 garlic cloves, finely chopped
1.75cm (½in) piece of ginger, grated and finely chopped
2 tbsp tandoori masala, shop-bought or homemade (see page 260)
2 tsp madras curry powder (see page 259 or shop-bought) or mixed powder (see page 258)
2 fresh green finger chilli peppers
½ large green or red (bell) pepper, roughly chopped
1 tomato, diced
2–4 tbsp unseasoned passata
225g (8oz) chicken thighs or breasts, skinned and cut into 2.5cm (1in) chunks
125ml (½ cup) water or chicken stock
1 tbsp cider vinegar
2 tbsp chopped coriander (cilantro)
Salt, to taste
Juice of ½ lime (optional)

Heat the oil or ghee in a frying pan (skillet) or balti pan over a high heat. Toss in the chopped onion and allow to fry for about 5 minutes, or until the onion is beginning to turn soft and translucent. Add the garlic and ginger and stir to combine. About 30 seconds should do the job – you just want to cook off the rawness.

Spoon in the tandoori masala and curry powder or mixed powder. Then add the green chillies, (bell) pepper, chopped tomatoes and passata. Give this all a good stir to combine.

Toss in the chicken pieces and brown them in the onion mixture. Stir continuously to brown the chicken evenly. Add about 125ml (½ cup) of water or chicken stock. You can add more to assist in cooking the chicken, but baltis are usually quite dry curries so try not to add too much. That is unless you prefer more sauce, of course. It's best to add the water or stock in small amounts until the chicken is cooked through and you have a thickish sauce.

Simmer for about 8 minutes, or until the chicken is cooked through. Add the cider vinegar and simmer for another minute. Just before serving, sprinkle the coriander (cilantro) into the curry. Season with salt to taste and then add the lime juice if you want a more sour flavour.

CHICKEN TIKKA MASALA

SERVES 4

You can really do so much with a chicken tikka masala to make it just right for your taste preferences. Some are very sweet and creamy. Others are more on the savoury side with less cream. Whatever your preference, you will get it here. Just taste as you go and adjust. Chicken tikka masala is usually a deep red colour, which is done with red food colouring. The colouring adds little to no flavour, so leave it out if you aren't bothered about eating a glowing red curry. I didn't add any food colouring in the photograph opposite.

PREP TIME: 10 MINS
COOKING TIME: 20 MINS

4 tbsp ghee or rapeseed (canola) oil
2 onions, finely chopped
2 tbsp garlic and ginger paste
2 tbsp ground almonds
2 tbsp coconut milk powder (see alternatives on page 11)
1 tbsp curry powder or mixed powder, shop-bought or homemade (see page 259 or 258)
1½ tbsp sweet paprika
2 tbsp tandoori masala, shop-bought or homemade (see page 260)
300g (10½oz) tinned (canned) chopped tomatoes
1 tsp sugar (more or less to taste)
250ml (1 cup) chicken stock or water
800g (1lb 12oz) cooked chicken tikka (see page 158 or 203) or cooked leftover or raw chicken, cut into bite-sized pieces
1–2 tsp red food colouring powder (optional)
200ml (generous ¾ cup) single (light) cream (more or less to taste)
Juice of 1 lemon
1 tbsp kasoori methi (dried fenugreek leaves)
Salt, to taste
1 tsp garam masala, shop-bought or homemade (see page 259)
4 tbsp fresh coriander (cilantro), finely chopped

Heat the ghee or oil in a large frying pan (skillet) over a medium–high heat. When visibly hot, stir in the chopped onions and fry for about 5 minutes, or until soft and translucent. Stir in the garlic and ginger paste and fry over a medium–high heat for about 30 seconds to cook out the rawness.

Now stir in the ground almonds, coconut milk powder, curry powder or mixed powder, paprika and tandoori masala. Stir this around in the pan to coat the onions. Because of all the spices used, it will look quite dry in the pan. Stir in the chopped tomatoes, sugar and about 125ml (½ cup) of the unsalted chicken stock or water. Take off the heat and allow to cool a little, then blend the sauce until really smooth.

Pour the blended sauce back into the pan over a medium–high heat. It will look way too thick, so add the remaining chicken stock or water and bring to a rolling simmer. Add the cooked or raw chicken. If using raw chicken, you will need to ensure it is cooked through in the bubbling sauce, so add a drop more water or stock if necessary. Only stir if the sauce is sticking to the pan. If you are not using a non-stick pan, it should caramelize on the side of the pan. Scrape that back into the sauce for added flavour.

When the chicken is heated/cooked through, it's time to fine-tune this curry! If your sauce is too runny, cook it down. If it's too thick, stir in a little more water or stock until you are happy. Add the red food colouring, if using. Stir in the cream and add the lemon juice. Add the kasoori methi by rubbing it between your fingers into the sauce and season with salt to taste. Dust with the garam masala and garnish with the chopped coriander (cilantro).

★ MAKE IT EASIER ★

Although blending the sauce ingredients will achieve a sauce that is much more like you would find at most curry houses, it is not necessary. You could skip this step and simply carry on with the recipe. Only add the stock/water in small amounts though until you are happy with the consistency.

CHICKEN KORMA
SERVES 4

British Indian kormas must be right up there with the most popular curry-house curries on the menu. They can be buttery, creamy, sweet and delicious when made exactly to your taste preferences. Cooking from a book like this is what cooking to preference is all about, as when you're the chef, you can do exactly that. As I am someone who really likes spicy curries, I often cook this up but add a few finely chopped green chillies to the oil at the beginning of the recipe. Most people who enjoy a korma, however, like them sweet and creamy, and just how sweet and creamy you make yours is really down to you. So use this recipe as a guide but feel free to add more sugar or cream as you like. There are several different types of coconut used in this curry. Please see page 11 for definitions and substitutes.

PREP TIME: 10 MINS
COOKING TIME: 20 MINS

4 tbsp ghee or rapeseed (canola) oil
2.5cm (1in) cinnamon stick
3 green cardamom pods, bruised
2 medium onions, finely chopped
½ carrot, grated
1 tbsp garlic and ginger paste
2 tbsp unseasoned passata
2 tbsp ground almonds
2 tbsp coconut milk powder (see alternatives on page 11)
1½ tbsp sugar
250ml (1 cup) water or chicken stock
100g (3½oz) block coconut (see alternatives on page 11)
800g (1lb 12oz) raw chicken breast, cut into thin slices at an angle
1 tsp garam masala, shop-bought or homemade (see page 259)
125ml (½ cup) single (light) cream
Salt, to taste
½ tsp rose water (optional, but popular in a korma)
Coriander (cilantro), to garnish (optional)

Heat the ghee or oil in a large frying pan (skillet) over a medium–high heat. When bubbling hot, add the cinnamon stick and cardamom pods to infuse for 30 seconds.

Stir in the chopped onions and grated carrot and fry for about 5 minutes, or until the onions are soft and translucent. If time allows, you could cook these veggies even longer over a low heat. The slower cooking will bring out their natural sweetness. Just be sure not to brown them. Add the garlic and ginger paste and fry for a further 30 seconds. Stir in the passata, ground almonds, coconut milk powder, sugar and 125ml (½ cup) of water or chicken stock. Allow the sauce to cool a little and remove the cardamom pods and cinnamon stick. Blend until really smooth.

Pour the blended sauce back into the pan. The sauce will be a bit thick, so add another 125ml (½ cup) of water or chicken stock and bring to a simmer over a medium–high heat. Only stir if the sauce is obviously sticking to the pan. If you're not using a non-stick pan, the sauce should begin to caramelize on the side of the pan as it cooks. Scrape this back in for added flavour. Add the block coconut and simmer until it melts into the sauce. Then add the sliced chicken and continue cooking until the chicken is cooked through. If the sauce is too thick, add more water or stock. If you add too much, just cook it down to your desired consistency.

To finish, add the garam masala and cream and season with salt to taste. If using rose water, stir it in now but be careful as it is really strong. Taste, taste, taste! If you like your korma a little sweeter, you could add more sugar. More creamy? I think you've got the idea. Garnish with the chopped coriander (cilantro) to serve, if liked.

★ MAKE IT EASIER ★

Blending your sauce will give it a smooth consistency, as in the opposite photograph, but it is not necessary. You could skip this step and simply carry on with the recipe. Only add the stock/water in small amounts until you are happy with the thickness and the chicken is cooked through. Remember that you can continue to cook the sauce down to your preferred consistency.

CHICKEN PASANDA
SERVES 4

Pasanda curries go back to the Mogul empire, before chillies were introduced to India. At the time, only the best cuts of mutton were used and they were tenderized by pounding the meat before slowly simmering in a nutty and fruity but not spicy sauce. There are many different versions. One thing they all had in common was pounded-flat meat. That isn't usually the case at British curry houses. Any meat, veggies or paneer can be added, and it is often cut tikka-style or into thin slices. The British-style pasanda is perfect for kids and those who don't like spicy curries. It's similar to a mild korma but fruitier.

PREP TIME: 10 MINS
COOKING TIME: 20 MINS

4 tbsp rapeseed (canola) oil
2 medium onions, finely chopped
3 tbsp coconut milk powder (see alternatives on page 11)
3 tbsp ground almonds
2 tbsp sugar
200g (7oz) tinned (canned) chopped tomatoes
250ml (1 cup) chicken stock or water
125ml (½ cup) red wine
125ml (½ cup) coconut cream
About 30 sultanas or raisins
800g (1lb 12oz) chicken breasts or thighs, thinly sliced
125ml (½ cup) single (light) cream
1 tsp garam masala, shop-bought or homemade (see page 259)
4 tbsp toasted almond flakes (optional)

Heat the oil in a large frying pan (skillet) over a medium–high heat. When visibly hot, stir in the chopped onions. Fry for about 5 minutes, or until soft and translucent but not yet browning. Add the coconut milk powder, ground almonds and sugar and stir it all together to coat the onions. Then add the chopped tomatoes and about 125ml (½ cup) of water or chicken stock. Bring to a simmer and then take off the heat to cool a little.

Transfer to a blender and blend into a smooth sauce. Then pour the blended sauce back into the pan and bring to a simmer over a medium–high heat. The sauce will look a bit too thick, so add about 125ml (½ cup) of red wine and up to 125ml (½ cup) of water or chicken stock. Only stir the sauce if it is sticking to the pan. If not using a non-stick pan, the sauce should caramelize on the sides of the pan. Scrape that back into the sauce for extra flavour.

Add the coconut cream and sultanas/raisins and stir into the smooth sauce. Now add the raw chicken. You might want to add a little water or stock at this point if the sauce is looking too thick or cook it down if too runny. Cook the chicken through and then add the single (light) cream. Sprinkle with the garam masala and serve garnished with the toasted almond flakes, if using.

★ MAKE IT EASIER ★

If you want your sauce to be like that in a curry house, you need to blend it, but this isn't necessary for a good pasanda. This curry was made for centuries without blending the sauce, so just make it as described and leave the blending step out if you like. If doing this, be sure to add the stock/water in small amounts so that it doesn't become too thin. If it does, just cook it down to your preferred consistency.

CHICKEN DHANSAK
SERVES 4

When it comes to curry house-style chicken dhansak, there are two groups of fans: those who like pineapple in their curry and those who don't. You can make this chicken dhansak just as you like it. You could leave the pineapple chunks out, but I do recommend adding the pineapple juice. British Indian restaurant dhansak curries are usually medium spiced, but they can also be quite spicy so be sure to add the chilli powder for this curry to taste. You also need to add cooked red lentils, which you can do by following the instructions on the packet. If you want to do this all in one pan, cook the lentils first and then carry on with the recipe. This flavourful curry is delicious simply served over white rice.

PREP TIME: 10 MINS
COOKING TIME: 20 MINS

4 tbsp rapeseed (canola) oil
2 onions, finely chopped
2 tbsp garlic and ginger paste
1 tsp ground turmeric
1 tbsp curry powder or mixed powder, shop-bought or homemade (see page 259 or 258)
1 tbsp Kashmiri chilli powder (more or less to taste)
½ tsp each of paprika, cumin and coriander
200g (7oz) tinned (canned) chopped tomatoes
125ml (½ cup) water or chicken stock
125ml (½ cup) pineapple juice
700g (1lb 9oz) cooked chicken tikka (see page 158 or 203) or raw chicken
1 tbsp tamarind sauce (see page 256 or shop-bought)
180g (1 cup) cooked red split lentils (use packet instructions)
3 tinned (canned) pineapple rings, cut into small pieces
1 tbsp lemon juice
3 tbsp chopped coriander (cilantro), to garnish
Salt, to taste

Heat the oil in a frying pan (skillet) and fry the onions over a medium–high heat until soft and translucent. About 5 minutes should do the job. Add the garlic and ginger paste and stir it in. Fry for about 30 seconds and then add the ground spices, chopped tomatoes and 125ml (½ cup) of water or chicken stock and the pineapple juice.

Allow to cool a little and blend this sauce until smooth. Pour the blended sauce back into the pan and bring to a simmer over a medium–high heat. Add a little stock or water if it is looking too thick. Add the chicken and tamarind sauce. Bring the cooked chicken up to heat or if using raw chicken, simmer in the sauce until cooked through. You might need to add more stock to aid in cooking.

Continue simmering the sauce, only stirring if it is sticking to the pan. If you're not using a non-stick pan, the sauce should caramelize on the sides as it cooks over the medium–high heat. Scrape it back into the sauce for added flavour. If your sauce is too thick, add more stock or water; if too thin, cook it down a little. Now add the cooked lentils and stir them into the sauce.

To finish, add the chopped pineapple, if using, and the lemon juice and chopped coriander (cilantro). Season with salt to taste. Serve garnished with more chopped coriander.

★ MAKE IT EASIER ★

Although I highly recommend blending the sauce to make a dish that is very close to curry-house dhansak, it is not essential. You could leave the blending step out and just carry on with the recipe. It will still be delicious, I promise!

CHICKEN CHASNI
SERVES 4

Chicken chasni is the now famous bright-red curry from Glasgow. The colour is achieved with red food colouring that adds no real flavour, so you can leave it out, but if you want that red glow it's got to go in. If you want this to look really authentic, either use red tandoori chicken pieces or try the pan-fried tandoori chicken on page 203 using the red food colouring before starting to cook the curry. In the photo opposite I used red food colouring and pre-cooked tandoori chicken, but these extras are all up to you. If you use raw chicken, no food colouring and decide not to blend the sauce, you'll still be left with a delicious chasni!

PREP TIME: 10 MINS
COOKING TIME: 20 MINS

3 tbsp rapeseed (canola) oil or ghee
2 medium onions, finely chopped
2 tbsp garlic and ginger paste
1 tsp ground cumin
1 tsp sweet paprika
Pinch of ground turmeric
200g (7oz) chopped tomatoes
3 tbsp mango chutney
2 tbsp mint sauce
3 tbsp ketchup
3 tbsp fresh chopped coriander (cilantro)
200ml (¾ cup) water or chicken stock
1 tsp red food colouring powder (optional and more or less to your preferred colour)
800g (1lb 12oz) pre-cooked tandoori chicken tikka (see page 158 or 203) or raw chicken breast or thigh cut into bite-sized pieces
200ml (generous ¾ cup) single (light) cream
Salt, to taste
1–2 tbsp lime or lemon juice
½ tsp garam masala, shop-bought or homemade (see page 259)

Heat the oil in a large frying pan (skillet) over a medium heat. When visibly hot, stir in the finely chopped onions and fry gently for about 8 minutes. The idea here is to soften the onions without actually browning them to bring out their natural sweetness. Stir in the garlic and ginger paste and allow to sizzle for about 30 seconds, and then add the ground cumin, paprika and turmeric. Stir these spices into the onions and then add the chopped tomatoes.

Take off the heat to cool a little and then blend to a smooth sauce with the mango chutney, mint sauce, ketchup, 2 tablespoons of the chopped coriander (cilantro) and 70ml (¼ cup) of the water or chicken stock.

Turn up the heat to medium–high and pour the blended sauce back into the pan to bring to a rolling simmer. Stir in the red food colouring, if using, and add either pre-cooked tandoori chicken (see page 158 or 203) or raw chicken pieces. If using pre-cooked chicken, heat it through in the sauce adding a little water or stock. If cooking from raw, stir in the remaining water or stock and simmer until cooked through.

Continue simmering the sauce, only stirring if it is sticking to the pan. If you're not using a non-stick pan, the sauce should caramelize on the sides as it cooks over the medium–high heat. Scrape it back into the sauce for added flavour. This should be a nice, thick sauce, but you are in control, so simmer until you are happy with the consistency, adding more water/stock if too thick or simmering it down if too thin. When you are happy with the consistency, stir in the cream.

Season with salt and lemon or lime juice to taste and sprinkle the garam masala over the top. Garnish with the remaining tablespoon of chopped coriander to serve.

★ MAKE IT EASIER ★

For a sauce that is very close to a curry-house chasni, I highly recommend blending the sauce, but it is not essential. You could leave the blending step out and just carry on with the recipe. It will still be delicious.

CHICKEN PATHIA

SERVES 4

Pathia curries were developed in Britain to compete with the hugely popular sweet and sour chicken served at Chinese restaurants. Indian chefs saw people opting for the Chinese dish and came up with something that they knew would get people in the doors of their restaurants. This curry has both sweet and sour flavours, both of which can easily be adjusted to taste. Like chicken tikka masala and chasni curries, pathia curries are often bright red in colour which is done with food colouring. I haven't included it in this recipe, but go ahead and add it to personal preference at the end of cooking, if you want.

PREP TIME: 10 MINS
COOKING TIME: 20 MINS

3 tbsp rapeseed (canola) oil
2 large onions, finely chopped
2 tbsp garlic and ginger paste
2 tbsp curry powder or mixed powder
1 tsp Kashmiri chilli powder
4 tbsp unseasoned passata
200g (7oz) chopped tinned (canned) tomatoes
2 tbsp sugar
1 tbsp mango chutney
250ml (1 cup) water or unsalted chicken stock
800g (1lb 12oz) pre-cooked tandoori chicken tikka (see page 158 or 203) or raw chicken
1 tsp kasoori methi (dried fenugreek leaves)
½ tsp tamarind paste
Juice of 1–2 lemons
Salt, to taste
3 tbsp chopped coriander (cilantro)

Heat the oil in a pan over a medium–high heat and stir in the chopped onions. Fry for about 5 minutes, or until the onion is soft and translucent but not browning. Stir in the garlic and ginger paste and fry for a further 30 seconds. Transfer about 4 tablespoons of the fried onions to a plate and set aside. Add the ground spices, passata, chopped tomatoes, sugar and mango chutney. Add about 125ml (½ cup) of chicken stock or water and bring to a simmer. Take off the heat to cool a little and then blend to a smooth sauce.

Pour the blended sauce back into the pan along with the chopped onion you set aside and bring it back to a simmer. Stir in the chicken. If using pre-cooked tandoori chicken, heat it through. If using raw chicken, be sure to cook it completely. Remember that if the sauce is too thick, add more water or stock. If it's too thin then cook it down, only stirring if the sauce is sticking to the pan. If not using a non-stick pan, the sauce should caramelize on the sides of the pan over the medium–high heat. Scrape this back in for added flavour.

Once the chicken is cooked/heated through, add the kasoori methi (dried fenugreek leaves) by rubbing them between your fingers. Then stir in the tamarind paste and lemon juice. Try it and adjust the sweet and sour flavours to preference and add salt to taste. Garnish with the chopped coriander (cilantro).

★ MAKE IT EASIER ★

If you want a smooth pathia sauce like those served at restaurants, you need to blend the sauce. That, however is up to you. You could leave the blending step out and just carry on with the recipe. It will still be delicious.

CHICKEN JALFREZI

SERVES 4

Jalfrezi curries are meant to be simple. Originally, they were cooked during the British Raj to use up leftovers from big hunts. These are quick stir fries and the addition of a curry house-style base sauce, or in this case a blended masala, helps cook the curry much faster. Jalfrezis have always been made with leftover cooked meat, so this is a good one to use tandoori chicken tikka in, but you can add raw chicken if you'd rather.

PREP TIME: 15 MINS
COOKING TIME: 15 MINS

3 tbsp rapeseed (canola) oil
1 medium onion, finely chopped
2 tbsp garlic and ginger paste
1 tbsp curry powder or mixed powder, shop-bought or homemade (see page 259 or 258)
1 tsp each of paprika, Kashmiri chilli powder, ground cumin and ground coriander
125ml (½ cup) unseasoned passata
250ml (1 cup) water or chicken stock
1 tsp black mustard seeds
20 fresh or frozen curry leaves
1 onion, thinly sliced
2 green finger chillies, thinly sliced
½ each green, red and yellow (bell) peppers, thinly sliced
700g (1lb 9oz) tandoori chicken tikka, cooked chicken or raw chicken
3 tomatoes, quartered
1 tsp kasoori methi (dried fenugreek leaves)
3 tbsp coriander (cilantro), finely chopped
Salt, to taste
2 limes, quartered

Heat half of the oil in a pan over a medium–high heat. When visibly hot, stir in the chopped onion and fry for about 5 minutes, or until soft and translucent. Stir in the garlic and ginger paste and fry for another 30 seconds. Then add the ground spices and the passata. Bring to a simmer and then add 125ml (½ cup) of water or unsalted chicken stock. Take off the heat and allow to cool a little. Blend this sauce until smooth and set aside.

Wipe the pan clean – no need to make it spotless! Then add the remaining oil over a medium–high heat. Stir in the mustard seeds and when they begin to crackle, add the curry leaves. Fry for about 30 seconds until fragrant. Add the thinly sliced onion, chillies and (bell) peppers and fry until the vegetables are about 70% cooked through. Then add the chicken tikka or raw chicken. Note that if you are using raw chicken, you might need to add more liquid to help it cook through.

Stir in the blended sauce. It may be a bit too thick, so add more water or stock if needed. If it's too runny, just cook it down until you are happy with the consistency. Add the tomatoes and push them right into the simmering sauce.

Once you are happy with how it all looks, sprinkle in the kasoori methi by rubbing it between your fingers. Then add the chopped coriander (cilantro) and season with salt to taste.

Serve with the quartered limes, which you can squeeze and drizzle over the curry to taste at the table.

★ MAKE IT EASIER ★

Curry-house jalfrezi curries really benefit from blending the sauce as described above. The smooth sauce together with those crunchy sliced vegetables is what takes them from the simple stir fry they were back in the British Raj to the curry-house favourite they are today. That said, you might decide to leave the blending out and go for that simple stir fry. To do so, you really can just wing it. Start by infusing the mustard seeds into the oil before adding the curry leaves. Then add the chopped onions and fry for about 5 minutes before adding the garlic and ginger paste and passata. Add the spices, sliced vegetables and chicken, and then gradually add stock or water to make the sauce. Carry on with the recipe as above.

CHICKEN CHILLI GARLIC
SERVES 4

If you like garlic and chillies, you're going to love this curry. It has a lot of both! Not only that, the garlic is prepared in three ways, which gives it different textures and flavours.

PREP TIME: 10 MINS
COOKING TIME: 20 MINS

4 tbsp rapeseed (canola) oil
15 garlic cloves, cut into thin slivers
3 medium onions, finely chopped
½ tsp salt
2 tbsp garlic and ginger paste
2 tsp Kashmiri chilli powder
1 tbsp curry powder or mixed powder, shop-bought or homemade (see page 259 or 258)
½ tsp each of ground coriander, cumin and paprika
2 tbsp tandoori masala, shop-bought or homemade (see page 260)
200g (7oz) tinned (canned) chopped tomatoes
250ml (1 cup) water or chicken stock
800g (1lb 12oz) pre-cooked tandoori chicken tikka (see page 158 or 203) or raw chicken breast or thigh cut into bite-sized pieces
Salt, to taste
1 tsp kasoori methi (dried fenugreek leaves)
Dried garlic flakes, to garnish (optional)
More thinly sliced green chillies, to garnish (optional)
Chopped coriander (cilantro), to garnish (optional)

Pour the oil into a frying pan (skillet) over a medium–high heat and stir in the garlic slivers. Fry, being very careful not to burn the garlic, until it is a light golden brown. Transfer to a plate with a slotted spoon. Now pour the finely chopped onions into the pan and add the salt to help release moisture. Fry for about 7 minutes, or until the onions are soft and golden brown. Transfer approximately one third of the chopped onions to the plate with the fried garlic. Returning to the pan, stir in the garlic and ginger paste and fry for about 30 seconds and then add the ground spices and chopped tomatoes.

Stir in about 125ml (½ cup) of water or chicken stock and bring to a simmer. Take off the heat and allow to cool a little. Blend the cooled sauce until smooth. Pour this thick sauce into the pan over a medium–high heat. It will be too thick, so add about 125ml (½ cup) of water or chicken stock and bring to a simmer. If the sauce is still looking too thick, add a little more stock or water. If it is too runny, just cook it down.

Add the cooked garlic slivers and onion to the sauce and stir them in. Now add either cooked chicken tikka or raw chicken. If using raw chicken, you may need to add a drop more water or stock and simmer until it cooks through. Continue simmering until you are happy with the consistency of the sauce.

To finish, taste it and add salt if needed. Sprinkle in the kasoori methi (dried fenugreek leaves) by rubbing them between your fingers. Serve topped with dried garlic flakes, some fresh chopped green chillies and/or chopped coriander (cilantro), if you like.

★ MAKE IT EASIER ★
Although I highly recommend blending the sauce, as described above, it is optional. If you prefer, you can simply fry the garlic slivers and transfer them to a side plate, then carry on with the recipe, leaving out the blending. If you add too much stock, just cook it down. If your curry is too dry, add more stock or water.

CHICKEN REZALA
SERVES 4

Chicken rezala is a lot like chicken tikka masala, though it is a bit spicier and there are fewer ingredients. This is probably my family's favourite curry house-style curry, so we make it often. Although adding raw chicken to cook in the sauce will work, I think rezalas definitely benefit from using tandoori-style chicken (see page 158 or 203). Please don't let that stop you from making this delicious curry though! Add raw chicken if more convenient and cook it through. Your rezala will be amazing.

PREP TIME: 15 MINS
COOKING TIME: 15 MINS

3 tbsp rapeseed (canola) oil or ghee
3–4 green finger chillies, finely chopped
3 onions, finely chopped
2 tbsp garlic and ginger paste
4 tbsp unseasoned passata
2 tbsp mixed powder or curry powder, shop-bought or homemade (see pages 258 or 259)
1 tsp Kashmiri chilli powder (more or less to taste)
200g (7oz) tinned (canned) chopped tomatoes
250ml (1 cup) water or chicken stock
800g (1lb 12oz) pre-cooked tandoori chicken tikka (see page 158 or 203) or raw chicken breast or thigh, cut into bite-sized pieces
125ml (½ cup) single (light) cream
½ tsp garam masala, shop-bought or homemade (see page 259)
2 tbsp coriander (cilantro), finely chopped
1–2 tbsp butter
Salt, to taste

Heat the oil in a pan over a medium–high heat. When visibly hot, stir in the chopped chillies and fry for about a minute. Transfer the chillies to a plate with a slotted spoon and set aside. Now add the chopped onions to the pan and fry for about 5 minutes, or until soft and translucent. Transfer approximately one third of the chopped onions to the plate with the chillies.

Now add the garlic and ginger paste to the remaining onions in the pan and fry for a further 30 seconds. Then stir in the passata along with the ground spices. Stir this really well into the onion mixture and then add the chopped tomatoes and 125ml (½ cup) of chicken stock or water. Allow to cool a little and then blend until smooth.

Pour the blended sauce back into the pan. It will look thick, so add some more water or chicken stock and then stir the cooked chopped onion and chillies back in. Bring to a simmer. If you are not using a non-stick pan, the sauce should caramelize on the sides of the pan. Scrape this back in, but only stir the sauce if it is obviously sticking to the pan.

Add the chicken and heat/cook it through. When your sauce has cooked down to how you like it, add the cream and stir it in. Then add the garam masala and the coriander (cilantro). Top it all with the butter and continue cooking until the butter melts into the sauce. Season with salt to taste before serving.

★ MAKE IT EASIER ★
Although I highly recommend blending the sauce as described above, it is optional. If not blending, there is no need to transfer the fried chillies and onion to a side plate. Add the stock/water in small amounts until the meat is cooked/heated through and you are happy with the consistency of the sauce.

CHICKEN DOPIAZA

SERVES 4

'Do' means two, and 'piaza' means onions. So dopiaza curries are cooked with onions in two ways. Every curry house-style dopiaza recipe I've ever tried calls for onions cooked in at least three ways, so the name doesn't really fit but that's just the way it is. All I know is that this is one of the most popular curries in the UK and India and I love it. The garnish is crispy fried onions, which you could do yourself. Just fry some onions in oil until crispy brown. Or you could purchase fried crispy onions, which do the job just fine.

PREP TIME: 10 MINS
COOKING TIME: 20 MINS

4 tbsp rapeseed (canola) oil
1 medium onion, quartered and broken up into individual petals
2 onions, finely chopped
3 tbsp garlic and ginger paste
1 tbsp curry powder or mixed powder, shop-bought or homemade (see page 258 or 259)
2 tsp ground cumin
1 tsp ground coriander
1 tsp paprika
1 tsp garam masala, shop-bought or homemade (see page 259)
1–2 tsp Kashmiri chilli powder
200g (7oz) chopped tinned (canned) tomatoes
375ml (1½ cups) water or chicken stock
1 tsp cumin seeds
1 tsp coriander seeds, roughly chopped
4 cardamom pods, bruised
2–4 green finger chillies, finely chopped
800g (1lb 12oz) cooked tandoori chicken (see page 158 or 203), leftover cooked chicken or raw chicken cut into bite-sized pieces.
2 tbsp natural yoghurt

TO SERVE
½ tsp garam masala, shop-bought or homemade (see page 259)
6 tbsp coriander (cilantro), finely chopped
Crispy fried onions

Heat 1 tablespoon of the oil in a large frying pan (skillet) over a medium–high heat. Place the onion petals in the pan and fry, turning regularly to char them in places. Transfer to a plate and set aside. Now add 2 tablespoons of the oil to the pan over a medium–high heat and add the chopped onions. Fry for about 10 minutes, stirring often until soft and a deep golden brown in colour. Stir in the garlic and ginger paste and fry for another 30 seconds. Then add the ground spices and stir again to coat the onions before pouring in the chopped tomatoes. Add 125ml (½ cup) of unsalted chicken stock or water and allow to cool a little.

Transfer the cooled onion mixture to a blender and blend until smooth. Wipe your pan clean with a paper towel. No need to make it spotless! Pour in the remaining tablespoon of oil and stir in the cumin seeds, coriander seeds, cardamom pods and green chillies to infuse for about 30 seconds. Now pour in the blended sauce. It will look too thick, so add about 250ml (1 cup) of chicken stock or water. Bring this to a rolling simmer and then add the cooked or raw chicken. You just need to heat the cooked chicken. If using raw chicken, be sure to cook it through. Only stir if the sauce is sticking to the pan. If you are not using a non-stick pan, the sauce should caramelize on the sides as it cooks. Stir this back into the sauce for more flavour.

Now let's finish this masterpiece of a curry off. If it's looking too thick, add more water or stock. If it is too thin, just cook it down to your liking. Stir in the yoghurt a tablespoon at a time and then add the fried onion petals. Season with salt to taste and sprinkle with the garam masala. Serve garnished with the chopped coriander and crispy fried onions.

★ **MAKE IT EASIER** ★
The blending of the sauce is recommended but not essential. To make this curry without blending the sauce, start at the beginning, frying the onion petals. Then transfer them to a plate and add the remaining oil. Infuse the cumin seeds, coriander seeds, cardamom pods and chillies in the oil as described and then carry on with the recipe. Only add the stock in small amounts until the chicken is cooked/heated through and you are happy with the consistency of the sauce. Add more stock/water if it's too dry, or cook it down if it's too watery.

CHICKEN VINDALOO
SERVES 4

Vindaloo just like you get at your local curry house but with no base sauce! This is one I make often and I think you might just like it better than my previous curry house-style vindaloo recipes. Vindaloos are spicy hot, too hot for some. That said, this is your creation so feel free to use fewer chillies and/or chilli powder.

PREP TIME: 10 MINS
COOKING TIME: 20 MINS

FOR THE SAUCE
2 tbsp rapeseed (canola) oil
2 onions, finely chopped
2 tbsp garlic and ginger paste
1 tsp ground turmeric
2 tbsp Kashmiri chilli powder
1 tbsp ground cumin
1 tbsp ground coriander
1 tsp paprika
1 tsp garam masala, shop-bought or homemade (see page 259)
1 tsp ground black pepper
1 tbsp Madras curry powder
1 tsp sugar (more or less to taste)
200g (7oz) tinned (canned) chopped tomatoes
375ml (1½ cups) water or unsalted chicken stock

FOR THE CURRY
2 tbsp rapeseed (canola) oil
6 green cardamom pods
2 star anise
1 Indian bay leaf
2 green finger chillies, finely chopped
2 scotch bonnet chillies, finely chopped
800g (1lb 12oz) pre-cooked tandoori chicken tikka or raw chicken
1 potato, peeled and cut into bite-sized pieces and boiled until cooked through (optional)
2 tbsp white distilled vinegar
1 tsp kasoori methi (dried fenugreek leaves)
Salt, to taste
3 tbsp coriander (cilantro), finely chopped
2 quartered limes, to serve

To make the sauce, heat the oil in a large frying pan (skillet) or karahi over a medium–high heat. When the oil begins to shimmer, stir in the chopped onions and fry for about 7 minutes, or until soft and light golden brown in colour. Stir in the garlic and ginger paste and fry for about 30 seconds and then add the ground spices. Move the spices around in the pan until the onions are nicely coated and then add the sugar and chopped tomatoes. Bring to a bubbling simmer and then add 125ml (½ cup) of water or chicken stock. Allow to cool a little and then blend until smooth.

Wipe the pan clean with a paper towel (no need to make it sparkly clean). Pour in the oil and place over a medium–high heat. Add the cardamom pods, star anise and Indian bay leaf, if using, and allow these spices to infuse into the oil for about 40 seconds. Then stir in the chopped chillies and fry for another 30 seconds. Pour in the blended sauce. At this stage, it will be a bit too thick. Pour in about 250ml (1 cup) water or chicken stock and bring to a simmer, only stirring if the sauce is sticking to the pan. If you are not using a non-stick pan, the sauce should begin to caramelize to the sides of the pan. When this happens, scrape it back into the sauce for additional flavour. Stir in the chicken and potato, if using, and continue simmering until they are heated through and the sauce is as you like it. If adding raw chicken, you might need to add a little more water or stock to help it cook. Remember that if your sauce is too runny, just cook it down. If it's too thick, add more water or stock.

When you are happy with how your vindaloo is looking, stir in the vinegar and add the kasoori methi by rubbing it between your fingers. Check for seasoning and add salt to taste. You can also add more sugar, chillies and/or chilli powder at this stage, again to taste. Serve hot, topped with chopped coriander (cilantro) and the quartered limes for additional sour flavour.

★ MAKE IT EASIER ★
Blending the sauce will get you a curry house-style vindaloo, but this step is optional. If you don't want to blend your sauce, infuse the cardamom pods, star anise and bay leaf in the oil first. Then add the chopped onions and continue with the curry recipe, omitting the blending step.

BEEF MADRAS
SERVES 4

You could use any protein in this madras. This time I used pre-cooked beef rump, fried and then stewed in water until tender. The idea is to get the meat super tender and, at the same time, produce a stock that adds so much more flavour than simply adding water to the curry. Madras curries are spicy, so I have used quite a lot of chilli powder and chillies. Reduce the amounts if you want to make this less spicy.

PREP TIME: 10 MINS
COOKING TIME: 30 MINS

FOR THE MEAT

2 tbsp rapeseed (canola) oil
700g (1lb 9oz) rump steak or stewing
  steak, cut into bite-sized pieces
2.5cm (1in) cinnamon stick
3 green cardamom pods, bruised
2 cloves
½ tsp ground cumin
½ tsp ground coriander
1 tsp paprika
1 onion, peeled and quartered
750ml (3 cups) water

FOR THE CURRY

4 tbsp rapeseed (canola) oil
2 medium onions, finely chopped
2 tbsp garlic and ginger paste
½ tsp ground turmeric
2 tbsp ground cumin
2 tsp ground coriander
½ tsp garam masala, shop-bought
  or homemade (see page 259)
  (optional)
1 tbsp Madras curry powder
1–2 tbsp Kashmiri chilli powder
1 tsp paprika
200g (7oz) tinned (canned) chopped
  tomatoes
1 tbsp smooth mango chutney, or to
  taste
2 dry Kashmiri chillies (optional)
Seeds from 2 green cardamom pods
2–4 green finger chillies, finely
  chopped
½ tsp kasoori methi (dried fenugreek
  leaves)
Salt, to taste
Juice of ½ lime
3 tbsp fresh coriander (cilantro),
  finely chopped

To cook the meat, brown it in a large frying pan (skillet) or karahi in the oil over a medium–high heat. This should only take a couple of minutes. Stir in the spices and quartered onion and then cover with 750ml (3 cups) of water. Allow to simmer until the meat is good and tender. This should take about 20 minutes, but don't rush it – the meat is ready when it's tender. When cooked to your liking, pour it through a sieve into a bowl, retaining the meat and stock but discarding the onion pieces and whole spices. Keep warm. The beef stock will taste amazing in this curry!

To make the curry, heat the same pan back up over a medium–high heat and add 2 tablespoons of oil. Stir in the chopped onions and fry for about 8 minutes, or until soft and translucent and just beginning to turn a light golden brown. Stir in the garlic and ginger paste and fry for a further 30 seconds. Then add the ground spices and stir them into the onion mixture. Add the chopped tomatoes and 125ml (½ cup) of the reserved beef stock from cooking the meat and bring to a simmer. Allow to cool a little and add the mango chutney. Blend until smooth.

Wipe your pan clean with a paper towel. It doesn't need to be spotless! Add 2 tablespoons of oil over a medium–high heat. When visibly hot, stir in the dried Kashmiri chillies and cardamom seeds and let these flavours infuse into the oil for about 30 seconds. Stir in the chopped chillies and fry for a further 30 seconds, then pour the blended sauce into the pan. At this stage, the sauce will be too thick. Add about 250ml (1 cup) more of the stock or water to thin it out a little and add the cooked beef. Bring to a rolling simmer, only stirring if the sauce is obviously sticking to the pan. If you aren't using a non-stick pan, the sauce should caramelize around the edges. Scrape this back into the sauce for more flavour.

Once your pre-cooked meat is heated through, it's time to finish this off. If your curry is too dry, add more water or stock. If it is too saucy, cook it down until you are happy with the consistency.

Sprinkle the kasoori methi (dried fenugreek leaves) into the sauce by rubbing it between your fingers. Then season with salt to taste, squeeze in the lime juice and garnish with coriander (cilantro) to serve.

★ MAKE IT EASIER ★

Blending the sauce will get you a curry house-style madras, but this step is optional. If you don't want to blend your sauce, infuse the dried chillies, cardamom seeds and fresh chillies in the oil first. Then add the finely chopped onions and continue with the curry recipe, omitting the blending step.

LAMB ACHARI
SERVES 4

In Hindi, achar means 'pickle', so lamb achari is a curry made with pickling spices such as panch poran and dried chillies. Mango chutney is added for sweetness and lime pickle is added to give the curry a well-rounded sweet-and-sour flavour. Panch poran is available prepared at Asian grocers, but you could just mix equal amounts of whole cumin seeds, fenugreek seeds, black mustard seeds, fennel seeds and nigella seeds (also known as 'black onion seeds', though they aren't actually onion seeds).

PREP TIME: 10 MINS
COOKING TIME: 35 MINS

FOR THE MEAT
1 tbsp rapeseed (canola) oil
700g (1lb 9oz) lamb leg meat, cut into
  bite-sized pieces
2.5cm (1in) cinnamon stick
3 green cardamom pods, bruised
2 cloves
½ tsp ground cumin
½ tsp ground coriander
1 tsp paprika
1 onion, peeled and quartered
750ml (3 cups) water

FOR THE CURRY
4 tbsp rapeseed (canola) oil
2 medium onions, finely chopped
2 tbsp garlic and ginger paste
2 green finger chillies, finely chopped
2 tbsp mixed powder or curry powder
1 tsp ground coriander
1 tsp Kashmiri chilli powder
200g (7oz) tinned (canned) chopped
  tomatoes
1 tbsp panch poran
2 dried Kashmiri chillies
1 onion, thinly sliced
2 tbsp lime pickle or 1 tbsp each of
  lime pickle and mango chutney
4 tbsp natural yoghurt
1 tsp garam masala, shop-bought or
  homemade (see page 259)
1 tsp kasoori methi (dried fenugreek
  leaves)
Salt, to taste
Juice of 1 lime or lemon
3 tbsp coriander (cilantro), finely
  chopped

To cook the meat, brown it in a large frying pan (skillet) or karahi in the oil over a medium–high heat. This should only take a couple of minutes. Stir in the spices and quartered onion and then cover with 750ml (3 cups) of water. Allow to simmer until the meat is good and tender. This should take about 20 minutes, but it's ready when it's tender so don't rush this. When cooked to your liking, pour this through a sieve into a bowl, retaining the meat and stock but discarding the onion pieces and whole spices. Keep warm.

Place your pan back on the hob over a medium–high heat and add 2 tablespoons of the oil. When hot, stir in the chopped onions. Fry for about 7 minutes, or until just beginning to brown and then stir in the garlic and ginger paste and the chopped chillies to fry for 30 seconds. Stir in the ground spices followed by the chopped tomatoes. Add about 125ml (½ cup) of the retained meat stock or water and bring to a simmer. Then allow to cool a little and blend until smooth.

Wipe your pan clean – no need to make it spotless – and add the remaining oil. Stir in the panch poran and dried chillies and temper these spices in the oil for about 30 seconds. Add the thinly sliced onion and fry for 5 minutes, or until it is soft and translucent. Pour the blended sauce into the pan. It will look quite thick, so thin it out with about 125ml (½ cup) of the meat stock or water. Bring to a simmer.

Stir in the cooked lamb and then add the lime pickle and mango chutney. Remember you can adjust the thickness of the sauce by adding more stock or cooking it down to your liking. Whisk in the yoghurt one tablespoon at a time, and then add the garam masala and the kasoori methi (dried fenugreek leaves) by rubbing the leaves between your fingers into the sauce. Season with salt to taste and squeeze in the lemon or lime juice. Garnish with the fresh coriander (cilantro) to serve.

NOTE
Any leftover meat stock can be frozen for up to six months to use in future curries or other recipes where meat stock is called for.

★ MAKE IT EASIER ★
For a curry house-style lamb achari you need to blend the sauce, but this step is optional. If not blending, temper the panch poran and dried chillies in oil first for about 30 seconds. Then add the thinly sliced and finely chopped onions and carry on with the sauce recipe as instructed, simply omitting the blending step.

LAMB BHUNA
SERVES 4

Bhunas are thick and therefore perfect for serving with naans or chapattis to soak up all that delicious sauce. To get the bhuna sauce consistency right, you will need to cook it down until the sauce is adhering to the meat. Unlike the other red meat curry-house curries in this book, where the meat is simmered until tender, in this recipe you use a classic bhuna braising technique to cook the meat. This cooking method could be applied to the other red meat curries, too. The advantage of cooking the meat by simmering, as in the other red meat curry recipes, is that you get a lot of nice stock that can be used in other curries. Cooking the meat 'bhuna' style like this, however, means one less step in the cooking process.

PREP TIME: 15 MINS
COOKING TIME: 30 MINS

4 tbsp ghee or rapeseed (canola) oil
1 large onion, finely chopped
2 tbsp garlic and ginger paste
200g (7oz) tinned (canned) chopped
    tomatoes
125ml (½ cup) unsalted beef or lamb
    stock or water
1 cinnamon stick
1 medium onion, very thinly sliced
700g (1lb 9oz) lamb, cut into bite-
    sized pieces
70ml (¼ cup) unseasoned passata
2 green finger chillies, finely chopped
2 tbsp coriander (cilantro) stems,
    finely chopped
1 tbsp curry powder or mixed powder
2 tbsp tandoori masala, shop-bought
    or homemade (see page 260)
½ tsp ground turmeric
1 tsp each of paprika, cumin and
    ground coriander
1 tbsp tamarind paste
Juice of 1 lemon
1 tsp kasoori methi (dried fenugreek
    leaves)
Salt, to taste
Sliced red chillies, to garnish

Heat half of the ghee/oil in a large frying pan (skillet). When visibly hot, stir in the chopped onion and fry until soft and translucent. This should take about 5 minutes. Now add the garlic and ginger paste and fry for a further 30 seconds before adding the chopped tomatoes and 125ml (½ cup) of water or unsalted beef/lamb stock. Bring to a simmer and then take off the heat to cool a little. Blend the cooled sauce until smooth and set aside.

Wipe your pan clean. No need to make it spotless! Add the remaining ghee/oil and add the cinnamon stick and the very thinly sliced onion. Fry for about 7 minutes, or until the onion is turning a golden brown. Add the lamb and brown it with the onion for a couple of minutes. Then add the passata, chopped chillies and coriander (cilantro) stems along with the ground spices. Pour in just enough water to cover and simmer until the water has almost evaporated. Check the meat. If it is still tough, add a little more water and continue cooking until tender. This is a dry curry, so be careful not to add too much water. Just enough!

Pour in half of the blended sauce and stir it in. Simmer a little longer until the sauce is really thick and clinging to the meat. Add the remaining sauce and continue cooking until you are happy with the consistency, only stirring if the sauce is sticking to the pan. If you are not using a non-stick pan, the sauce should caramelize on the sides. Scrape this back in for added flavour.

Stir in the tamarind paste and lemon juice. Add the kasoori methi (dried fenugreek leaves) by rubbing it between your fingers, season with salt to taste and top with sliced red chillies to serve.

★ MAKE IT EASIER ★

I highly recommend blending the sauce to give it a texture that is closer to a curry house-style bhuna, but this step is optional. You could just add all the oil/ghee at the beginning with the cinnamon stick and then carry on with the recipe, leaving the blending step out.

LAMB KEEMA SHIMLA MIRCH
SERVES 4

If you have my other books that feature lamb keema, you'll notice that this version is simplified. The keema meat is usually prepared ahead of service at restaurants, so that it is readily available to add to a keema curry when ordered. If you have one of those books, you could use the pre-cooked keema in this recipe – but this time, I have used a more authentic and traditional keema which will get you fantastic results in a lot less time.

PREP TIME: 15 MINS
COOKING TIME: 25 MINS

FOR THE KEEMA
600g (1lb 5oz) minced (ground) lamb
1 onion, finely chopped
1 tsp salt
500ml (2 cups) water
1 tbsp rapeseed (canola) oil

FOR THE CURRY
3 tbsp rapeseed (canola) oil
2 medium onions, finely chopped
2 tbsp garlic and ginger paste
1–2 tbsp mixed powder or curry powder, shop-bought or homemade (see page 258 or 259)
1 tsp ground cumin
1 tsp ground coriander
2 tsp Kashmiri chilli powder
½ tsp ground turmeric
200g (7oz) tinned (canned) chopped tomatoes
250ml (1 cup) water or meat stock
1 medium red onion, roughly chopped
1–2 green finger chillies, finely chopped
2 large green (bell) peppers, roughly chopped
200ml (generous ¾ cup) thick coconut milk
2 medium tomatoes, quartered

TO GARNISH
5cm (2in) piece of ginger, peeled and julienned
4 spring onions (scallions), roughly chopped
5 tbsp coriander (cilantro), finely chopped

Place the minced (ground) lamb, finely chopped onion and salt in a mixing bowl and pour in the water. Mix well, breaking the meat apart as best you can. It should look like a meaty porridge. Add the oil to a frying pan (skillet) over a medium–high heat. Simmer the lamb in the pan, stirring regularly and breaking apart any big chunks. Continue cooking until most of the water has evaporated and the meat has browned. This could take about 10 minutes, so continue until the meat is cooked. It's difficult to overcook keema. Transfer the cooked keema to a bowl and set aside.

Wipe your pan clean – no need to make it spotless. Pour in 2 tablespoons of the oil and heat over a medium–high heat. Add the chopped onions and fry for about 5 minutes, or until soft and translucent. Then stir in the garlic and ginger paste and continue frying for 30 seconds. Stir in the ground spices and the chopped tomatoes along with 125ml (½ cup) of water or stock. Bring to a simmer and then take off the heat and allow to cool a little. Blend all the contents of the pan into a smooth sauce.

Give the pan another wipe clean, pour the remaining oil into the pan and add the chopped onion, chillies and (bell) peppers. Fry for about 3 minutes, stirring regularly to soften. Then pour in the blended sauce. It will look quite thick, so add about 125ml (½ cup) of water or stock and bring it all to a simmer, only stirring if the sauce is obviously sticking to the pan. If you are not using a non-stick pan, the sauce should caramelize on the sides of the pan. If it does, scrape that back into the sauce for additional flavour. Stir in the cooked keema and continue cooking the sauce, adding more liquid if too thick or cooking it down if too thin. Then add the thick coconut milk and continue simmering until you are happy with the consistency. Add the quartered tomatoes by pushing them right into the sauce and meat to heat through.

Season with salt to taste and garnish with the julienned ginger, spring onions (scallions) and chopped coriander (cilantro).

★ MAKE IT EASIER ★
This recipe benefits greatly from the blended sauce but you could leave the blending out if you prefer. Stir all the ingredients into the cooked keema and simmer until you are happy with the consistency of the sauce.

LAMB SAAG

SERVES 4

You could use the protein of your choice with this curry-house classic. Here I have used lamb and pre-cooked it, using the stock to flavour the curry. Other popular options are tandoori chicken (see page 203) and paneer, which would cut the cooking time in half. I recommend serving this with white rice, naans and/or chapattis.

PREP TIME: 15 MINS
COOKING TIME: 35 MINS

FOR THE MEAT
1 tbsp rapeseed (canola) oil
700g (1lb 9oz) lamb leg meat, cut into
    bite-sized pieces
2.5cm (1in) cinnamon stick
3 green cardamom pods, bruised
2 cloves
½ tsp ground cumin
½ tsp ground coriander
1 tsp paprika
1 onion, peeled and quartered
750ml (3 cups) water

FOR THE CURRY
4 tbsp ghee or rapeseed (canola) oil
2 onions, finely chopped
2 garlic cloves, roughly chopped
3 tbsp garlic and ginger paste
1 generous tbsp ground coriander
1 tbsp Madras curry powder or mixed
    powder
1 tbsp garam masala, shop-bought or
    homemade (see page 259)
1 tsp paprika
1 tsp Kashmiri chilli powder (more or
    less to taste)
200g (7oz) tinned (canned) chopped
    tomatoes
225g (8oz) baby spinach leaves,
    washed and roughly chopped
3–6 finger chillies
60g (2oz) fresh coriander (cilantro),
    roughly chopped
2 tbsp natural yoghurt
Salt, to taste
Juice of 1 lemon

To cook the meat, brown it in a large frying pan (skillet) or karahi in the oil over a medium–high heat. This should only take a couple of minutes. Stir in the spices and the quartered onion, then cover with 750ml (3 cups) of water. Allow to simmer until the meat is tender. This should take about 20 minutes but it's ready when it's tender, so don't rush this. When cooked to your liking, pour through a sieve into a bowl, retaining the meat and stock but discarding the onion pieces and whole spices. Keep warm.

Wipe your pan clean and add the ghee or oil over a medium–high heat. When bubbling hot, stir in the chopped onions and fry for about 5 minutes, or until soft and translucent. Now add the chopped garlic and garlic and ginger paste and stir it into the onions to fry for another 40 seconds. Stir in the ground coriander, curry powder, 2 teaspoons of the garam masala, the paprika and chilli powder. Using a large spoon, stir this into the onion mixture and then add the chopped tomatoes and 125ml (½ cup) of the stock from the cooked lamb (or water). Take off the heat and allow to cool a little before blending until smooth.

Pour the blended onion sauce into the pan over a medium–high heat. The sauce will be quite thick, so stir in about 250ml (1 cup) of the cooking stock from the lamb or water and bring to a simmer, only stirring if the sauce is sticking to the pan. If you are not using a non-stick pan, the sauce will begin to caramelize around the edges. Be sure to scrape this back in for additional flavour.

Add the cooked lamb pieces. If the sauce is looking too thick, add more stock or water; if too thin, cook it down. Meanwhile, place the spinach, green chillies and coriander (cilantro) in a food processor or blender and blend to a smooth paste, using just enough water to do so. The spinach purée should be quite thick. Set aside.

When the sauce is looking like you would expect a good curry house-style saag sauce to look, stir in the spinach purée and swirl it around until you have a green sauce. Be sure to add more stock or water if it is looking too thick. To finish, add the yoghurt one tablespoon at a time, stirring it into the sauce as you do. Season with salt to taste and squeeze in the lemon juice. Sprinkle over the remaining garam masala and serve.

NOTE
Any leftover meat stock can be frozen for up to six months to use in future curries or other recipes where meat stock is called for.

★ MAKE IT EASIER ★
Blending the sauce will achieve a smooth sauce like you get at curry houses, but it is optional. For that matter, you don't have to blend the spinach either. The curry will look different to the photograph opposite but it will still be delicious.

LAMB ROGAN JOSH
SERVES 4

You won't be able to tell the difference between this new version of my lamb rogan josh and the curry-house version with base sauce in my earlier books. Rogan josh is quite mild and gets its red colouring from the paprika. The flavour of the stock – made by simmering the lamb – gives the dish a deeper flavour that is closer to the classic Indian rogan josh than most quickly made curry-house versions. This rogan josh, however, can be made with the protein of your choice. Use raw chicken or paneer and you can cook this even faster.

PREP TIME: 15 MINS
COOKING TIME: 25 MINS

FOR THE MEAT
1 tbsp rapeseed (canola) oil
700g (1lb 9oz) lamb leg meat, cut into bite-sized pieces
2.5cm (1in) cinnamon stick
3 green cardamom pods, bruised
2 cloves
½ tsp ground cumin
½ tsp ground coriander
1 tsp paprika
1 onion, peeled and quartered
750ml (3 cups) water

FOR THE CURRY
4 tbsp rapeseed (canola) oil
2 onions, finely chopped
2 tbsp garlic and ginger paste
2½ tbsp paprika
1 tsp Kashmiri chilli powder
1½ tbsp mixed powder or Madras curry powder (see page 258 or 259 or shop-bought)
½ tsp each of ground cumin and ground coriander
8 cashews
200g (7oz) tinned (canned) chopped tomatoes
2 tomatoes, quartered
3 tbsp natural yoghurt
1 tsp kasoori methi (dried fenugreek leaves)
1 tsp garam masala, shop-bought or homemade (see page 259)
3 tbsp fresh coriander (cilantro), finely chopped
Salt, to taste
Chopped red onion, to garnish

To cook the meat, brown it in a large frying pan (skillet) or karahi in the oil over a medium–high heat. This should only take a couple of minutes. Stir in the spices and quartered onion and then cover with 750ml (3 cups) of water. Allow to simmer until the meat is good and tender. This should take about 20 minutes but it's ready when it's tender, so don't rush this. When cooked to your liking, pour it through a sieve into a bowl, retaining the meat and stock but discarding the onion pieces and whole spices. Keep warm.

Now wipe the pan clean – no need to make it spotless. Heat the oil for the curry in the pan over a medium–high heat. When visibly hot, add the chopped onions and fry for about 7 minutes, or until soft and just beginning to brown. Add the garlic and ginger paste and fry for a further 30 seconds, and then add the paprika, chilli powder, curry powder, ground cumin and coriander and the cashews. Stir this into the onion mixture to coat and then stir in the chopped tomatoes. Pour in 125ml (½ cup) of the stock from cooking the lamb (or water) and allow to cool slightly.

Blend this sauce until smooth. Pour it all back into the pan over a medium–high heat and bring to a simmer. It will look too thick at this point, so stir in about 250ml (1 cup) of lamb stock or water. If the sauce is looking too thin, cook it down. If too dry, add more water or stock. Stir in the cooked lamb and heat through.

To finish, push the quartered tomatoes right into the hot sauce and stir the yoghurt into the sauce one tablespoon at a time. Sprinkle in the kasoori methi (dried fenugreek leaves) by rubbing them between your fingers. Dust the top with garam masala. Season with salt to taste and garnish with chopped coriander (cilantro) and chopped red onions to serve.

NOTE
Any leftover meat stock can be frozen for up to six months to use in future curries or other recipes where meat stock is called for.

★ MAKE IT EASIER ★
Blending the sauce will achieve a smooth sauce like you get at curry houses, but it is optional. You could just cook the recipe without blending.

CURRIES, STEWS AND SAUCE-BASED DISHES

In this chapter, you'll find some of my favourite curries, stews and sauce-based dishes from around the world. Some of the recipes require blending the sauces or making specially prepared pastes, but they are all pretty straightforward recipes and, as with all the recipes in the book, cook in just one pan.

WHAT EXACTLY IS A CURRY AND HOW DOES IT DIFFER FROM A STEW?

Put simply, a curry is any saucy dish of Indian influence. There are, of course, countless examples. Indian merchants and indentured servants brought their recipes with them as they traded and migrated through South East Asia, China, Tibet, Nepal, Africa, Europe and as far away as the Caribbean. These recipes were then changed and adapted to local ingredients and cooking techniques. You will find a lot of delicious curries on the following pages.

It's believed by many food historians that the word 'curry' dates back to the 18th century, when members of the British East India Company were trading with Tamil merchants. The British misheard the word *kari*, which means 'sauce' in the Tamil language, and the word 'curry' was born. Although the word curry may not be used in any Indian language, it is used a lot in Sri Lanka, South East Asia, Europe and the Americas, even if only to entice curry-loving tourists into restaurants.

Stews, on the other hand, can often resemble a curry but they are not influenced by Indian cuisine. As this is a book of spicy dishes from around the world, you'll find that many of these recipes include the same or similar ingredients to curries. In fact, some of the recipes include ingredients that pre-date their use in curries, such as chillies, chilli powder, tomatoes and potatoes.

THINGS TO CONSIDER WHEN A RECIPE CALLS FOR A PASTE...

I learned to make some delicious homemade spice pastes while researching for this book. Trying the different curries abroad and making the pastes at home really opened my eyes to just how amazing a curry can be. Although the traditional method of pounding the paste ingredients in a pestle and mortar really brings out their flavours, I usually just blend them, which only takes about five minutes. You can prepare the pastes ahead of time or as you cook. They also freeze well if you want to make more to have on hand for future cooking.

You can often substitute a shop-bought paste and you'll still get a good curry, but if you decide to do this, be careful with how much you add! The reason for this is simple: shop-bought pastes are usually packed with chillies and salt. All of the other delicious ingredients rarely come through in the end dish like they should, even if they are in the ingredients list on the package. The pastes you will make from the following recipes are quite substantial and are anywhere from 250ml to 500ml (1–2 cups) in volume and sometimes even more. If you added that much of a shop-bought curry paste, you would taste nothing but chillies and salt. So if you do decide to use a shop-bought paste, I recommend using far less, perhaps 2–3 tablespoons to start and then more if needed at the end of cooking.

The homemade pastes can be added in larger amounts because they are a delicious blend of ingredients such as lemongrass, shallots, chillies, garlic, ginger and galangal, just to name a few. When these ingredients are blended together and hit the pan, they taste great together and none of them overpowers the others. They make the curry!

One last thing... If you purchase a curry paste, look at the side of it. There are usually recipe instructions on how much to use and how to prepare a curry with them. You don't need a cookbook for that. So I really hope you try these recipes in their entirety but if you must, go ahead and use a shop-bought paste. Shop-bought pastes are also sometimes good added just at the end of cooking, when you desire a little more spicy or salty flavour – so as a seasoning, rather than in the curry itself.

AYAM MASAK MERAH

SERVES 4

Popular in Malaysia and Singapore, ayam masak merah translates as 'red cooked chicken'. The first time I tried it, I was hooked! This is a truly unique chicken curry. The chicken is first shallow-fried and then cooked in the same wok or pan into an amazing, bright red sauce.

PREP TIME: 15 MINS
COOKING TIME: 30 MINS

FOR THE CHICKEN

1kg (2lb 2oz) chicken thighs on the
  bone, skin-on
1 tsp ground turmeric
120g (1 cup) plain (all-purpose) flour
1 tsp salt

FOR THE PASTE

10 dried red chillies, soaked in hot
  water for 10 minutes
1 medium red onion, roughly
  chopped
6 garlic cloves, roughly chopped
5cm (2in) piece of ginger, roughly
  chopped
2.5cm (1in) piece of galangal, skin
  removed and roughly chopped
2 lemongrass stalks, white part only,
  thinly sliced

FOR THE CURRY

250ml (1 cup) rapeseed (canola) oil,
  for shallow-frying
1 star anise, broken into pieces
3.75cm (1½in) cinnamon stick
2 cardamom pods, smashed
2 cloves
400ml (1¾ cups) unseasoned passata
400ml (1¾ cups) thick coconut milk
Salt and black pepper, to taste

Place the chicken in a mixing bowl and rub the turmeric, flour and salt all over the skin. You might want to do this with plastic kitchen gloves so you don't stain your fingers with the ground turmeric. Set aside while you prepare the paste.

The paste can be done a day or so ahead of cooking if more convenient. Place all of the paste ingredients in a food processor or blender and blend with just enough water to make a thick paste. Set aside.

When ready to cook, heat the oil in a wok or large frying pan (skillet) over a medium–high heat. The oil is hot enough for frying when lots of bubbles form instantly when you place a wooden chop stick or spatula in. Fry the chicken pieces until crispy on the exterior – you might need to do this in batches. Transfer to a metal rack to drip off any excess oil and set aside.

Discard all but about 70ml (¼ cup) of the oil in the wok and place it back over a medium–high heat. You could cook this curry with less oil, although at many Malaysian food stalls they use even more oil, so do as you like. When visibly hot, stir in the star anise, cinnamon, cardamom and cloves and swirl around in the oil for about 30 seconds or until fragrant.

Stir in the prepared curry paste and fry it for about a minute to cook out the rawness. Add the passata and coconut milk and bring to a simmer. Cook for a few minutes to thicken the sauce, then add the fried chicken and simmer in the sauce until it is cooked through. Season with salt and black pepper to taste.

★ MAKE IT EASIER ★

Although the flavour will be slightly different, you could get away with purchasing shop-bought crispy fried chicken and heating that through in the sauce instead.

KARI AYAM
SERVES 4

The first meal I had in Kuala Lumpur simply had to be kari ayam. I had made it many times at home but I wanted to see how it compared. The kari ayam I ordered for breakfast at my hotel that morning was quite a lot spicier than mine and it was so good! Luckily I became friends with the chef that week and he explained to me something I already knew about Malaysian food but that he really brought home – namely that many recipes like this are a combination of several different influences, chiefly Indian, Malay and Chinese. There is a heavy use of curry powder in this one but believe me, it works! He used homemade Malaysian curry powder that was really just like the curry powder on page 259 minus the fenugreek seeds. You won't be disappointed with the fenugreek flavour if you already have some made and want to try this recipe, but any good-quality curry powder will do.

PREP TIME: 15 MINS
COOKING TIME: 40 MINS

FOR THE AROMATIC PASTE
4 garlic cloves, smashed
2.5cm (1in) piece of ginger, roughly chopped
4 banana shallots
125ml (½ cup) water

FOR THE RED CHILLI PASTE
4 generous tbsp Madras (see page 259) or Malaysian curry powder, shop-bought or homemade
1–2 tbsp Kashmiri chilli powder
125ml (½ cup) water

FOR THE CURRY
3 tbsp rapeseed (canola), coconut or peanut oil
5cm (2in) cinnamon stick
2 star anise
3 green cardamom pods, bruised
2 garlic cloves, finely chopped
5cm (2in) piece of ginger, peeled and julienned
3 banana shallots, thinly sliced
20 fresh or frozen curry leaves
2 lemongrass stalks, tough outer layer removed, white parts only, lightly bruised
½ tsp tamarind paste (see page 256 or shop-bought)
700g (1lb 9oz) chicken thighs and/or legs, skinned or unskinned
2 large potatoes, peeled and cut into bite-sized pieces
250ml (1 cup) thick coconut milk
Salt, to taste

To make the aromatic paste, place the garlic, ginger, shallots and water in a blender and blend until smooth, Set aside.

Now prepare the chilli paste. Spoon the curry powder and chilli powder into a bowl and pour in the water. Stir with a spoon until smooth and set aside.

To cook the curry, heat the oil in a large pan or wok that has a lid over a medium–high heat. When the oil begins to shimmer, add the cinnamon stick, star anise and cardamom pods and stir for 30 seconds to infuse their flavours into the oil. Now add the garlic, ginger and shallots and fry for a minute, then add the curry leaves and lemongrass stalks and fry for another minute. Add the prepared aromatic paste and the chilli paste and stir well. If you are at all concerned about the spiciness of the chilli paste, add less of it and then stir in more if you want. The paste does give the curry its characteristic red glow, so you might want to substitute some paprika for colouring. Continue frying for about 3 minutes, at which time the sauce will have darkened a few shades. Stir in the tamarind paste.

Add the chicken and potatoes and stir well to coat with all the other ingredients. Fry for a few minutes, or until the meat is turning white. Then add just enough water to cover the chicken. Cover the pan and allow to simmer over a medium heat for 20 minutes. Take off the lid, add the coconut milk and continue simmering until the potatoes are soft. This should only take another 10 minutes or so. Don't rush it, though! You want the potatoes to be fall-apart perfect.

Once the potatoes have cooked through, season with salt to taste and serve immediately.

HAITIAN CHICKEN CURRY
SERVES 4–6

If you enjoy spicy chicken dishes, you're going to love this Haitian chicken curry called poul nan sos. If spicy sauces aren't your thing, you can just leave out the chillies and it will still be superb! This mouthwatering Haitian recipe calls for a blend of ingredients that is called an 'epis'. If you like the recipe, you might like to make more of it to keep on hand for next time – the coarsely ground epis freezes well. The chillies in this recipe are quite spicy, so it's a good idea to use plastic gloves and not touch your eyes until you remove them. You will need an ovenproof pan for best results, but you could just simmer the curry until the meat is cooked and the sauce has thickened. This dish is great with white rice or a crusty loaf of bread.

**PREP TIME: 15 MINS, PLUS
MARINATING TIME
COOKING TIME: 1 HOUR
20 MINS**

1.5kg (3lb 5oz) chicken thighs on the bone
1 tsp fine sea salt

FOR THE EPIS
2 tbsp orange juice (optional, for a sweeter flavour)
2 tbsp lime juice
2 scotch bonnet or habanero chillies, halved and seeded
1 green (bell) pepper, roughly chopped
5 garlic cloves, smashed
1 medium onion, roughly chopped
30g (1 packed cup or small bunch) parsley
4 tbsp fresh thyme
3 spring onions (scallions), roughly chopped
2 tbsp light olive oil

FOR THE CURRY
3 tbsp light olive oil
1 medium onion, thinly sliced
1 red (bell) pepper, thinly sliced
1 yellow (bell) pepper, thinly sliced
2 tbsp tomato purée (paste)
500ml (2 cups) unsalted chicken stock, homemade (see page 250) or shop-bought
Salt and pepper, to taste
3 tbsp parsley or coriander (cilantro), finely chopped
1 red scotch bonnet or habanero chilli, thinly sliced

Place the chicken in a large mixing bowl and sprinkle the salt all over it, rubbing it into the skin. Set aside. This can be done up to a day ahead of cooking, storing the salted chicken covered in the fridge until needed.

To prepare the epis, place all the ingredients in a food processor and blend until you have a chunky paste. You want a bit of texture, so don't go blending a vegetable smoothie! Rub this into the chicken too, ensuring you get it right into the flesh. Allow to marinate for at least 30 minutes, or up to 4 hours.

When ready to cook, preheat the oven to 200°C (400°F/Gas 6). Heat 2 tablespoons of the olive oil in a large frying pan (skillet) or wok over a medium–high heat. When visibly hot, rub as much of the epis marinade off the chicken as you can, retaining the marinade. Place the chicken skin-side down in the hot oil and fry for 8–10 minutes until crispy and browned. Transfer to a plate and set aside.

Add the remaining oil to the pan and stir in the sliced onion and (bell) peppers and fry for 3 minutes. Add the tomato purée (paste) to the pan and stir it all up well to combine. Then add the retained epis marinade and fry for 30 seconds before returning the fried chicken, skin-side up, and meat juices along with the chicken stock.

Bring to a rolling simmer, then transfer the pan to your preheated oven and cook for 1 hour, basting with the sauce every 15–20 minutes. By this time the chicken will be really tender and the skin will be deliciously crispy. Remove from the oven and season with salt and pepper to taste. Garnish with the parsley and sliced chilli to serve.

TRINI CHICKEN AND POTATO CURRY
SERVES 6

I'm a big fan of curries from Trinidad and Tobago. Curry was introduced to the country after slavery was abolished and the landowners were in desperate need of workers to pick cotton. Many workers came from India, and they of course brought their curry recipes with them, but they had to change the recipes to use ingredients that were available. The resulting curries were delicious but quite different from the curries found in India. This is a hot one! Feel free to use fewer chillies.

PREP TIME: 10 MINS, PLUS
    MARINATING TIME
COOKING TIME: 40 MINS

1kg (2lb 2oz) chicken thighs on the
    bone, skin removed

FOR THE GREEN PASTE
60g (2oz) coriander (cilantro)
30g (1oz) parsley
15g (½oz) thyme
5 spring onions (scallions), roughly
    chopped
2 heads of garlic, cloves separated but
    skin left on
1 green (bell) pepper
2 jalapeño chillies
1–2 habanero chillies
2.5cm (1in) piece of ginger
3 tbsp lemon juice

FOR THE MARINADE
80ml (⅓ cup) green paste
1 tsp ground cumin
½ tsp curry powder
1 tsp black pepper

FOR THE CURRY
2 tbsp rapeseed (canola) oil
1 onion, finely chopped
3 garlic cloves, finely chopped
1 jalapeño chilli, finely chopped
2 tbsp curry powder
1 tsp ground cumin
½ tsp ground turmeric
1 large potato, peeled and diced
1 whole red habanero chilli
3 tbsp green paste (more or less to
    taste)
Salt, to taste
½ tsp garam masala, shop-bought or
    homemade (see page 259)

Start by preparing the green paste. Blend all of the ingredients into a thick paste, adding a little water if needed to help blending, and set aside. Now make the marinade by whisking all of the ingredients together. Add the chicken pieces to the marinade and allow to marinate for at least 30 minutes, or up to 4 hours.

When ready to cook the curry, heat the oil in a large pan or wok over a medium–high heat. Add the chopped onion and fry for about 5 minutes, or until the onion is soft and a light golden brown. Stir in the chopped garlic and jalapeño and fry for a further minute. Add the ground spices. Stir in the marinated chicken and fry for about a minute before adding 80ml (⅓ cup) of water. Cover the pan and simmer for about 10 minutes. Take the lid off and continue cooking, stirring from time to time for another 5 minutes. The sauce will thicken as you do this.

Now add the diced potato and the whole habanero chilli and just enough water to cover the chicken and potato pieces. Simmer for another 8–10 minutes until the chicken and diced potato are cooked through. To finish, add 3 tablespoons or more of the green paste. Stir well to combine and simmer until you are happy with the consistency of the sauce. Season with salt to taste and sprinkle with the garam masala to serve.

MALAYSIAN DEVIL CURRY
SERVES 4

This is traditionally a very spicy curry, hence the name, but as with all of these spicy recipes, you can always tone it down a bit by adding fewer chillies. The dish is often referred to as 'Eurasian', as it was made popular by the Portuguese in Malaysia. It is generally eaten on special occasions around Christmas by the Christian community, and often with leftover meat from Christmas – I make devil curry with leftover turkey, sausages and roast potatoes. This recipe cooks from fresh, but go ahead and substitute leftover Christmas turkey, pork or beef if you like.

PREP TIME: 15 MINS
COOKING TIME: 30 MINS

1kg (2lb 2oz) bone-in chicken thighs
2 tbsp light soy sauce (gluten-free brands are available)
3 tbsp white wine vinegar
Leftover meats, sausage, roast potatoes (optional)

FOR THE PASTE

15 dried red chillies soaked in water for 20 minutes
2 fresh red finger or spur chillies, roughly chopped
10 shallots, roughly chopped
5 candlenuts or 8 macadamia nuts
6 garlic cloves, roughly chopped
2 lemongrass stalks, thinly sliced
2.5cm (1in) piece of ginger, roughly chopped
2.5cm (1in) piece of galangal, roughly chopped
1 tsp ground turmeric

FOR THE CURRY

2 tbsp rapeseed (canola) oil
1 tbsp mustard seeds
4 whole green finger chillies (optional)
1 tsp cracked black pepper
2 tbsp unseasoned passata
Salt, to taste
Pinch of sugar (optional)

Marinate the chicken pieces in the soy sauce and vinegar while you prepare the rest of the ingredients; set aside. Place all of the ingredients for the paste in a blender and mix until smooth, adding just enough water to blend. Set aside.

Now heat the oil in a large saucepan for a minute and add the mustard seeds. When they begin to pop, stir in the whole chillies and cracked black pepper and continue cooking for about 30 seconds. Add the paste to the pan and heat through for 2 or 3 minutes while continually stirring, until nicely fragrant and the oil starts to separate and rise to the top.

Add the passata to the pan and stir well to combine. Stir in the chicken pieces and add just enough water to cover. Simmer until the chicken is about half cooked through and the sauce has thickened a little. Then cover the pan and simmer for an additional 15–20 minutes.

Remove the lid. If you have any leftovers such as sausages or roast potatoes, this is a good time to add them and heat them through.

To finish, season with salt to taste. You can also add a little sugar if you prefer a sweeter flavour. I usually add a bit more vinegar, too.

CHICKEN KAPITAN
SERVES 4

The first time I tried chicken kapitan it was made with potatoes, which helped give the curry its classic thick sauce. That was in San Francisco and I really liked it, but I was eager to try the curry cooked in a more traditional way with candlenuts when my wife and I visited Malaysia. The nuts have a mild, nutty flavour and also work as a sauce thickener. They are easily sourced online and at speciality Asian shops. This is a simple Nyonya curry popular in Malaysia, Singapore and Indonesia, with Chinese, South East Asian and Indian influences. There are far too many unverified explanations as to how the curry got its name to list here – all you need to know is that it is delicious and one you've simply got to try. I like to serve this with white rice or a crusty loaf of bread.

PREP TIME: 20 MINS
COOKING TIME: 30 MINS

8 chicken thighs, on the bone
1 tsp ground turmeric
3 tbsp peanut oil or rapeseed (canola) oil
500ml (2 cups) water
3 fresh lime leaves, stems removed and thinly sliced
4 tbsp thick coconut milk
Salt, to taste
1 tsp sugar (optional)
Juice of 1 lime

FOR THE PASTE
15 dried red finger chillies
8 banana shallots, peeled
6 garlic cloves, smashed
3 fresh lime leaves, stems removed and thinly sliced
2 lemongrass stalks, peeled and white parts only, thinly sliced
4 fresh red finger chillies
5cm (2in) piece of galangal, roughly chopped
1.25cm (½in) piece of ginger, roughly chopped
4 candlenuts or macadamia nuts
½ tsp belacan (fermented shrimp paste)

Start by making the paste. Soak the dried red chillies in boiling water for about 10 minutes to soften. Place the soaked chillies in a food processor or spice grinder and retain the soaking water. Add the remaining ingredients and blend to a smooth paste, adding a little of the soaking water if needed to help it blend. Set aside.

Now rub the chicken all over with the ground turmeric. Both this step and making the paste can be done a day ahead of cooking if more convenient. When ready to cook, heat the oil in a large saucepan or wok over a medium–high heat. Add the prepared paste and fry for about 2 minutes, or until fragrant. Then add the chicken thighs and fry to brown for a couple of minutes, ensuring that the chicken is nicely and evenly coated with the paste. Stir in the water and sliced lime leaves and bring to a simmer.

Reduce the heat to medium and simmer the chicken in this sauce for about 20 minutes, or until the chicken is cooked through and the sauce has thickened. If you find that the sauce is becoming too thick, add a drop more water.

To finish, stir in the coconut milk. This is supposed to be a dry curry, but if you prefer more sauce, go ahead and add more coconut milk. Taste the curry and add salt to taste and sugar if you would like it sweeter. Squeeze the lime juice over the top before serving.

JAPANESE CHICKEN CURRY
SERVES 4

This is a completely homemade version of a Japanese chicken curry. You will be preparing an essential roux, which will thicken the sauce. In Japan, packet curry kits are really popular because they are good and very easy to prepare. I like homemade best, but if you're curious, source a Japanese curry kit and try that too. You will find these curry kits at most Asian grocers, including a roux. There are several different brands and they all taste a bit different. Try this homemade version first, though. I have never been disappointed by the outcome. I recommend serving this with white rice. To make this vegetarian, omit the chicken and add more vegetables such as aubergine (eggplant), courgette (zucchini) and mushrooms. Tofu is also good in this curry.

PREP TIME: 10 MINS
COOKING TIME: 20 MINS

FOR THE ROUX
2 tbsp unsalted butter
2 tbsp plain (all-purpose) flour
1 generous tbsp Japanese curry powder (homemade, see page 261, or S&B Oriental) or any curry powder
1 tsp garam masala, shop-bought or homemade (see page 259)
1 tsp paprika or chilli powder
2 tbsp light soy sauce
1 tbsp mirin (optional but authentic)
1 apple, grated and pounded or blended to a paste*
4 tbsp chicken stock

FOR THE CURRY
2 tbsp rapeseed (canola) or peanut oil
1 large onion, thinly sliced
1 large potato, skinned and cut into small cubes
1 carrot, cut into small bite-sized pieces at an angle
700g (1lb 9oz) chicken thighs or breasts, cut into bite-sized pieces
1 litre (4 cups) chicken stock

Start by making the roux. Melt the butter over a medium heat in a large, high-sided frying pan (skillet) and add the flour. Stir continuously until the roux turns a light beige. Then stir in the curry powder, garam masala and paprika. As you stir, the roux will take on a milk chocolate-brown colour from all the spices.

Now stir in the soy sauce, mirin (if using) and apple paste. Be sure to stir quickly so that you are left with a dark, wet paste. Stir in about 3 tablespoons of stock to thin it a bit. You want the roux to be a bit runny and well combined, so add more stock if needed but not too much! Once you have a nice, runny roux that literally oozes off your spoon, transfer it to a bowl and set aside. It will solidify like jelly as it cools.

Wipe your pan clean with a paper towel and place over a medium heat. Add the oil to the pan and then the sliced onion. Stir well to combine and allow to fry for about 4 minutes until the onion is soft and translucent but not at all browned.

Add the potato and fry over a medium heat for about 5 minutes and then add the chopped carrot. Continue cooking until the potato is about 60% cooked through. This should take about 10 more minutes.

Now add the chicken and stir it into the onion mixture. Cook until the chicken is turning white on the exterior and then return the roux to the pan. Again, stir well to combine and stir in about 250ml (1 cup) of chicken stock. Stir it all up. As you do, the stock will thicken quickly because of the roux. Slowly add more stock when the sauce thickens. It is essential that you don't just pour all the stock in at once, as it may not all be needed. Add it in small amounts until the sauce is thick and creamy.

Continue simmering and adding chicken stock in small amounts until the potatoes, carrots and chicken are cooked through and you have a delicious, thick curry sauce. Season with more salt or soy sauce if needed.

NOTE
*Alternatively, you could use about 3 generous tablespoons of unsweetened, shop-bought apple sauce.

BALOCHI CHICKEN KARAHI
SERVES 4

If you're looking for a light dish, this isn't it. It is, however, much lighter than the way I saw it demonstrated by a friend a few years back. There's a lot of ghee in that pan but it isn't served as you would other curries. The thick, buttery sauce literally sticks to the meat, which is meant to be eaten by hand. Any sauce that is left over in the karahi can be soaked up with naans or chapattis, or left if you don't want the calories. I usually don't want the calories but end up consuming them anyway. The sauce is garlicky, with just enough heat added to not be considered mild. We're talking just under madras-hot here, but of course how spicy hot you make this is completely up to you.

PREP TIME: 10 MINS, PLUS OPTIONAL MARINATING TIME
COOKING TIME: 20 MINS

900g (2lb) whole chicken, skinned and cut into 8 pieces

FOR THE MARINADE
Juice of 2 lemons
1 tsp salt
1 tsp ground turmeric

FOR THE CURRY
250ml (1 cup) ghee
6–8 garlic cloves, skinned and roughly chopped
7 medium green chillies, left whole and seeded if you prefer it less spicy
3 tbsp natural yoghurt
2 tsp ground coriander
2 tsp ground cumin
1 tsp ground black pepper
1 tbsp Kashmiri chilli powder
1 tsp chaat masala, shop-bought or homemade (see page 260)
4 green finger chillies, finely chopped
1 tbsp kasoori methi (dried fenugreek leaves)
Salt, to taste
4 tbsp coriander (cilantro), finely chopped
1 thumb-sized piece of ginger, julienned

Marinate the chicken pieces with the lemon juice, salt and turmeric for about 20 minutes. If you're in a rush, just get cooking.

When ready to cook, heat the ghee in a frying pan (skillet) or karahi over a high heat. When visibly hot and bubbling, add the marinated chicken and stir it around in the ghee to brown for a few minutes. When the chicken is about half cooked, stir in the garlic and whole chillies and fry for a few more minutes until the chillies are beginning to blister. Transfer the chicken, garlic and chillies to a plate using a slotted spoon and set aside.

Now add the yoghurt to the pan. You don't need to worry about it curdling, just stir hard and fast until it has cooked into the ghee. Stir in the ground spices, finely chopped chillies and kasoori methi. The ghee mixture will become red in colour.

Return the chicken, chillies and garlic to the karahi and cook until the chicken has completely cooked through and you are left with a thick and buttery sauce that coats the meat. Season with salt to taste and garnish with coriander (cilantro) and the julienned ginger to serve.

★ MAKE IT EASIER ★
Although I recommend removing the chicken, garlic and chillies before adding the yoghurt, finely chopped chillies and spices, this is optional. I like to do it so I can concentrate on stirring and thickening the sauce. You could just carry on with the recipe and it will still be delicious.

NADAN CHICKEN CURRY
SERVES 4–6

Nadan chicken curry is so good! This is a recipe I learned while in Kerala a couple of years back. It was supposed to go in another book, but I forgot I had it. Thankfully, while writing this book I found it again in my notes and I'm so happy it wasn't lost for good. Nadan curry is different and unique. The onions are first slowly shallow-fried, which brings out their natural sweetness. Then you continue to slowly simmer the curry, which produces a thick and delicious sauce that soaks into the chicken. Slivered fresh coconut is also added at the end for texture. This isn't a dry curry, but it is thick and tastes amazing served over white or matta rice. In Kerala, they also serve it topped with a freshly fried hot poppadum.

PREP TIME: 15 MINS
COOKING TIME: 1 HOUR

70ml (¼ cup) coconut oil or rapeseed oil
1 tsp black mustard seeds
5cm (2in) cinnamon stick
2 cloves
30–40 fresh or frozen curry leaves
4 red onions, thinly sliced
1 tsp salt
3 tbsp garlic and ginger paste
1 tbsp garam masala, shop-bought or homemade (see page 259)
½ tsp ground fennel (optional)
½ tsp ground turmeric
1 tbsp Kashmiri chilli powder
2 tbsp ground coriander
2 medium tomatoes, finely chopped
1kg (2lb 2oz) chicken thighs, bone in or out
2 cups water or chicken stock
100g (3½oz) fresh coconut, slivered
5 tbsp thick coconut milk
Salt and pepper, to taste

Heat the oil over a high heat in a large pan or wok. When visibly hot, stir in the mustard seeds. When the seeds begin to pop, stir in the cinnamon stick and cloves and fry for about 20 seconds to infuse these flavours into the oil. Add half the curry leaves and fry for a further 20 seconds.

Now reduce the heat to medium–low and add the sliced red onions. This is an important step for making the sauce. Stir in about a teaspoon of salt and simmer on this low heat for at least 15 minutes, or until the onions are beginning to break down into a paste. Stir regularly.

Add the garlic and ginger paste and stir it into the onion mixture, then stir in the ground spices. Add the tomatoes, followed by the chicken thighs. Cook the chicken over a low heat until the exterior begins to turn white and then add just enough water or stock to cover. Don't add too much, as you don't want the sauce to be too thin.

Cover the pan and simmer over a medium heat for 20 minutes. By this time, the sauce should be quite thick but still pourable. Add the slivered coconut and cover again to simmer for another 10 minutes. To finish, stir in the remaining curry leaves and the coconut milk. Season with salt and pepper to taste.

MUMBAI-STYLE CHICKEN CURRY
SERVES 4–6

This is one to save for a special curry night. It's not one of the light ones, as the use of ghee is quite heavy, but it's deliciously indulgent. This is just like a curry I had in Mumbai, and it's kind of a mix between north and south Indian cooking. The use of ghee is more of a northern thing, while grated coconut and coconut milk are much more southern. The mix works, though, as I found out when I first tried it. This is my interpretation of the dish, and it tastes just like the original. You can serve this with rice, naans or chapattis, although rice is what I usually serve it with.

PREP TIME: 15 MINS
COOKING TIME: 30 MINS

FOR THE SPICE BLEND
½ tsp coriander seeds
½ tsp cumin seeds
½ star anise
Seeds from 2 green cardamom pods
¼ tsp ajwain (carom) seeds

FOR THE CURRY
6 tbsp ghee (use less if you like)
75g (½ cup) cashews
5cm (2in) cinnamon stick
5 black peppercorns
3 green cardamom pods
1 tsp cumin seeds
1 Indian bay leaf
20 curry leaves
2 red onions – ½ onion sliced thinly
    and the rest finely chopped
1 tbsp garlic and ginger paste
2–4 green finger chillies, finely
    chopped
1 tsp ground turmeric
2 tsp prepared spice blend or
    garam masala, shop-bought or
    homemade (see page 259)
1–2 tsp Kashmiri chilli powder
1 tbsp tomato purée (paste)
45g (2oz) fresh coconut, grated
4 skinned chicken breasts, cut
    diagonally against the grain into
    bite-sized pieces
400ml (1¾ cups) coconut milk
Salt, to taste

Place the spice blend ingredients in a pan over a medium–high heat and toast, stirring continuously for about 40 seconds or until warm to the touch and fragrant. Transfer to a pestle and mortar or spice grinder and grind to a fine powder. Set aside. You could just substitute 2 teaspoons of garam masala, but this toasted spice blend will be better.

In the same pan, melt half of the ghee and toss in the cashews. Fry them, stirring regularly over a medium–high heat until golden brown all over. This should only take about 3 minutes. Transfer the cashews to a plate and set aside.

Add the remaining ghee to the pan and stir in the cinnamon stick, peppercorns, cardamom pods, cumin seeds, Indian bay leaf and curry leaves and temper them in the hot ghee for about 30 seconds. Stir in the finely chopped onions and fry for 5 minutes, or until soft and translucent.

Now add the garlic and ginger paste, green chillies, ground turmeric, the prepared spice blend or garam masala and chilli powder and fry to combine with the onions for about a minute. Stir in the tomato purée (paste) until it has combined with the other ingredients, and then add the grated coconut and continue frying and stirring for another minute.

Add the chicken pieces and stir them around in the pan until they are beginning to turn white, and then and add just enough water or chicken stock to cover. Bring to a simmer over a medium–high heat. Add the coconut milk and cook for a further 7–10 minutes, or until the chicken is cooked through. Continue simmering over a medium heat until you are happy with the sauce consistency. Season with salt to taste.

To serve, top with the roasted cashews and remaining sliced onion.

BUNNY CHOW
(DURBAN CHICKEN CURRY)
SERVES 4

One of my many jobs when I first moved to the UK was working in a ring-binder factory in London. The receptionist there was from South Africa, and knowing my love for a good curry she gave me her mother's recipe for a classic Durban curry. Durban is the third-largest city in South Africa and it has the largest Indian population in South Africa. During apartheid Black people were not allowed to eat in Indian restaurants, so many of the Durban chefs would hide this and other curries in hollowed-out bread loaves and serve them out of the back door. The word 'bunny' referred to the Indian merchants at the time and 'chow' means food. So roughly speaking, 'bunny chow' means Indian food. This is a spicy one!

PREP TIME: 10 MINS
COOKING TIME: 50 MINS

3 tbsp ghee
1 tsp cumin seeds
5cm (2in) cinnamon stick
20 fresh or frozen curry leaves
2 medium onions, finely chopped
2 tbsp garlic and ginger paste
2 green finger chillies, finely chopped
1 tbsp ground cumin
1 tbsp ground coriander
1 tsp cayenne chilli powder
1 tbsp Kashmiri chilli powder
1 tbsp tomato purée (paste)
2 medium tomatoes, diced
2 medium potatoes, diced into 2.5cm (1in) cubes
225g (8oz) swede (rutabaga) diced into 2.5cm (1in) cubes
500ml (2 cups) unsalted chicken stock or water
900g (2lb) chicken thighs, cut into bite-sized pieces
Salt, to taste
1 tsp garam masala, shop-bought or homemade (see page 259)
Fresh coriander (cilantro) leaves, for garnish (optional)
4 small loaves of bread, hollowed out (optional)

Melt the ghee in a pan over a medium–high heat. When visibly hot, stir in the cumin seeds, cinnamon stick and curry leaves and move these around in the ghee until fragrant. About 30 seconds should do. Stir in the chopped onions and fry for about 5 minutes, or until soft and translucent.

Now add the garlic and ginger paste and chillies and stir them around in the onions for about 30 seconds. Then add the ground spices, chilli powder, tomato purée (paste) and tomatoes and stir some more to combine.

Add the chunks of potato and swede (rutabaga) and then add just enough stock or water to cover. Simmer for 20–30 minutes, or until both the potatoes and swede are turning soft.

Stir in the chicken and top with more stock or water if needed. You only want to add enough to almost cover the meat so that it cooks through. Continue simmering until the chicken is cooked through and you have a thick sauce. Taste it and season with salt to taste.

To serve, sprinkle in the garam masala and garnish with chopped coriander (cilantro). Serve as it is, or bunny chow-style in hollowed-out bread loaves.

CHICKEN AND MUSTARD CURRY

SERVES 4

One of the most memorable days of our time in Sri Lanka was at Cinnamon Lodge, Habarana, where chef Senaka Jayasinghe and his team cooked up a feast for us, village style! As is common with many Sri Lankan dishes, the recipes were quite simple but amazing. Everything was cooked in clay pots over log fires and we filmed it all so that we could bring the recipes back with us. This recipe was prepared with a homemade coconut mustard. I have used Dijon and added a little coconut water at the end to bring out the subtle coconut flavour we experienced that day. The chicken is meant to be eaten by hand with a mound of matta rice (see page 249) that soaks up the juices deliciously, but any cooked rice will do.

PREP TIME: 10 MINS, PLUS
    MARINATING TIME
COOKING TIME: 20 MINS

700g (1lb 9oz) skinned chicken
    thighs, on the bone and cut in half

FOR THE MARINADE
1 generous tsp red chilli powder
1½ tsp black pepper
½ tsp salt
1½ tsp unroasted curry powder
    (see page 258)
1 tsp ground turmeric
2 green finger chillies, finely chopped
5cm (2in) real cinnamon stick, broken
    into many pieces, or a pinch of
    ground cinnamon
3 garlic cloves, finely chopped
20 fresh or frozen curry leaves

FOR THE CURRY
3 tbsp coconut oil
1 tsp black mustard seeds
½ red onion, thinly sliced
4 garlic cloves, thinly sliced
1 green cardamom pod, smashed
2.5cm (1in) cinnamon stick
½ tsp fenugreek seeds
5cm (2in) square piece of pandan leaf,
    cut into 3 pieces
2 tsp Dijon mustard
5 fresh or frozen curry leaves
½ tsp ground turmeric
1 large tomato, cut into about 8 pieces
70ml (¼ cup) water or coconut water
    (optional)
Salt, to taste

Place the chicken in a large mixing bowl and add all the marinade ingredients. Using your hands, get right in there and rub it all deep into the flesh. Cover to marinate for at least 20 minutes, or let it marinate overnight.

When ready to cook, heat the coconut oil over a medium–high heat in a large saucepan or clay pot. When visibly hot, stir in the mustard seeds. When they begin to crackle, stir in the sliced red onion and fry for about 5 minutes, or until soft and translucent. Stir in the garlic, cardamom, cinnamon stick and fenugreek seeds. The fenugreek seeds not only flavour the chicken but also work as a thickener for the sauce, which is a common practice in Sri Lankan cooking.

Fry for about 30 seconds and then add the pandan leaf, mustard, ground turmeric and curry leaves and continue frying and stirring it all together for another minute. Now add the marinated chicken and stir well so that it is nicely covered in the coconut oil and spice mixture. Reduce the heat to medium and cook until the chicken has turned white on the exterior.

Add the chopped tomato and continue cooking and stirring regularly for another 10 minutes. The chicken and tomatoes will release moisture into the pan as you do. At this point, you could add the water or coconut water, if using, and continue cooking until the chicken is completely cooked through. This is a dry curry, so don't add too much coconut water. To finish, season with salt to taste.

CHICKEN MASSAMAN
SERVES 4

Beef massaman is most popular in the West, but in Thailand chicken massaman is eaten much more often. In fact, the dish was originally developed with chicken by Indian Muslims who had made their way to a new life in Thailand. Halal chicken was easier to come by than beef, or so I've been told. So massaman curries are a mix of Indian and Thai cuisines. The spices used are different to what you find in most Thai curries. If you don't have the time or the will to make the spice paste, substitute a good-quality shop-bought massaman paste to taste. Start with about 2–3 tablespoons and then adjust to your own taste preferences.

PREP TIME: 15 MINS
COOKING TIME: 25 MINS

FOR THE MASSAMAN PASTE
1 tbsp coriander seeds
1½ tbsp cumin seeds
5 whole cloves
1 tbsp black peppercorns
1 whole nutmeg
Seeds from 6 green cardamom pods
5cm (2in) piece of cinnamon stick
6–12 dried red finger chillies, soaked in water for 30 minutes and then cut into small pieces
8 garlic cloves, smashed
4 small shallots, thinly sliced
1 long lemongrass stalk (white part only), thinly sliced
1 thumb-sized piece of galangal, sliced into thin rounds
Zest of ½ lime
3 makrut lime leaves (fresh or frozen)
1 tsp shrimp paste

FOR THE CURRY
2 tbsp rapeseed (canola) oil
½ red onion, quartered
Handful of roasted peanuts
2 potatoes, peeled and cut into bite-size pieces
300ml (1¼ cups) water or unsalted chicken stock
900g (2lb) chicken thighs, on or off the bone
400ml (1¾ cups) thick coconut milk
1 tbsp palm sugar
1 tsp tamarind paste (see page 256 or shop-bought)
3 tbsp Thai fish sauce (gluten-free brands are available)
Thai holy basil, to garnish

Place the paste ingredients in a food processor or spice grinder and blend to a fine paste. You can add a little water if needed to blend. Set aside.

When ready to cook, heat the oil in a large wok or frying pan (skillet). When visibly hot, add the onion and peanuts and stir well into the oil. Pour in the prepared paste and fry for about a minute, stirring regularly to cook out the rawness.

Now add the potatoes and about 250ml (1 cup) of water or chicken stock. Bring to a simmer and then stir in the chicken thighs. If needed, add just enough water or stock to cover and simmer the chicken until cooked through and the potatoes are soft. This should take about 12 minutes. Stir in the coconut milk and bring to a simmer. Then add the sugar, tamarind paste and fish sauce. Taste it and add more sugar for a sweeter flavour, more tamarind to make it more sour and/or fish sauce for a savoury flavour.

Continue simmering until you are happy with the consistency. Serve topped with Thai basil leaves.

THAI BEEF GREEN CURRY

SERVES 4

Beef green curry is incredibly delicious and, personally, I prefer it to the more popular chicken green curry. The most important thing is to use the right cut of beef. I used skirt steak in this recipe, which is flavourful and cooks quickly when cut as described below. You could also use thinly sliced strips of ribeye or sirloin which is easier to find at supermarkets but pricier. This curry is delicious served with jasmine rice. I also like to drizzle on a little homemade basil oil (see page 258) as a garnish and for extra flavour.

PREP TIME: 10 MINS
COOKING TIME: 20 MINS

FOR THE CURRY PASTE
1 tsp cumin seeds
1 tsp coriander seeds
1½ tsp white pepper
About 20 green finger chillies, roughly
    chopped (more or less to taste)
2 lemongrass stalks (white parts
    only), thinly sliced
8 garlic cloves, smashed
1 thumb-sized piece of galangal,
    thinly sliced
3 small shallots, roughly chopped
10 Thai sweet basil stalks
5 coriander (cilantro) stalks
Zest of ½ lime
5 makrut lime leaves (fresh or frozen)
1 tsp shrimp paste

FOR THE CURRY
2 tbsp coconut or rapeseed (canola)
    oil
450g (1lb) beef skirt steak, cut into
    thin strips against the grain
250ml (1 cup) unsalted Thai beef or
    chicken stock (or shop-bought
    stock)
400ml (1¾ cups) thick coconut milk
About 250g (9oz) vegetables such
    as baby corn, bamboo shoots,
    aubergine (eggplant), asparagus,
    broccoli, sliced lotus root
3 tbsp fish sauce, preferably Thai
    (gluten-free brands are available)
2 spur chillies, thinly sliced to garnish
3 makrut lime leaves, stalks removed
    and thinly sliced, to garnish
1 handful of Thai sweet basil, roughly
    chopped, to garnish (optional)

Prepare the curry paste by placing all of the paste ingredients in a food processor or blender and blending to a paste. You can add a drop of water if needed to assist blending. There will be a lot of paste, and yes, you do use it all in this recipe.

Heat the oil in a wok or large frying pan (skillet) and when visibly hot, stir in the beef and fry for about 8 minutes, or until almost tender enough to eat. Add the green curry paste, stirring so that the beef is coated with it.

Add the stock and bring to a simmer. Continue simmering for about 5–10 minutes, or until the beef is tender. Don't rush this! The beef is ready when it's ready.

Stir in the coconut milk and the vegetables and continue stirring until the vegetables are cooked to your liking. I prefer my vegetables a bit on the crunchy side and not too mushy. Add 3 tablespoons of fish sauce or to taste.

Garnish with the sliced spur chillies, thinly sliced lime leaves and perhaps some basil leaves.

★ MAKE IT EASIER ★

If you don't have time to make the green curry paste in this recipe, you could substitute 2–3 tablespoons of shop-bought paste, or add it to taste.

BEEF BIBIMBAP
SERVES 3–4

Bibimbaps are rice bowls that can consist of whatever you want to throw in. The version I have for you here is quite common. Many of the ingredients are cooked in Korean spices and are therefore packed with amazing flavours. Although the ingredient list is long, these are only suggestions so you could substitute other vegetables or even leftover beef bulgogi (see page 208) for the minced (ground) meat. Often these bowls are topped with a fried egg. At one restaurant I went to in LA, a raw egg yolk was added to the top and we were instructed to mix it in, cooking the egg yolk and ensuring every bite was spectacular.

PREP TIME: 15 MINS, PLUS
OPTIONAL MARINATING TIME
COOKING TIME: 25 MINS

FOR THE BEEF MARINADE
450g (1lb) minced (ground) beef
2 tbsp soy sauce★
1 tsp sugar
1 tbsp sesame oil
1 tbsp sesame seeds
1 tbsp rice wine
4 garlic cloves, finely chopped
4 spring onions (scallions), thinly sliced

FOR THE MAYONNAISE
6 generous tbsp mayonnaise
1 tbsp gochujang (Korean hot pepper paste)★
1 tsp finely chopped garlic
Juice of 1 lime

FOR THE CUCUMBER
1 English cucumber, slit down the middle and thinly sliced
2 tbsp soy sauce★
2 tbsp rice wine vinegar
1 tbsp sugar
½ tsp sesame seeds
1 tsp gochugaru (Korean chilli powder)
3 spring onions (scallions), finely chopped

FOR THE VEGETABLES
Approx. 2–3 tbsp rapeseed (canola) oil or sesame oil
3 garlic cloves, finely chopped
A selection of vegetables, such as julienned carrots, sliced mushrooms, shredded spinach leaves, as much as you want
Salt, to taste

TO FINISH
800g (4 cups) cooked white rice, hot
4 egg yolks (optional)
Chopped spring onions (scallions)
Salt and pepper, to taste

Start by marinating the minced (ground) beef. Place the meat in a bowl and cover with the marinade ingredients. Really work it in with your hands then set aside while you prepare the rest of the dish (or overnight).

To make the bibimbap mayonnaise, simply whisk all the mayo ingredients together and place in the fridge until required. To make the pickled cucumber, place the sliced cucumber in a mixing bowl and cover with the dressing ingredients. This can be done a couple of days ahead of serving for more flavour, but it isn't necessary.

For ease, you could just fry a handful or two of your chosen vegetables all together until cooked through. For presentation reasons, I recommend frying each vegetable separately so that you have more control over the doneness of each vegetable and they can all have their own place in the bowl when served. It's looks more authentic and is very colourful as you will see in the photo opposite.

To fry vegetables such as carrots and mushrooms, place your pan over a medium–high heat and add a little oil and some of the chopped garlic. Fry for about 5 minutes, or until the vegetables are starting to caramelize a bit. Season with salt to taste and transfer to a plate and keep warm. To cook leafy greens such as spinach, fry in the same way until lightly wilted. Season and transfer to a plate to keep warm.

Clean the pan with a paper towel and add the marinated beef over a medium–high heat. Stir regularly to break the meat down as it cooks, so that there are no large lumps. When cooked through, set aside and keep warm.

To serve, divide the rice among four bowls. Next to the rice, add a scoop of the meat. Then add some pickled cucumber, the spinach, fried mushrooms and fried carrots. Squirt or spoon some of the mayonnaise dressing over each bibimbap and top each with a raw egg yolk, garnished with more spring onions (scallions) and salt and pepper to taste. Mix it all up and dig in.

NOTE
★Some soy sauces and gochujang pastes contain gluten, but gluten-free brands are available.

KOREAN BRAISED BEEF SHORT RIBS
SERVES 6

Like so many Asian recipes, the meat for stews and soups is usually brought to a boil in water for about 10 minutes. Then it's strained, and all the blood and other impurities are cleaned from the meat. I'd like to stress that this step isn't essential, but it will benefit the appearance of the final dish. Juicy and tender Korean braised beef short ribs are amazing. They're spicy, sweet and just a bit sticky: I simply can't get enough of them, and I hope you love this recipe and want to make it as often as I do. Ask your butcher to cut the short ribs into small 5cm (2in) chunks. Failing that, just use larger, Western-style cuts of beef short ribs.

PREP TIME: 20 MINS
COOKING TIME: 90 MINS

1.5kg (3lb 5oz) beef short ribs, cut into 5cm (2in) pieces
175ml (¾ cup) light soy sauce or tamari (gluten-free)
125ml (½ cup) Chinese cooking wine or dry sherry
Approx. 1 litre (4 cups) unsalted beef stock or water
4 tbsp honey
2 tbsp gochujang (Korean hot pepper paste; gluten-free brands are available)
2 tbsp sesame oil
2–4 tbsp gochugaru (Korean hot pepper flakes)
15 garlic cloves, finely chopped
5cm (2in) piece of ginger, finely chopped
2 large carrots, cut into 2.5cm (1in) chunks
2 large potatoes, cut into large, bite-sized pieces
12 spring onions (scallions), sliced lengthwise down the centre
2 medium onions, quartered and divided into petals
Salt and pepper, to taste
4 tbsp toasted or untoasted sesame seeds, to garnish
5 red finger chillies, cut at an angle in half, seeds removed for less heat, to garnish

Bring a large saucepan of water to a boil over a high heat and add the short ribs. Bring back to a boil and simmer for 10 minutes, skimming off any impurities that rise to the top. After 10 minutes of boiling, drain the meat in a colander and rinse it with cold water. Wipe your pan clean and then wash each piece of meat to remove any blood or other impurities and return them to the pan.

Pour the soy sauce/tamari and Chinese rice wine/sherry over the meat and then add just enough water or unsalted beef stock to cover and bring to a rolling simmer over a high heat. Stir in the honey, gochujang, sesame oil and gochugaru. If you are not sure about the spiciness, add less of the gochujang and gochugaru. You can always add more later to taste, if needed.

Simmer, covered, over a high heat for 30 minutes and then uncover and continue simmering over a medium heat for an additional 30 minutes, or until the meat is fall-off-the-bone tender.

To finish, stir in the garlic, ginger, carrots and potatoes. If needed, you can add a drop more water if it is looking too dry. Continue simmering over a medium heat until the carrots and potatoes are cooked through. Stir in the spring onions (scallions) and onion petals and let them cook in the hot sauce for about a minute. Your braised beef ribs are ready when everything is cooked through and you have a thick but still-liquid sauce. Season with salt if needed and freshly ground pepper, to taste.

To serve, divide between six bowls and garnish with the sesame seeds and more thinly sliced spring onions and red chillies.

BEEF RENDANG
SERVES 4

It is believed that beef rendang, and other rendangs for that matter, have Indian origins because of the cooking process and spices used. Indian merchants brought the recipe to Indonesia and there it was adjusted to local taste using local ingredients. Ginger was probably originally added instead of galangal, and in some beef rendang recipes it still is. Modern-day rendang originated in West Sumatra by the Minangkabau people. Originally it was prepared to take on long journeys, as the spices and salt helped preserve the curry.

PREP TIME: 15 MINS
COOKING TIME: 1–1½ HOURS

FOR THE PASTE
6 shallots, roughly chopped
6 garlic cloves, smashed
2.5cm (1in) piece of galangal, roughly chopped
2 lime leaves, stemmed and roughly chopped
2 lemongrass stalks, white parts only, thinly sliced
12 dried red chillies, soaked in water for 20 minutes

FOR THE CURRY
70ml (¼ cup) coconut or rapeseed (canola) oil
5cm (2in) cinnamon stick
2 star anise
4 cloves
4 cardamom pods, lightly bruised
2 lemongrass stalks, white parts only, thinly sliced
800g (1lb 12oz) beef short ribs, sirloin or stewing steak
400ml (14oz) thick tinned (canned) coconut milk
250ml (1 cup) water
1½ tsp tamarind paste (see page 256 or shop-bought)
6 tbsp toasted fresh or frozen grated coconut (kerisik)*
1 tsp palm sugar (or more to taste)
5 lime leaves, stems removed and thinly sliced
Salt, to taste
2 red spur chillies, thinly sliced, to garnish
3 spring onions (scallions), thinly sliced, to garnish

Start by preparing the rendang paste. Place all of the ingredients in a blender and blend to a paste. You can add a little water to assist with blending. Set aside until ready to use.

To make the curry, heat the oil in a clay pot, wok or large pan over a medium–high heat. When visibly hot, stir in the whole spices and allow to infuse into the hot oil for about 30 seconds.

Stir in the prepared rendang paste and fry for about a minute to cook out the rawness.

Now add the thinly sliced lemongrass and the beef and stir well to combine. Fry for about 5 minutes to brown and then add the coconut milk and enough water to cover. I usually add about 250ml (1 cup) of water and then top it up during cooking as required.

Stir in the tamarind paste, toasted coconut (kerisik), sugar and lime leaves and allow to simmer for 60–90 minutes, depending on the cut of beef you use. Don't rush this, as you want the meat to be deliciously tender before serving. When cooked, season with salt to taste and add more sugar if you want, also to taste. Serve garnished with the sliced spur chillies and spring onions (scallions).

NOTE
*To toast the grated coconut, simply pour it into a pan and dry-fry over a medium–high heat until light golden brown. You can also purchase toasted grated coconut, which is called kerisik.

CALIFORNIA-STYLE CHILLI CON CARNE
SERVES 6–8

Anyone can make chilli con carne using chilli powder or a shop-bought spice blend. If that's what you'd rather do, skip to the third paragraph of this recipe and take it from there. However, this is how I was taught to make chilli con carne in my teens. Roasting, soaking and then blending the whole dried chillies gives the sauce a flavour boost that is far superior to ground chilli powder. This chilli is so thick, you can stick a spoon in it and it will stand up! I used pinto beans rather than kidney beans because I think they're much better in a chilli con carne. If you cook dried beans you can use the cooking stock for flavour, but tinned (canned) beans will do fine. You can easily make this vegetarian by leaving out the beef and adding more beans.

PREP TIME: 40 MINS
COOKING TIME: 60 MINS

FOR THE SAUCE
6 dried ancho chillies, torn open and
    seeds removed
6 dried guajillo chillies, torn open
    and seeds removed
8 garlic cloves, smashed and roughly
    chopped
1 medium onion, roughly chopped
400g (14oz) tinned (canned) chopped
    tomatoes
3 tbsp chipotle chillies in adobo
    sauce, or to taste
1 tbsp dried oregano
1½ tbsp ground cumin

FOR THE CHILLI
3 tbsp light olive oil
1kg (2lb 2oz) minced (ground) beef
1 onion, finely chopped
3 green jalapeño chillies, finely
    chopped and to taste
4 garlic cloves, finely chopped
400g (14oz) tinned (canned) chopped
    tomatoes (optional)
Approx. 500ml (2 cups) beef stock
    (optional)
2 handfuls of plain corn crisps (chips)
2 bay leaves
5 tbsp fresh coriander (cilantro),
    finely chopped
Cayenne chilli powder, to taste
    (optional)
500g (1lb 2oz) cooked pinto beans,
    with some of the cooking stock

TO SERVE
Grated cheese
Fresh coriander (cilantro), chopped
Sour cream
Corn tortillas, fried and thinly sliced

Start by making the sauce. Heat a large, heavy-based saucepan over a medium–high heat and toss in the dried chillies. Push them down with a wooden spoon or spatula until they become fragrant from the toasting. This should only take a few seconds. Then flip them over to toast the other side. The chillies will turn a couple of tones darker while toasting, but try not to burn them and turn the exterior black or they will become bitter. Transfer the toasted chillies to a large mixing bowl and pour boiling water over them. Allow to sit in the water for 30 minutes.

After 30 minutes, the chillies will be soft and rehydrated. Transfer them, one by one, to a blender, removing any seeds you might have missed earlier. Taste the soaking water. If it has a strong, bitter flavour, discard it, but if it is sweet and only mildly bitter, keep it. Top the chillies in the blender with the remaining sauce ingredients and blend to a smooth paste. You can add some of the soaking water or fresh water to assist blending, if necessary. Set aside.

Returning to the saucepan, heat the oil for the chilli over a medium–high heat and add the minced (ground) beef. Fry for about 5 minutes, or until the meat is completely cooked through, stirring and breaking the meat apart as you do so that there are no large lumps. Once cooked, add the chopped onion and chillies and continue frying and stirring for 5–8 minutes, or until the onion is turning a golden brown. Stir in the chopped garlic and fry for a further minute before adding the prepared chilli sauce, the additional chopped tomatoes, if using, and some beef stock, retained chilli soaking water and/or retained cooking liquid from the beans if you cooked them from dried, to cover. If you want to add beef stock but don't have any fresh, you could add water and a beef stock cube.

Toss in two handfuls of corn crisps (chips), the bay leaves and chopped coriander (cilantro) and bring to a simmer, stirring occasionally for about 30 minutes. You could turn the heat right down to low and simmer for longer, adding more liquid if required for more depth of flavour.

After cooking for about 30 minutes, the corn crisps (chips) will have disintegrated and thickened the sauce. Taste it and season with salt and pepper if needed. You could also up the heat some by stirring in a bit of cayenne chilli powder. Stir in the beans and simmer for another minute to heat them through. Spoon this thick chilli into bowls and serve with cheese, coriander, sour cream and fried, sliced corn tortillas.

BIRRIA DE RES
SERVES 8

Birria de res is an amazing Mexican stew that takes me right back to my childhood. Friday night was always taco night in my neighbourhood, when everyone would get together for, you guessed it... tacos. Everyone would bring a taco filling to one house and we would all dig in. Birria de res was eaten as a stew, like chilli con carne, but we often fried tortillas, dipped them in the sauce and topped them with the meat, cheese and salsas. Nowadays, frying birria-sauce dipped tortilla is how the famous birria tacos are prepared. To do that, you'll need another pan though. Simply dip corn tortillas in the birria de res sauce and top with some of the meat and cheese, fold them over and fry in a little oil to heat through, turning a couple of times as you do. Birria tacos are some of the best out there, but this is also amazing served as a simple beef stew, as described here. If you have any birria de res left over, try cooking up some instant ramen noodles and adding them to the liquid. Birria ramen is one of my favourite quick, after-work meals.

PREP TIME: 25 MINS
COOKING TIME: 6 HOURS*

2kg (4½lb) beef cheek or chuck, cut
    into large 10cm (4in) pieces
1½ tsp salt
6 dried guajillo peppers
6 dried ancho chillies
1 large onion, cut into about 8 pieces
8 garlic cloves
2 large tomatoes
2.5cm (1in) real cinnamon stick or
    1–2 pinches of ground cinnamon
1 tsp freshly ground black pepper
1 tbsp ground cumin
1 tsp marjoram
1 tbsp Mexican oregano
70ml (¼ cup) cider vinegar
1 beef stock cube
3 tbsp rapeseed (canola) oil or light
    olive oil
Water, beef or chicken stock, as
    needed
Salt and pepper, to taste

OPTIONAL GARNISHES (ALL
    TO TASTE)
Chopped coriander (cilantro)
Pickled onions (see page 262)
Pickled jalapeño slices
Sour cream
Grated cheddar

Season the meat with the salt and set aside.

Remove the stems from the dried chillies and tear them down the centre, removing the seeds. Then place the dried chillies in a saucepan over a medium heat and toast them, turning regularly for about 3 minutes, or until fragrant. Be very careful not to burn them, or it will make the stew bitter. Transfer to a bowl and cover with boiling water for about 15 minutes, or longer if more convenient.

Returning to the saucepan, add the chopped onion, garlic cloves and tomatoes and roast over a medium–high heat until fragrant and charred slightly on the exterior. This should take about 5 minutes. Transfer to a blender to cool a little. Add the cinnamon, black pepper, ground cumin, marjoram, oregano, vinegar, stock cube and the soaked chillies to the blender. Taste the water that the chillies were soaking in. If it is bitter, discard it and add 125ml (½ cup) of fresh water to the blender. If it's not bitter, use that instead of fresh water. Blend until really smooth. You can add more of the soaking water or fresh water if needed to help blend. Set aside.

Pour the oil into your saucepan over a medium–high heat and fry the meat until lightly charred on the exterior. This will take about 10 minutes. You don't want to overcrowd your pan, so do this in batches if necessary.

Pour the blended sauce over the top and add enough water or stock to cover. Bring to a rolling simmer and then reduce the heat, covering the pan and simmering lightly for about 4–5 hours, or until the meat is really tender and shreds easily. You can always add more stock or water if necessary.

Once the meat is good and tender, serve it up topped with your garnishes of choice.

★ MAKE IT FASTER ★
*If you have a countertop pressure cooker, you can cook the meat in a fraction of the time. About an hour in a pressure cooker set to high should make it nice and tender.

CAPE MALAY BOBOTIE
SERVES 4

Bobotie is thought by many to be South Africa's national dish. It offers a combination of sweet, spicy and savoury flavours, none of which should overpower the others. The dish has both European and Malay/Indian roots. The creamy topping on the mildly spiced beef is similar to moussaka, and the spicing has Indian and Malay origins. Many versions of this recipe call for soaked white bread, which thickens the sauce, but the original bobotie curries did not include this. So bread is optional for any of you who are on a gluten-free diet. It is usually served with white or yellow rice.

PREP TIME: 10 MINS
COOKING TIME: 45 MINS

2 slices of white bread, crusts removed (optional)
200ml (¾ cup) full-fat milk
100g (3½oz) raisins or sultanas
3 tbsp ghee or rapeseed (canola) oil
2.5cm (1in) cinnamon stick
2 medium onions, finely chopped
2 tbsp garlic and ginger paste
1 tbsp curry powder
½–1 tsp cayenne chilli powder (to taste)
1 tsp ground cumin
1 tbsp ground ginger (optional)
½ tsp ground turmeric
800g (1lb 12oz) minced (ground) beef (preferably 85:15 meat-to-fat ratio)
4 tbsp apricot jam or mango chutney (more or less to taste)
2 tbsp Worcestershire sauce
2 tbsp tomato purée (paste)
3 tbsp toasted almond flakes
Salt and pepper, to taste
6 bay leaves

FOR THE CUSTARD
4 eggs
½ tsp ground turmeric
1 tsp ground cumin
½ tsp black pepper
Salt, to taste

Preheat the oven to 180°C (350°F/Gas 4).

Place the slices of white bread in a bowl and cover with the milk. The bread is optional, but you will need the milk to make the custard topping. Pour the raisins into another bowl and cover with cold water. Set aside. Now heat the oil in a large, ovenproof frying pan (skillet) over a medium–high heat. When visibly hot, add the cinnamon stick and infuse its flavour into the oil for about 30 seconds. Then add the chopped onions and fry until soft and translucent – about 5 minutes should suffice. Stir in the garlic and ginger paste and fry for a further 30 seconds.

Add the ground spices and stir to coat the onion mixture and then stir in the minced (ground) beef. Cook for about 10 minutes while pushing the meat down with your spoon to break up any large lumps. When cooked through, stir in the apricot jam or mango chutney, Worcestershire sauce and tomato purée (paste) and continue cooking for about 5 minutes.

Take the bread out of the milk it is soaking in and squeeze out the liquid, keeping the milk for the custard. Add the bread to the beef. Remove the raisins from the soaking water and add them to the pan along with the toasted flaked almonds, stirring well to combine. The bread will break down and thicken the sauce.

Now flatten the beef mixture into the pan lightly and smooth it over on top. Take off the heat. In a bowl, whisk the eggs, turmeric, cumin, milk, salt and pepper together until creamy smooth. Then pour it over the meat mixture, decorate with the bay leaves and place in the oven. Bake for 30 minutes, or until the custard is set and golden brown on top.

HUNGARIAN GOULASH
SERVES 4–6

Hungary was part of the Silk Road routes, and chillies and other spices will have made their way through the region. It wasn't until the early 19th century, however, that chillies really caught on and that was in the use of paprika. Now Hungary produces some of the best paprika in the world and it plays a big part in their national dish, beef goulash, and other recipes. So if you can get hot Hungarian paprika for this recipe, do it. You can adjust the spiciness by replacing the sweet paprika with hot paprika if you like. This can be eaten on its own, or served with a crusty loaf of bread or buttered tagliatelle.

PREP TIME: 15 MINS
COOKING TIME: 80 MINS

4 tbsp pork lard
4 carrots, cut into thin rounds
3 red (bell) peppers, seeded and cut into bite-sized pieces
2 green (bell) peppers, seeded and cut into bite-sized pieces
2 medium onions, finely chopped
½ tsp caraway seeds, lightly crushed
2 bay leaves
6 garlic cloves, finely chopped
800g (1lb 12oz) stewing beef, cut into bite-sized pieces
2 tbsp sweet paprika
2 tbsp hot paprika (or more sweet paprika)
1.25 litres (5 cups) water or unsalted beef stock
400g (14oz) tinned (canned) chopped tomatoes
2 potatoes, cut into bite-sized pieces
Salt and pepper, to taste
Chopped parsley, to serve

Melt the pork lard over a medium–high heat in a large saucepan. When bubbling hot, add two of the sliced carrots and half of the red and green (bell) peppers and fry until the vegetables are just cooked through and have a nice shine to them. Transfer to a plate with a slotted spoon and set aside.

Now add the chopped onions and fry for about 8 minutes, or until lightly browned. Add the crushed caraway seeds, bay leaves and garlic and fry, stirring continuously, for 30 seconds to combine. Add the beef and continue cooking and stirring for about 10 minutes, or until the beef is browned all over. Stir in the sweet paprika and, if you are sure you are okay with the heat, the hot paprika too. You can always add this to taste at the end.

Pour in the water or beef stock and the chopped tomatoes and bring to a boil. While this is heating up, tie the remaining raw carrots and (bell) peppers tightly in a muslin cloth and add this to the stock. When the stock reaches boiling point, reduce the heat and simmer for about 45 minutes.

Add the cubed potatoes and continue cooking until the meat is really tender and the potatoes are cooked through. This should take about 30 minutes, but don't rush it – the meat is ready when it's ready. Remove the muslin and bay leaves and then return the cooked carrots and peppers to the stock.

Add salt and pepper to taste and add more paprika (hot or sweet) to your liking. Serve hot, garnished with the chopped parsley.

★ MAKE IT EASIER ★
The two separate stages for cooking the carrots and green (bell) peppers, are done for both presentation and extra flavour. However, for ease, you could simply add all of the carrots and bell peppers when you add the chopped onion and then carry on with the recipe.

EASY SRI LANKAN BEEF CURRY
SERVES 4–6

As easy recipes go, this is a good one! My wife and I learned this recipe at a little restaurant/hotel in Habarana, Sri Lanka called Inspire. We were out on a walk one day and just happened to find it, enjoying a spectacular lunch. The owner invited us back the next day to learn how to make all of the dishes that we ordered, and we jumped at the chance. Sri Lanka is the cinnamon capital of the world. The 'real' cinnamon (see page 9) in this recipe is just broken up by hand and then added. The paper-thin pieces actually dissolve into the sauce. It's really worth sourcing some, but you can use cinnamon cassia. This curry is delicious served with white basmati rice or red matta rice (see page 249).

PREP TIME: 15 MINS
COOKING TIME: 45 MINS

900g (2lb) stewing beef, cut into bite-sized pieces
2 generous tsp ground cumin
1 generous tbsp Kashmiri chilli powder or another of choice
2 tsp black pepper
1 tsp salt
5cm (2in) real cinnamon stick or cassia, broken up
2 tbsp coconut oil
5 garlic cloves, finely chopped (approx. 2 generous tbsp)
5cm (2in) leek, thinly sliced
15 fresh or frozen curry leaves
¼ red onion, thinly sliced
1 tsp fenugreek seeds

Place the beef in a mixing bowl and add the cumin, chilli powder, black pepper, salt and broken-up piece of real cinnamon. If using cassia instead of real cinnamon, add it later in the cooking process, when instructed. Mix well with your hands so that the meat is equally coated and then pour in 250ml (1 cup) of water. Stir it all up and set aside to marinate for a few minutes or even overnight. The longer, the better.

When ready to cook the curry, heat the oil in a large saucepan over a medium–high heat and stir in the garlic. Stir until fragrant, about 30 seconds, and then add the sliced leek, curry leaves, red onion and fenugreek seeds. If using cassia instead of real cinnamon, it can be added to the oil at this stage too. Fry this veggie mixture for about 5 minutes to soften and flavour the oil and then pour in the marinated beef. Brown the beef in the oil for a couple of minutes and then pour in just enough water to cover. Place the lid on the pan and simmer over a medium heat for about 40 minutes, or until the beef is good and tender. Don't rush this! It's ready when it's ready. If needed, you can always add a drop more water if the sauce is drying up. Serve hot.

Clockwise from top left: Easy Sri Lankan beef curry; aubergine curry (page 142); Sri Lankan dal curry (page 143)

LANDI KOTAL LAMB KARAHI
SERVES 4

Landi Kotal is a town in Pakistan where this karahi curry originates, although I have to say I have seen very similar curries from other cities. Street vendors will either stew large quantities of the meat or grill it over an open flame until tender, and then cook up this karahi in minutes for hungry customers. Here I offer my version, which you can cook up from scratch in your own kitchen.

PREP TIME: 10 MINS
COOKING TIME: 35 MINS

3 tbsp rapeseed (canola) oil or ghee
2 medium onions, thinly sliced
1 tsp salt
2 tbsp garlic and ginger paste
1kg (2lb 2oz) lamb leg, cut into bite-sized pieces
3 large tomatoes, diced
½ tsp ground turmeric
1–2 tsp Kashmiri chilli powder
4–6 green bird's eye chillies, roughly chopped
Salt, to taste
3 tbsp coriander (cilantro), finely chopped

Heat the oil or ghee in a karahi or wok over a medium–high heat and fry the onions for about 7 minutes, or until golden brown. Add the salt while the onion cooks, which will draw out some of the liquid. Stir in the garlic and ginger paste and fry for a further 30 seconds. Then add the meat and continue cooking until it is browned all over. This should take about 5 minutes.

Add the diced tomatoes, turmeric and chilli powder and stir to combine. Pour in enough water to cover the meat and bring to a boil. Lower the heat and simmer until you have a thick sauce and the meat is cooked through and tender. This should take about 20 minutes, but don't rush this step. The meat is ready when it's ready. Stir in the chillies and simmer for another minute or so and then season with more salt to taste, if required. Garnish with the coriander (cilantro) to serve.

LAMB CURRY WITH SWEET POTATO

SERVES 4–6

This is a straightforward, no-fuss curry that is so easy to prepare. I have used sweet potato here, but you could substitute normal baking potatoes or even swede (rutabaga) if you aren't a fan of sweet potatoes. The curry simmers slowly and can also be prepared a day or two ahead of serving, making it really convenient. The depth of flavour intensifies as the curry sits in the fridge. All you'll need to do is heat it up. After tempering the spices and frying the onions in the ghee, you could even pour everything into a slow cooker and cook on low for eight hours if more convenient. This is good served over white rice or with naans or chapattis.

PREP TIME: 20 MINS
COOKING TIME: 60 MINS

2 tbsp rapeseed (canola) oil or ghee
5cm (2in) cinnamon stick
3 black cardamom pods or 6 green
    cardamom pods, lightly crushed
10 black peppercorns
1 star anise
2 Indian bay leaves
3 onions, finely chopped
1 tsp salt
2 tbsp garlic and ginger paste
5 plum tomatoes, diced
1 leg of lamb, cut into 5cm (2in)
    chunks (retain the bone if you
    have it)
1 tbsp ground cumin
1 tbsp ground coriander
1–2 tbsp Kashmiri chilli powder
2 medium sweet potatoes, peeled and
    cut into 2.5cm (1in) dice
3 tbsp natural yoghurt
1 tsp garam masala, shop-bought or
    homemade (see page 259)
Salt, to taste
3 tbsp fresh coriander (cilantro),
    finely chopped
Lime wedges, to serve

Heat the oil or ghee in a large saucepan over a medium–high heat. When visibly hot, stir in the cinnamon, cardamom pods, black peppercorns, star anise and bay leaves and temper them in the hot oil, stirring regularly for about a minute. Stir in the chopped onion and sprinkle in the salt and fry for about 8 minutes, or until lightly browned and soft. Stir in the garlic and ginger paste and let it sizzle into the onion mixture for about a minute.

Now add the diced tomatoes, followed by the lamb chunks. If you have the bone, go ahead and throw that in, too. Let the meat sizzle for a couple of minutes, moving it around often to brown it all over. Add the ground cumin, ground coriander and chilli powder and then pour in just enough water to cover. Bring this to a simmer and cook for 20 minutes and then add the cubed sweet potato. Cover the pan and simmer over a medium heat for about 30 minutes, or until the meat and sweet potato are tender. When ready, stir in the yoghurt one tablespoon at a time. Then sprinkle the garam masala over the top and stir it in too.

Season with salt to taste and garnish with the fresh coriander (cilantro). Serve with the lime wedges, which can be squeezed over the curry to taste.

TRINI CURRY GOAT
SERVES 4

Goat meat is highly underrated, so unfortunately it's not something you can just run out to the supermarket and pick up. At least not where I live. You can get it at most Indian grocers and butchers, though, so put it on your shopping list and give this delicious curry from Trinidad and Tobago a try. You can usually get it cut off the bone for you, but I purchase a whole leg and use the bone in the curry too, for flavour. Lamb can be substituted. I recommend using a saucepan with a light-coloured base for this recipe so that you can better judge when the brown sugar is ready. I like to serve this with white rice or a crusty loaf of bread.

PREP TIME: 15 MINS, PLUS
 OPTIONAL MARINATING TIME
COOKING TIME: 40–60 MINS

1kg (2lb 2oz) goat meat, cut into
 2.5cm (1in) cubes

FOR THE MARINADE
5 tbsp dark rum
2 tbsp garlic and ginger paste
3–4 bay leaves
3 spring onions (scallions), roughly
 chopped
4 sprigs of fresh thyme
3 sprigs of fresh oregano

FOR THE CURRY
2–3 tbsp coconut oil
2 cinnamon sticks
3 cloves
1 heaped tbsp light brown sugar
1.25 litres (5 cups) water or beef stock
1 onion, finely chopped
2 carrots, chopped
2 tbsp chopped celery
2 tomatoes, diced
200g (7oz) block coconut or 200g
 (7oz) thick coconut milk
100g (3½oz) butter

FOR THE CURRY PASTE
1 large bunch of fresh coriander
½ onion
5 garlic cloves, roughly chopped
2 tbsp curry powder
1 tsp ground turmeric
2 tbsp ground cumin and coriander
1 scotch bonnet chilli, roughly
 chopped
¼ tsp allspice
½ tbsp salt
¼ tsp black pepper

In a large bowl, cover the goat meat in the rum, garlic and ginger paste, bay leaves, spring onions (scallions), thyme and oregano and marinate for 24–48 hours. If you must, you can just start cooking immediately with good results, but the longer marinating time will benefit the curry.

When ready to cook the curry, melt the coconut oil over a medium–high heat and then toss in the cinnamon and cloves. Temper these spices in the oil for about a minute. Now add the light brown sugar and stir until it melts and turns a few shades darker. Have the water or stock ready and to hand. As soon as the sugar is a deep chocolate brown, carefully pour in the water or stock followed by the marinated meat. Don't let the sugar turn black or it will be burnt and you will have to start over again!

Bring to a simmer over a medium–high heat and continue simmering, covered, until the meat is tender. This will take about 45–60 minutes. While the meat is simmering, prepare the curry paste. Blend all of the paste ingredients in a blender or food processor into a smooth paste. Set aside.

When the meat is tender, stir in the chopped onion, carrots, celery and tomatoes and continue simmering until the carrots are cooked through and the sauce has reduced a little. Pour in the prepared curry paste and then add the block coconut or coconut milk. Continue cooking until you are happy with the consistency. The sauce should be quite thick but still quite liquidy.

Add the butter and stir until it has melted into the sauce. Check for seasoning, adding more salt and spices to taste, then serve.

WILD BOAR JUNGLE CURRY

SERVES 3–4

I featured a duck jungle curry in my cookbook *The Curry Guy Thai*, and there was no way I could write this book without featuring at least one jungle curry. Jungle curries are traditionally made with game meat and I love the gamey flavour that wild boar gives to this recipe, though you could just use pork if you have trouble sourcing the wild stuff. Unlike most popular Thai curries, jungle curry does not call for coconut milk. This is a spicy curry that I make often. Jungle curry could easily be made vegetarian by using vegetable stock and more vegetables, and/or fried or raw tofu that can be added to the sauce at the end of cooking. I like to serve this with jasmine rice.

PREP TIME: 15 MINS
COOKING TIME: 15 MINS

2 tbsp rapeseed (canola), peanut or coconut oil
600g (1lb 5oz) wild boar (or farmed pork), preferably shoulder, cut into thin slices across the grain
6 tbsp Thai red curry paste (see page 153 or shop-bought, to taste)
500ml (2 cups) chicken stock (see page 250 or shop-bought) or water
10 green (string) beans, cut into 2.5cm (1in) pieces
1 x 227g (8oz) tin (can) bamboo shoots, drained and cut into matchsticks
150g (5½oz) small Thai aubergines (eggplants) or courgettes (zucchini)
3 tbsp fresh green peppercorns
2–3 tbsp Thai fish sauce (gluten-free brands are available)
6 lime leaves, stalks removed and leaves thinly sliced
Juice of ½ lime
1 tsp palm sugar (optional)
Coriander (cilantro) leaves, to garnish
Thai sweet basil leaves, to garnish

Heat the oil in a large pan or wok over a medium–high heat. When visibly hot, add the meat and fry for about 5 minutes, or until nearly cooked through. Stir in the curry paste and fry for about a minute, until really fragrant. Pour in the stock or water and bring to a rolling simmer.

Stir in the veggies and green peppercorns and simmer until cooked to your liking. I usually only cook mine for about 3 minutes, as the vegetables will continue cooking in the hot curry sauce. Add the fish sauce, sliced lime leaves and lime juice. Taste the sauce and adjust, adding more fish sauce for a saltier flavour, sugar if you prefer it sweeter and more lime juice for sourness.

This is a spicy curry, so you could add a little more red curry paste or chilli powder, too. Once you have the flavour you are looking for, garnish with coriander (cilantro) and Thai sweet basil leaves.

BABI KECAP
SERVES 4

Travelling around Bali for four weeks was a culinary experience I want to do again really soon. A lot of what was on offer, however, was pretty much expected: the dishes everyone knows and goes to Bali to try. Every now and then we came across something new and exciting, and this babi kecap was one of them. This dish is so easy to prepare. The pork is simmered in a delicious sweet, sour, savoury and spicy sauce until it literally melts in your mouth. Although it may not be one of the best-known Indonesian dishes, babi kecap is definitely one of my favourites from our trip and one you need to put on your 'must try' list. If you like spicy food, consider serving this with homemade (see page 252) or shop-bought sambal oelek.

PREP TIME: 10 MINS
COOKING TIME: 45 MINS

FOR THE SAMBAL PASTE
5 banana shallots
3 candlenuts or macadamia nuts
3 red finger chillies, roughly chopped
4 garlic cloves, peeled and smashed
5cm (2in) piece of ginger, roughly chopped
½ tsp ground turmeric

FOR THE STEW
2 tbsp rapeseed (canola) oil
700g (1lb 9oz) pork belly, cut into 5cm (2in) chunks
2 makrut lime leaves, stems removed and thinly sliced
1 tbsp medium hot sauce (of your choice)
1 tsp palm sugar or light brown sugar
6 tbsp kecap manis*
1 tbsp tamarind paste (see page 256 or shop-bought)
1 tbsp lemon juice
2 red spur chillies, thinly sliced, to garnish

Place the shallots, candlenuts/macadamia nuts, chillies, garlic, ginger and ground turmeric in a food processor and blend to a smooth paste. You might need to add a little water to assist blending. Set aside.

Now heat a large, high-sided frying pan (skillet) that has a lid over a medium–high heat and add the oil. When the oil is visibly hot, add the pork belly pieces and brown the meat for about 5 minutes. Depending on the size of your pan, you might need to do this in two batches. Then add the prepared sambal paste to the pan and stir well to combine. Continue cooking for another 3 minutes to cook out the rawness of the sambal and then stir in the fresh, thinly sliced lime leaves and the hot sauce.

Add just enough water to cover the meat and bring to a simmer over a medium heat. Stir in the sugar and cover the pan to simmer for 30 minutes. Remove the lid and stir in the kecap manis and tamarind paste and bring to a boil over a medium–high heat. Reduce the heat to low and simmer, stirring occasionally, for 30 minutes, or until the pork is fall-apart tender. To finish, stir in the lemon juice and continue cooking until you have a thick sauce that literally clings to the meat. Garnish with the sliced spur chillies and serve immediately as it is, or with white rice.

NOTE
*Most, if not all, shop-bought kecap manis contains gluten. If you are on a gluten-free diet, you can still make this recipe using my kecap manis recipe on page 258, using a gluten-free soy sauce such as tamari.

SRI LANKAN BLACK PORK CURRY
SERVES 4–6

Out of all the curries I tried in Sri Lanka – and there were a lot of them – this was my favourite. You can purchase good-quality dark-roasted Sri Lankan curry powder online and at specialist shops, but making your own will take this recipe to the most amazing level. We're talking just as good as you will find anywhere in Sri Lanka, here! Preparing the dark-roasted curry powder is a bit of a chore, but it's worth doing if you have time.

PREP TIME: 15 MINS, PLUS MARINATING TIME
COOKING TIME: 60 MINS

900g (2lb) belly pork, cut into bite-sized pieces

FOR THE MARINADE
2 tsp red chilli powder (or to taste)
½ tsp ground turmeric
1 tbsp ground black pepper
70ml (¼ cup) distilled white vinegar
1 tbsp garlic and ginger paste
1 tsp salt

FOR THE CURRY
2 tbsp coconut oil or rapeseed (canola) oil
20 fresh or frozen curry leaves
5cm (2in) square piece of pandan leaf (optional)
2 medium red onions, finely chopped
2 tbsp garlic and ginger paste
1 lemongrass stalk, white part only, cut into about 8 pieces
5 green finger chillies, slit lengthwise down the middle
3 tbsp dark-roasted curry powder (see page 261 or shop-bought)
1 whole head of garlic, smashed but left in the skins
2 tsp jaggery or light brown sugar
2 tsp tamarind paste (see page 256 or shop-bought)
Salt, to taste

Put the pork pieces in a mixing bowl and add the marinade ingredients. Mix well with your hands or a spoon. You might want to wear plastic gloves if mixing by hand because of the chilli powder. Cover and leave to marinate for 3 hours or overnight – the longer, the better.

When you're ready to cook the curry, heat the oil in a large pan over a medium–high heat. When visibly hot, stir in the curry leaves and pandan leaf and allow them to infuse into the oil for about 30 seconds. Now add the chopped red onions and fry for about 5 minutes, or until soft and translucent. Stir in the garlic and ginger paste, lemongrass and chillies and fry for a further 30 seconds. Add the dark-roasted curry powder and stir well to combine.

Now pour in the pork with all of the marinade and stir until the meat is nicely coated with the other ingredients. Fry over a medium heat for about 10 minutes to brown the pork and then add just enough water to cover the meat completely. Stir in the smashed garlic, sugar and tamarind paste and simmer, covered, for 30 minutes.

After 30 minutes, lift the lid and take a look. This is a dry curry, so if it's looking really saucy cook a little longer until the delicious thick sauce is coating the meat. Taste the curry and if needed add more sugar for sweetness or tamarind for sourness, to taste. Complete by adding salt to taste.

BICOL EXPRESS

SERVES 4

Bicol express is amazing. There's really no other way to put it. It has a creamy, coconut sauce that's mildly spiced with red and green chillies. The pork belly is cooked to perfection, so tender it dissolves in your mouth. There are a good number of explanations for the name of this 'curry', but the one I believe most is that it was named by a woman called Cely Kalaw. She had developed her own version of a similar curry for a cooking competition she entered in the 1970s. Cely's brother heard the Bicol express train passing her restaurant and suggested she call it that. The rest is history, though you might find other explanations.

PREP TIME: 10 MINS
COOKING TIME: 45 MINS

2 tbsp rapeseed (canola) or coconut oil
1 large onion, finely chopped
6 garlic cloves, finely chopped
1 thumb-sized piece of ginger, finely chopped
1kg (2lb 2oz) pork belly, cut into bite-sized pieces
2 tbsp ginisang bagoong shrimp paste★
400ml (1¾ cups) thick coconut milk
250ml (1 cup) water
5 red finger chillies, finely chopped
150g (5½oz) block coconut (see page 11 for substitutes)
5 green chillies, cut into rings
Salt and pepper, to taste

Heat the oil in a large frying pan (skillet) over a medium–high heat. When visibly hot, stir in the chopped onion and fry for about 5 minutes, or until soft and translucent. Stir in the chopped garlic and ginger and fry for another 30 seconds.

Now add the pork and fry with the onion mixture until lightly browned. This should take about 3 minutes. Stir in the ginisang bagoong and fry for a further couple of minutes, stirring regularly. Add the coconut milk and water and bring to a simmer. Stir in the chopped red chillies and simmer, covered, for about 20 minutes. Remove the lid and add the block coconut and continue simmering for another 20 minutes, or until the pork is really tender and the sauce has thickened. The block coconut will melt into the sauce as you do.

Add the sliced green chillies and continue simmering until you have a nice thick sauce. Season with salt and pepper to taste.

NOTE

★Ginisang bagoong shrimp paste is popular in Filipino cooking and is available online and at specialist shops. The paste is prepared by frying shrimp paste, onions, tomatoes, garlic, spices and vinegar in pork fat. You could substitute about 2 teaspoons of Chinese shrimp paste, but the ginisang bagoong will give you a more authentic look and flavour.

KIMCHI JJIGAE
SERVES 4

This one is savoury, spicy, mildly sweet and sour. When it comes to a mouthful of deliciousness, kimchi jjigae ticks all the boxes. I learned this recipe back when I was at university and often used to stay with friends in LA. A couple of guys I knew from school studied at UCLA, and their room-mates were from South Korea. This recipe brings back great memories of those days, drinking way too much beer and gulping down bowls of kimchi jjigae.

PREP TIME: 10 MINS
COOKING TIME: 35 MINS

375g (¾lb) pork belly, cut into small bite-sized pieces
1 tsp ground black pepper
1 tbsp light soy sauce (gluten-free brands are available)

FOR THE JJIGAE
70ml (¼ cup) kimchi brine
450g (1lb) aged kimchi, cut into bite-sized pieces
3 spring onions (scallions), roughly chopped
1 onion, thinly sliced
3 tsp gochugaru (Korean hot pepper flakes)
1½ tbsp gochujang (Korean hot pepper paste; gluten-free brands are available)
1 tbsp toasted sesame oil
500ml (2 cups) chicken stock or water
200g (7oz) tofu, sliced into bite-sized pieces
Salt and sugar, to taste
2 spring onions (scallions), thinly sliced

Place the pork belly pieces in a bowl and mix with the black pepper and soy sauce. Set aside until needed, or allow to marinate for longer if you like.

Pour the kimchi brine into a saucepan that is large enough to contain all the ingredients. Add the kimchi, spring onions (scallions) and sliced onion. Press it all down and then arrange the marinated pork on top. Add the gochugaru, gochujang, sesame oil and chicken stock or water. Ensure that all the ingredients are completely submerged in the stock.

Place the pan over a medium–high heat and bring to a simmer. Cover and cook for about 20 minutes. Then take the lid off and add the tofu, being sure to spoon some of that delicious sauce over it. Cover the pan again and simmer for another 15 minutes. Taste the sauce and add salt and sugar to taste. I usually add about a teaspoon of salt and a teaspoon of sugar, but you need to add these to your preference. Be careful with the salt as kimchi is already salty.

Serve with white rice topped with the thinly sliced spring onions.

GOAN-STYLE PORK KEEMA VINDALOO

SERVES 3–4

Goan vindaloo is one of my favourite curries from India. This recipe gives the awesome flavour of a traditional vindaloo but it can be cooked so much faster. Instead of chunks of pork shoulder, you cook minced (ground) pork. So you still get the pork flavour, but the dish is ready in less than 30 minutes if you don't add the optional sautéed garlic cloves. You can serve this vindaloo over rice, or wrap it up into a tortilla or chapatti.

PREP TIME: 10 MINS, PLUS
   OPTIONAL MARINATING TIME
COOKING TIME: 40 MINS

750g (1lb 10oz) minced (ground) pork

FOR THE MARINADE
1 tbsp Kashmiri chilli powder
1½ tbsp ground cumin
1½ tbsp ground coriander
½ tsp ground fenugreek
½ tsp ground cloves
1 tbsp ground black pepper
½ tsp ground turmeric
¾ tsp ground cinnamon
½ tsp ground cardamom
4 green chillies, finely chopped
5 tbsp red wine vinegar
2 tbsp soft brown sugar
1 tbsp tamarind paste
3 tbsp garlic and ginger paste

FOR THE CURRY
3–4 tbsp coconut oil
1 head of garlic, cloves separated and
   smashed lightly (optional)
1 tsp brown mustard seeds
20 fresh curry leaves
2 medium red onions, finely chopped
2 tomatoes, finely diced
Salt, to taste
3 tbsp coriander (cilantro), finely
   chopped
2 limes, quartered

Start with the marinade. Place all the marinade ingredients in a large mixing bowl and stir into a smooth paste. Add the minced (ground) pork to the marinade and mix well to combine. Cover and set aside or place, covered, in the fridge for 30 minutes or overnight. The longer, the better.

Adding the whole garlic cloves is optional, so skip this paragraph if you're not adding them. Heat the coconut oil in a saucepan over a low heat. Add the garlic cloves and allow to cook gently for about 20 minutes. It is important not to burn the garlic, so watch carefully. The garlic should be squishy soft and translucent when ready. Transfer the garlic from the saucepan to a plate and set aside, leaving as much of the oil in the pan as possible.

Pour about 400ml (1¾ cups) of water over the marinated minced pork and break it down with your hands. It should have the same consistency as a thick porridge. If not, add a little more water. Now heat the oil over a medium–high heat. If you cooked the garlic, just top it up a little, if needed, so that you have about 3 tablespoons of oil in the pan. When visibly hot, stir in the mustard seeds. When they begin to pop, add the curry leaves and sauté for 30 seconds before adding the chopped onions. Fry for about 10 minutes until the onions are soft, translucent and golden brown in colour.

Add the prepared meat and fry for 8–10 minutes, breaking the meat down so that there are no big lumps. As the meat fries, the water will slowly evaporate and you will be left with a pan of very fine minced pork. Stir in the tomatoes and continue simmering for another 3 minutes until you have a keema consistency that you are happy with. It should not be dry but also not really saucy.

To finish, stir in the garlic cloves if you sautéed them earlier. Check the seasoning and add salt to taste. Serve immediately, garnished with the chopped coriander (cilantro) and the quartered limes, which can be squeezed over the top at the table to taste.

GF

MALAYSIAN FISH CURRY
SERVES 4

One of my favourite seafood curries I tried in Kuala Lumper was fish-head curry. Fish heads are slowly simmered into a delicious curry sauce and then you just need to pick the meat off and enjoy. At home I have started making this curry with halibut instead of fish heads, which isn't cheap but is one of the most delicious fishes on the planet. You could, however, use any white, meaty fish for this recipe. Although I do love the fish-head version, you could be in for a rather painful surprise if you bite into one of those toothy jaws the wrong way, as I unfortunately found out the hard way.

PREP TIME: 15 MINS
COOKING TIME: 20 MINS

FOR THE PASTE

8 banana shallots
5 garlic cloves, smashed
2.5cm (1in) piece of galangal, roughly
    chopped
2.5cm (1in) piece of ginger, roughly
    chopped
2 green finger chillies
2 lemongrass stalks
½ tsp shrimp paste

FOR THE CURRY

3 tbsp rapeseed (canola) or coconut
    oil (I use coconut oil for this one)
5cm (2in) cinnamon stick
2 star anise
20 fresh or frozen curry leaves
2 tbsp unroasted curry powder (see
    page 258 or shop-bought)
2½ tsp tamarind paste (see page 256
    or shop-bought)
6 makrut lime leaves, stems removed
    and quartered
200g (1½ cups) green (string) beans,
    cut into 2.5cm (1in) pieces
250ml (1 cup) water or fish stock
400ml (1¾ cups) thick coconut milk
6–10 fried tofu puffs (optional)*
700g (1lb 9oz) halibut or another
    white, meaty fish like cod, codling
    or swordfish, cut into large chunks
3 medium tomatoes, quartered or
    even cut smaller
1 tsp palm sugar or white sugar (or
    to taste)
Salt and pepper, to taste
Lime wedges, to serve

Put all of the paste ingredients in a blender or spice grinder and blend to a smooth paste. You can add a drop of water if needed to blend. Set aside.

Heat the oil in a large pan or wok over a medium–high heat. When visibly hot, throw in the cinnamon stick and star anise and move them around to infuse into the oil for about 30 seconds. Now add the curry leaves and fry for a further 30 seconds, or until fragrant. Stir in the prepared spice paste and fry for about 2 minutes to cook out the rawness. Add the curry powder, tamarind paste, makrut lime leaves and green (string) beans and stir well to combine. Then add the water or stock. Simmer for about 5 minutes, or until the green bean are almost cooked through but still a bit crisp. Add the coconut milk, tofu puffs (if using) and fish and simmer gently for about 5 minutes. Do not stir! Instead, pick up your pan and swirl it around from time to time, which will do the same job but will stop the fish from falling apart.

Once the fish is cooked through, add the quartered tomatoes and push them into the simmering sauce. Taste the sauce and add sugar, salt and pepper to taste. You can also add more tamarind paste if you prefer a more sour flavour, but I find that a squeeze or two of lime juice is all this needs. Serve immediately with lime wedges over white rice or with crusty bread.

NOTE

*Tofu puffs are available at many Asian grocers and online but are also easy to make. Pat a block of fresh, firm tofu dry and cut into bite-sized cubes. Heat about 10cm (4in) of vegetable oil in a wok over a medium–high heat. Your oil is ready for cooking when thousands of little bubbles form on contact when you place a wooden chopstick or spatula in it. Fry in small batches for about 10–15 minutes, or until the tofu is light brown, puffed and spongy. After about 5 minutes of frying, the tofu will begin to float to the top, which is a good indication that it is becoming light and airy.

MEEN MOLEE
SERVES 4

I make this salmon meen molee often as it is delicious, quick and easy to prepare. You can literally cook this meal in less than 20 minutes. Meen molee may be a quick meal, but the flavours work so well together. It really will taste like you've been slaving over a hot stove for hours! I watched this curry being prepared in Kerala where kingfish is the fish of choice, but salmon is a perfect substitute.

PREP TIME: 5 MINS
COOKING TIME: 15 MINS

2 tbsp coconut oil
1 tbsp black mustard seeds
20 fresh or frozen curry leaves
1 onion, finely chopped
2 tbsp garlic and ginger paste
2–5 fresh green chillies, finely
    chopped (optional)
1½ tsp Kashmiri chilli powder
½ tsp ground cumin
1 tsp ground turmeric
2 medium tomatoes, finely chopped
400ml (1¾ cups) thick coconut milk
4 x 150g (5½oz) salmon fillets
Salt and pepper, to taste
Juice of 2 limes
4 tbsp coriander (cilantro), finely
    chopped

Heat the oil in a large frying pan (skillet) over a medium–high heat. When visibly hot, stir in the mustard seeds. When they begin to crackle, stir in the curry leaves and fry until fragrant – this should take about 30 seconds. Stir in the chopped onion and fry for about 5 minutes, or until soft and translucent. Then add the garlic and ginger paste and chopped chillies and stir them around in the pan for about 30 seconds.

Now add the ground spices and stir well to combine. Add the chopped tomatoes and stir again. Then pour in the coconut milk and bring to a rolling simmer. Add the salmon fillets to the pan and cover. Simmer, covered, for about 4 minutes, or until almost cooked through to your liking. I like my salmon a bit pink in the centre, but you could cook it longer if you prefer yours more well done. Be careful not to overcook it.

Take the lid off the pan. If the sauce is too thin, remove the salmon and cook it down a little. Season with salt and pepper to taste. To serve, add some lime juice to taste and garnish with fresh coriander (cilantro).

FISH VINDAYE
SERVES 4

Fish vindaye is a pickled fish curry from Mauritius, although I didn't learn this recipe there. This one came to me in Sri Lanka. One of the chefs at the hotel I was staying at was from Mauritius, and my wife and I had just enjoyed his signature chilli crab dish. Hearing that we both loved seafood and spice, he scribbled down this recipe on a cocktail napkin and told me I had to try it. The ingredients are simple and it's really easy to make, too. It kind of reminds me of Goan pork vindaloo, but with fish and far fewer ingredients. This is great served simply with white rice or with crusty bread on the side.

PREP TIME: 15 MINS
COOKING TIME: 10 MINS

FOR THE PASTE
1 tsp black mustard seeds
½ tsp fenugreek seeds
3–6 Kashmiri dried red chillies
1 tsp ground turmeric
5 garlic cloves
2.5cm (1in) piece of ginger, roughly chopped

FOR THE CURRY
700g (1lb 9oz) fresh tuna or any meaty fish, cut into 2.5cm (1in) cubes
½ tsp salt
1 tsp ground turmeric
1 tsp black pepper
70ml (¼ cup) coconut oil
2 medium red onions, thinly sliced
Green finger chillies, slit down the middle, to your preference
80ml (⅓ cup) distilled white vinegar

Place the mustard seeds, fenugreek seeds and dried Kashmiri chillies in a pestle and mortar and pound until broken down into a powder. Add the turmeric, garlic and ginger and keep pounding until you have a thick and fragrant paste. Add about 3 tablespoons of water and grind it some more until smooth. Set aside. This could all be done in a small food processor if it's more convenient.

Sprinkle the fish with the salt, ground turmeric and pepper and toss so that it is evenly coated. Then heat the oil in a wok or large pan over a high heat and add the fish. Fry, stirring occasionally and delicately, for about 5 minutes to brown the exterior. You should see some crispy bits, too. Transfer the cooked fish to a bowl with a slotted spoon, leaving what oil remains in the pan. Set aside.

Now add the paste to the oil over a medium–high heat and fry it for about a minute to cook off the rawness. Add the cooked fish back into the pan and stir to combine. Then add the sliced onion and as many chillies as you like and stir some more until the onion and chillies have softened a little and are covered in the paste mixture. A couple of minutes should do the trick. Pour in the vinegar and stir again to combine.

Eat immediately or keep in the fridge for up to three days, stirring once daily. This will intensify the flavour.

GOAN FISH CURRY
SERVES 3–4

It's so easy to lose track of time on a beach in southern Goa. Sitting there with cold beers in hand and watching the sun go down was our favourite time of day. All of the beach restaurants would fire up their barbecues and cook the fresh fish that had only been brought in from the sea a few hours earlier. We must have had seafood cooked in every way possible during our stay and this simple fish curry, which was cooked in a clay pot over fire, was incredible. It was served simply over a bed of matta rice (see page 249). Although this curry is obviously a main course, it became a beautiful starter as the grilled fish on offer was too good to pass up.

PREP TIME: 10 MINS
COOKING TIME: 15 MINS

500g (1lb 2oz) swordfish, skinned and sliced thickly
1 tsp flaky sea salt

FOR THE PASTE
10 dried Kashmiri chillies, soaked in water for 30 minutes
1 medium red onion, roughly chopped
6 large garlic cloves, peeled and smashed
2.5cm (1in) piece of ginger, roughly chopped
1 tsp cumin seeds
½ tsp freshly cracked black pepper
¼ tsp ground turmeric
2.5cm (1in) cinnamon stick or pinch of ground cinnamon

FOR THE CURRY
2 tbsp coconut or rapeseed (canola) oil
10 fresh or frozen curry leaves
1 medium brown onion, finely chopped
200g (7oz) chopped tomatoes
2 green chillies, sliced lengthwise
2 tbsp tamarind paste (see page 256 or shop-bought)
Salt, to taste
2 tbsp chopped coriander (cilantro), to garnish

In a bowl, sprinkle the salt over the fish and set aside while you make the sauce. Blend all of the curry paste ingredients with just enough water to make a thick and smooth paste. Set aside.

Heat the oil in a large frying pan (skillet) or wok over a medium–high heat. When hot, add the curry leaves and temper them in the oil for about 30 seconds. Then add the onion and fry for about 5–7 minutes until lightly browned.

Add the curry paste and tomatoes and give it all a good stir for about a minute to combine. Now add enough water to make a sauce that is to your preferred consistency. I used about 250ml (1 cup). Add the green chillies and the fish and push the fish down into the simmering sauce to cook. It should only take about 3–5 minutes to cook through.

To finish, stir in the tamarind paste a tablespoon at a time. Tamarind paste gives the curry a nice sour flavour. I recommend tasting the sauce after one tablespoon and then adding more if you like.

Season with salt to taste and garnish with the chopped coriander (cilantro).

SRI LANKAN CRAB CURRY
SERVES 3–4

This is one I learned at Cinnamon Hikka Tranz hotel on the west coast of Sri Lanka. We filmed it being made for my YouTube channel and I couldn't wait to give it a go at home. Chef Pasan Attanayaka was great! He showed me how to cook so many different curries and they were all amazing. He prepared this curry using fresh mud crabs, which you can find in the freezer section of many Sri Lankan shops, but any crab will do. The brown crabs we get off the coast of the UK work perfectly. You could use just the claws and crack them so that the flavour of the crab gets right into the sauce. Unroasted curry powder is available online and at Sri Lankan grocers. It plays an important part in Sri Lankan seafood curries. I have given a recipe on page 258, but you could just use a good-quality curry powder for ease.

PREP TIME: 15 MINS
COOKING TIME: 25 MINS

FOR THE COCONUT AND RICE MIX
3 tbsp raw matta or basmati white rice
4 tbsp (¼ cup) grated coconut
200ml (¾ cup) thick coconut milk
½ tsp ground turmeric

FOR THE CURRY
3 tbsp coconut oil
10 curry leaves
5cm (2in) square piece of pandan leaf, cut into 4 strips
5cm (2in) real cinnamon stick, broken into small pieces, or whole cassia if you must
3 shallots or ¼ red onion, roughly chopped
2.5cm (1in) piece of ginger, roughly chopped
3 garlic cloves, roughly chopped
2 green finger chillies, thinly sliced or to taste
1 medium tomato, diced
1 generous tbsp Kashmiri chilli powder
1 generous tbsp unroasted curry powder (see page 258) or good-quality shop-bought
2 raw mud crabs, cleaned and cut in half, or the equivalent of another variety
400ml (14oz) tinned (canned) thick coconut milk
70ml (¼ cup) water or coconut water
1 tsp each salt and pepper (or more to taste)
Juice of 1 or 2 limes, to taste
Fresh curry leaves, to garnish (optional)

Heat a large saucepan or clay pot over a medium heat. You will need a pot large enough to be able to stir in the crabs. When hot, add the rice and grated coconut and dry-fry until lightly browned and charring in places and fragrant. Transfer to a spice grinder or pestle and mortar and grind to a fine powder. Then stir it into the coconut milk in a bowl along with the ground turmeric. Set aside.

Add about 2 tablespoons of coconut oil to your pan over a medium–high heat. Add the curry leaves, pandan leaf, cinnamon, shallot/onion, ginger, garlic, chillies and tomato and sauté for a few minutes until the onion has softened.

Now add the chilli powder and curry powder and stir these into the other ingredients for about 30 seconds. Your pan will be looking quite dry because of the powders and they will roast a little over the heat, so be careful not to burn them. Add the crabs and stir well to coat them with everything in the pan. Then stir in the coconut milk and water or coconut water and bring to a simmer. Add the salt and pepper and then cover the pan to cook. If using raw crabs, simmer for about 10–15 minutes. If you purchased cooked crabs or crab parts, 5 minutes will do. Uncover the pan, pour in the rice and coconut mixture and then bring it back to a simmer.

To finish, cook the sauce down until you are happy with the consistency. Check for seasoning, adding more salt and pepper if you like, and then squeeze in the lime juice and garnish with fresh curry leaves, if you like. Serve warm with steamed rice or bread.

SRI LANKAN PRAWN CURRY
SERVES 2–4

This is a prawn (shrimp) curry recipe I watched being prepared by Chaminda Kumara, Executive Chef at Cinnamon Bey Beruwala hotel on the west coast of Sri Lanka. Chef Chaminda showed me how to prepare several dried fish curries that are popular in Sri Lanka, and the flavour was intense! All of the dishes prepared that day were spectacular and this giant prawn curry was one of our favourites. If you want this dish to go further, use about 700g (1lb 9oz) of medium-sized prawns instead of the large prawns.

PREP TIME: 10 MINS
COOKING TIME: 15 MINS

2 tbsp coconut oil
½ red onion, thinly sliced
1 tbsp roughly chopped garlic
1 tbsp roughly chopped ginger
1 tbsp thinly sliced lemongrass
2–3 green finger chillies, thinly sliced
20 curry leaves
5cm (2in) square piece of pandan
    leaf, cut into 4 strips
5cm (2in) cinnamon stick
1 tbsp unroasted curry powder (see
    page 258) or good-quality shop-
    bought
½ tsp ground turmeric
1 tbsp Kashmiri chilli powder
2 tomatoes, diced
1 tbsp Dijon mustard mixed with 1 tsp
    melted coconut oil
4 extra large jumbo prawns (shrimp)
    with shell and heads, deveined
250ml (1 cup) coconut milk
Salt and freshly ground black pepper,
    to taste
2 limes, quartered

Heat the coconut oil in a frying pan (skillet) or wok over a medium–high heat and then add the sliced onion. Fry for a couple of minutes and then stir in the chopped garlic and ginger and sliced lemongrass and green chillies.

Stir this all around in the oil and then toss in the curry leaves, pandan leaf and cinnamon stick. If using real cinnamon, you can break it up into the sauce – it's really good! Fry for another 30 seconds and then add the curry powder, ground turmeric, chilli powder, chopped tomatoes and the mustard and coconut oil mixture and give it all a good stir.

Add the prawns (shrimp) and cook, turning and stirring regularly, until the prawns are just cooked through. The cooking time will vary depending on the size of your prawns. Add the coconut milk and bring to a simmer. Season with salt and pepper to taste and serve with the lime wedges, which can be squeezed over the curry, to taste, at the table.

CAJUN PRAWN MACARONI AND CHEESE

SERVES 8–10

This is party food. It's also some of the best comfort food you'll ever eat. When my kids were growing up, this is what they would request for their birthday meals. On one occasion, we quadrupled the recipe and served it to 30 hungry teenagers. There wasn't one piece of macaroni left over. My son would always request that the prawns weren't added as he hates them, so if you're not a fan of seafood, you can leave them out. By the way… if you're on a diet, skip this recipe. Don't even look at it.

PREP TIME: 20 MINS
COOKING TIME: 15 MINS

225g (8oz) baby or medium prawns (shrimp), peeled, deveined and chopped
4 generous tbsp Cajun seasoning, shop-bought or homemade (see page 262)
1kg (2lb 2oz) dry macaroni
115g (4oz) butter
720g (9 cups) grated strong and/or medium cheddar
1 large onion, finely chopped
12 garlic cloves
500ml (2 cups) milk
425ml (1½ cups) double (heavy) cream
250ml (1 cup) sour cream
240g (3 cups) grated fresh Parmesan
3 egg yolks, beaten
2 spring onions (scallions), finely chopped, to garnish

Place the prawns (shrimp) in a bowl and sprinkle with 2 tablespoons of the Cajun seasoning. Mix well and set aside.

Bring a large saucepan of lightly salted water to a boil. When boiling, pour in the macaroni and cook for about 15 minutes, or until the texture is to your liking. Strain the macaroni and place it in a large bowl. Stir in 2 tablespoons of the butter and about 3 large handfuls of the cheddar. Mix well and set aside.

Place the onion and garlic in a food processor and blend until you have a smooth paste. Now melt the remaining butter in the same pan you used to cook the macaroni and add the remaining Cajun spice blend. Stir to combine and then add the onion and garlic mixture. Allow this to sizzle for about 2 minutes.

Pour in the milk, cream and sour cream and bring to a simmer over a medium heat. Add the rest of the cheese to this sauce one handful at a time while whisking constantly, until you have added all the cheese.

Simmer for about 5 minutes to thicken the sauce while continuing to whisk. Don't stop whisking! Reduce the heat a little and stir in the beaten egg yolks and prawns. Then slowly pour the prepared macaroni into the sauce, continuing to stir as you do. At first it might look like the macaroni is drowning in the sauce, but don't worry, you're on your way to cheesy, macaroni heaven. Once all of the macaroni is coated with that thick cheese sauce, turn off the heat and serve, garnished with the spring onions (scallions) and a little more Cajun spice blend, if you like.

NOTE

When we make this recipe ahead of big parties, we find that it's easiest to make the cheese and macaroni early, leaving out a little of the cheese. Cook the pasta until al dente before adding to the sauce, then pour it all into one or several casserole dishes. Put a packet of cheese crackers in a food processor and blitz it to crumbs. Dust the top of the macaroni with the cheese cracker crumbs and a bit of grated cheese. Cover the casserole dishes tightly with foil and place in the oven at 200°C (400°F/Gas 6) for 30 minutes. Take it out of the oven and allow to sit for 10 more minutes, covered with the foil. Remove the foil and dig in!

CAJUN SHRIMP BOIL
SERVES 4

This is the dish that first got me into seafood during our family trips to Louisiana as a kid. It became a family favourite and my parents made it regularly. I like this really spicy hot, but you can of course adjust the spicing to taste. In the UK, prawns are much easier to source than shrimp so that's how I cook this recipe at home. Although it's messier, I prefer to cook the prawns/shrimp with the shell on, as it adds more flavour, but you could also cook these with the shell off.

PREP TIME: 10 MINS
COOKING TIME: 15 MINS

1 tbsp salt (optional)
1–2 tbsp Cajun seasoning, shop-bought or homemade (see page 262)
3 ears of corn, each cut into 5 pieces
2 potatoes, cut into 7.5cm (3in) pieces
375g (13oz) unsalted butter
1 medium onion, finely chopped
10 garlic cloves, thinly sliced
1 tbsp smoked paprika
2 tsp dried chilli flakes
1 tsp cayenne chilli powder
1 tsp coarsely ground black pepper
1kg (2lb 2oz) medium prawns (shrimp), deveined
400g (14oz) cooked smoked sausage, such as andouille sausage or another European smoked sausage
4 tbsp fresh parley, finely chopped
Salt, to taste
1–2 tbsp lemon juice

Bring a large, high-sided frying pan (skillet) of water to a boil over a high heat and stir in about 1 tablespoon of salt and 1 tablespoon of the Cajun seasoning. Add the corn and potatoes and simmer for about 15 minutes, or until the potatoes are cooked through and soft. Pass through a colander and set aside. Keep warm.

Now, using the same pan, add the butter and melt it over a medium–high heat. Once melted, stir in the onion and fry for about 5 minutes, or until the onion is soft and translucent. Add the garlic and fry for another minute to soften. Stir in the rest of the Cajun seasoning along with the other ground spices, followed by the prawns (shrimp) and sausage. Fry, stirring often, for about 5 minutes, or until the prawns are cooked through and the sausages are browning in places. The sausages are already cooked, so you just need to lightly char them to your liking.

Pour the cooked corn and potatoes back into the pan and stir well to combine.

To finish, add the chopped parsley and season with salt to taste. At this point, you could also adjust the other seasoning, stirring more in to taste. Squeeze in lemon juice to taste, then serve immediately in the pan or on a serving platter and dig in.

PUNJABI SAAG

SERVES 4

This is a truly delicious version of saag curry. Although it is vegetarian, you could add other ingredients such as cooked lamb or chicken to make a lamb or chicken saag. You could also add other veggies to it such as cooked potatoes or chickpeas or stir in cubed paneer to heat through just before serving, for a delicious saag paneer. I really love the addition of mustard leaves, which can be found at Indian grocers and online. You can also find the fine cornmeal flour in the same shops and online. This saag is delicious over rice, but in the Punjab it is traditionally served with chapattis. It is pictured on page 141.

PREP TIME: 15 MINS
COOKING TIME: 30 MINS

2 bunches (approx. 150g/5½oz) of mustard leaves, chopped
240g (9oz) spinach leaves, chopped
½ bunch (approx. 80g/3oz) of fresh fenugreek leaves, chopped
2 tbsp rapeseed (canola) oil
1 tsp cumin seeds
1 medium white onion, roughly chopped
6 garlic cloves, roughly chopped
2.5cm (1in) piece of ginger, roughly chopped
2–3 green finger chillies
2 tomatoes, diced
2 tsp ground coriander
1½ tsp ground cumin
½ tsp Kashmiri chilli powder (more or less to taste)
¼ tsp ground turmeric
125ml (½ cup) water
1 tbsp fine cornmeal flour
Salt, to taste
2 tbsp butter or ghee

Prepare the greens by washing thoroughly under cold running water to remove any dirt or sand.

Heat the oil over a medium–high heat in a large saucepan and stir in the cumin seeds. Infuse the cumin seeds into the oil for about 30 seconds, then the add the chopped onion and fry for about 3 minutes to soften. Add the garlic, ginger and chillies and continue frying for another minute or two. Stir in the diced tomatoes and the ground spices. Then add the greens in small amounts until they have wilted. Add the water and bring to a simmer, then blend it all together. I find it easier to do this in a countertop blender, but a stick blender will also work.

Add the cornmeal flour and stir it in. Then cover the pan and simmer over a low heat for about 15–20 minutes, or until you are happy with the consistency. Season with salt to taste and stir in the ghee.

INDIAN

PANEER MAKHANI

SERVES 4

This is a classic Punjabi version of paneer makhani. The sauce works so well with paneer but you aren't limited to that! You could add tandoori-style chicken to this sauce and you will have butter chicken. Want a vegan curry? No problem! Stir in some sliced mushrooms and peas and leave the cream and butter out or use vegan cream and butter substitutes. It's very good and I'm not even vegan. Back to this recipe, cooking the paneer in the butter just plain gets it! It will literally melt in your mouth when you serve it. It's one of my favourite ways to serve paneer. Some people prefer a sweeter makhani sauce. This is not a sweet curry, but you can stir in a little sugar to taste when you add the salt.

PREP TIME: 15 MINS
COOKING TIME: 30 MINS

FOR THE SAUCE

2 x 400g (14oz) tinned (canned)
  chopped tomatoes
70ml (¼ cup) water
1 medium red onion, roughly
  chopped
6 garlic cloves, roughly chopped
2.5cm (1in) piece of ginger, roughly
  chopped
4 green cardamom pods, lightly
  crushed
4 cloves
5cm (2in) cinnamon stick
4 green finger chillies
1 tbsp Kashmiri chilli powder
2 tbsp butter
10 cashews
½ tsp salt

FOR THE CURRY

2½ tbsp unsalted butter
1.25cm (½in) piece of ginger, finely
  chopped
2 green finger chillies, sliced
  lengthwise down the centre
500g (1lb 2oz) paneer, cut into bite-
  sized cubes
1 tsp Kashmiri chilli powder
  (optional)
1 tsp kasoori methi (dried fenugreek
  leaves)
125ml (½ cup) single (light) cream
Salt, to taste
Sugar to taste (optional)

Place all of the sauce ingredients in a saucepan and stir well to combine. Cover and simmer over a medium heat for 20 minutes, lifting the lid once or twice to stir and add a drop of water if needed. After 20 minutes, take off the lid and turn off the heat. Most, if not all, of the whole spices will have risen to the top. Pick them out and allow the sauce to cool a little before pouring it all into your blender and blending until very smooth. Set aside.

Wipe your pan clean. No need to make it spotless, but you can if you want. Place the pan over a medium–high heat and add the butter. When it melts, stir in the finely chopped ginger, chillies and then the paneer cubes. Cook over a medium heat until the paneer is turning soft and is about one tone darker from the frying. Be sure to turn the paneer from time to time so that it cooks on all, or at least two, sides. If you like a spicier curry, add a teaspoon of Kashmiri chilli powder and fry for about 15 seconds, then pour in the blended sauce. Bring to a simmer and add the kasoori methi (dried fenugreek leaves) by rubbing the leaves between your fingers over the curry. Stir in the cream, then add salt and sugar to taste to serve.

Top left: Punjabi saag (page 139)
Bottom right: Paneer makhani

SWEET, SOUR AND SPICY AUBERGINE CURRY

SERVES 4–6

Aubergine (eggplant) curries are very popular in the Indian subcontinent, and this one is similar to what you might find in southern India. The spicy, sour and sweet flavours all work so well together with the crispy fried aubergine and shallots. Another way to prepare the aubergines is to slice them into thin strips like French fries rather than cutting them into cubes. This dish is pictured on page 111 with the easy Sri Lankan beef curry.

PREP TIME: 15 MINS
COOKING TIME: 30 MINS

2 medium aubergines (eggplants),
    cut into 2.5cm (1in) pieces
½ tsp ground turmeric
1 tsp salt
Rapeseed (canola) oil, for shallow-
    frying
10 shallots
2 tbsp coconut oil
1 tsp black mustard seeds
2.5cm (1in) cinnamon stick
3 green cardamom pods, bruised
20 fresh or frozen curry leaves
2.5cm (1in) square piece of pandan
    leaf (optional)
1 red onion, finely chopped
10 green finger chillies, split
    lengthwise
1 tbsp ground coriander
2 tsp ground cumin
2 tsp Kashmiri chilli powder
2 tsp light brown sugar
2 tbsp distilled white vinegar or
    coconut vinegar
1 tsp tamarind paste (see page 256 or
    shop-bought)
250ml (1 cup) thick coconut milk

Place the aubergine (eggplant) pieces in a large mixing bowl and sprinkle with the ground turmeric and salt. Mix well to coat and allow to sit while you heat the oil. Heat about 2.5cm (1in) of rapeseed (canola) oil in a large frying pan (skillet) or wok until visibly hot and then add the aubergine. You should do this in two batches to maintain the heat of the oil. Fry until golden brown and then transfer to paper towels to soak up any excess oil. Discard the oil from the pan. Fry the shallots in the same way, but these should only be lightly browned to soften. Transfer these to paper towels, too.

Wipe the pan clean and then place it back over a medium–high heat. Add the coconut oil and when it melts, stir in the mustard seeds. When the mustard seeds begin to crackle, reduce the heat to medium and add the cinnamon, cardamom pods, curry leaves and pandan leaf, if using. Infuse the ingredients into the oil for about 30 seconds and then add the chopped onion. Fry this for about 5 minutes, or until the onion is soft and translucent. Stir in the chillies and fry for 30 seconds, and then add the remaining ingredients.

Simmer the sauce for a minute or two and then taste it. It should be a nice combination of sweet, sour and spicy. At this stage you can adjust the flavour to taste by adding more sugar, vinegar or tamarind. If you think it is too spicy, just add more coconut milk.

Once you're happy with the sauce, add in the fried aubergines and shallots. Bring up to heat, stirring it all together to combine. Season with salt to taste and serve.

SRI LANKAN DAL CURRY
SERVES 4

Curry and rice is on the menu of almost every restaurant in Sri Lanka. You'll get a nice mound of rice that is served with a selection of mouthwatering curries, and dal curry is always one of them. This one-pot curry is so easy to make. If you like a good curry house-style dhansak (see page 47) that requires cooked lentils, you could use some of this if you have any left over. It usually all goes at my house, though! This recipe does include coconut milk, so your dhansak will be different but equally as good, if not better. You can see this dish photographed on page 111.

PREP TIME: 10 MINS
COOKING TIME: 15 MINS

600ml (2¼ cups) light coconut milk
1 tsp black mustard seeds, lightly
    crushed
200g (1 cup) red (masoor) dal, soaked
    for 10 minutes
1 tsp Kashmiri chilli powder
½ tsp ground turmeric
¼ red onion, roughly chopped
3 garlic cloves, roughly chopped
5cm (2in) square piece of pandan
    leaf, cut into 3 pieces
20 curry leaves, fresh or frozen
Salt, to taste

In a mixing bowl, mix the coconut milk with the crushed mustard seeds and set aside.

Place the soaked lentils in a saucepan or clay pot and add the chilli powder, ground turmeric, onion, garlic, pandan leaf and curry leaves. Pour the coconut milk and mustard seed mixture over the lentils and then place over a medium–high heat. Bring to a simmer and cook for about 15 minutes, or until the coconut milk has reduced and the lentils are soft. Season with salt to taste and serve over rice.

SRI LANKAN SQUASH CURRY
SERVES 4

I learned to make this curry using green pumpkin in Habarana, Sri Lanka. Green pumpkin isn't very easy to come by where I live, so I often use butternut squash, which works equally well. This is an interesting curry as there is no frying – instead, the pumpkin is simmered in the coconut milk with the other ingredients. It's simple and delicious.

PREP TIME: 10 MINS
COOKING TIME: 20 MINS

1½ tsp mustard seeds, lightly crushed
600ml (2¼ cups) light coconut milk
1 generous tbsp roughly chopped garlic
1 generous tbsp roughly chopped ginger
1 small, unpeeled green pumpkin or a small butternut squash, seeded and cut into bite-sized pieces
½ tsp ground turmeric
20 curry leaves, fresh or frozen
2.5cm (1in) leek, thinly sliced, white part only
½ red onion, thinly sliced
Salt, to taste

Start by preparing the sauce. Mix together the crushed mustard seeds, coconut milk, garlic and ginger and set aside.

Place the cut pumpkin/squash in a clay pot or large, flat-bottomed saucepan and cover with the prepared sauce. Bring to a simmer over a medium–high heat. Add the turmeric, curry leaves, leek and red onion. Simmer for around 20 minutes, or until soft. Season with salt to taste and serve.

GREEN BEAN CURRY
SERVES 4

Caroline and I learned to make this green bean curry while in Sri Lanka, at a little restaurant called Inspire. We just happened upon the place and loved the meal we had so much that we asked for the recipes. This was just one of a few curries we learned the following day. It makes a really nice and light vegetarian main, or it can also be served as a side or with other curries.

PREP TIME: 10 MINS
COOKING TIME: 15 MINS

225g (8oz) green (string) beans, sliced at an angle into 5cm (2in) pieces
1 tsp ground turmeric
1 tsp salt, plus more to taste
2 tbsp coconut oil
1 tsp black mustard seeds
3 garlic cloves, roughly chopped
15 curry leaves, fresh or frozen, roughly chopped
2.5cm (1in) square piece of pandan leaf, cut into thin strips
½ red onion, thinly sliced
5cm (2in) piece of leek, thinly sliced
1 tsp red chilli powder
3 tbsp light coconut milk

Put the sliced green (string) beans into a bowl and mix in the turmeric and salt with your hands. Set aside.

Heat the coconut oil in a clay pot or saucepan over a medium–high heat. When visibly hot, stir in the mustard seeds. When they begin to crackle in the hot oil, stir in the chopped garlic. Fry the garlic for about 30 seconds and then add the curry leaves, pandan leaf, onion, leek and chilli powder. Continue cooking for about 5 minutes, or until the onion is soft and translucent.

Stir in the green beans and coat them with the oil and other ingredients. Stir-fry for about 3 minutes and then add the coconut milk. Continue cooking until the beans are cooked through to your liking, then add salt to taste to serve.

Top: Green bean curry
Bottom: Sri Lankan squash curry

BOMBAY ALOO

SERVES 3–4

There are many recipes for Bombay aloo. I have featured other versions in earlier books and on my blog, but this is the one I've been making most often lately. It is a bit oil-heavy, but it's supposed to be. If you prefer, you could pour some of the oil out after frying the potatoes and then carry on with the recipe.

PREP TIME: 15 MINS
COOKING TIME: 25 MINS

1½ tsp ground turmeric
1 generous tsp salt
20 new potatoes, cut in half
190ml (¾ cup) rapeseed (canola) oil
1 tsp black mustard seeds
5 fenugreek seeds (optional)
3 dried red Kashmiri chillies
2 medium onions, thinly sliced and cut into 2.5cm (1in) pieces
6 garlic cloves, finely chopped
2 green finger chillies, finely chopped
2 tsp curry powder (see page 259)
1–2 tsp Kashmiri chilli powder
1 tsp ground cumin
1 tsp ground coriander
2 medium tomatoes, diced
1 tsp tamarind paste (see page 256 or shop-bought)
3 green finger chillies, left whole (optional)
3 tbsp coriander (cilantro), finely chopped
½ tsp garam masala, shop-bought or homemade (see page 259)
Lime wedges, to serve

Fill a high-sided frying pan (skillet) with enough water to cover the potatoes (don't add them yet) and bring to a boil over a high heat. Stir in one teaspoon of the ground turmeric, the salt and the potatoes and simmer until tender but still a bit too undercooked to eat. This should take about 10 minutes. Strain through a colander.

Dry your pan and place it back over a medium–high heat and pour in the oil. When the oil is visibly hot, add the par-cooked potatoes and fry for about 3–5 minutes, or until they are golden brown. Using a slotted spoon, transfer the potatoes to a plate and set aside.

Add the mustard and fenugreek seeds to the hot oil. When the mustard seeds begin to crackle and pop, add the dried Kashmiri chillies and let them flavour the oil for about 30 seconds, then add the thinly sliced onions and fry for about 8 minutes, or until they are turning golden brown. Add the chopped garlic and green chillies and fry for a further 45 seconds, while stirring continuously.

Now add the curry powder, chilli powder, cumin and coriander along with 70ml (¼ cup) of water and the diced tomatoes. Continue to simmer for another 5 minutes to let the tomatoes break down a little, and then stir in the tamarind paste and the whole green finger chillies, if using. Simmer the sauce for another minute and then stir in the crispy fried potatoes. Cover the pan and simmer for another 5 minutes, lifting the lid a few times to give it all a good stir.

Add 250ml (1 cup) of hot water and bring to a rolling simmer. Then cover the pan and continue simmering for 5–8 minutes, or until you are happy with the consistency of the sauce. To finish, taste it and add more salt, if needed. Add half of the chopped coriander (cilantro) and the garam masala and stir it all in. Garnish with the remaining coriander and serve with the lime wedges, which you can squeeze over it all, to taste, at the table.

SAAG ALOO
SERVES 4

I wanted to include this recipe, not only because it is a popular way of preparing saag aloo, but also because I wanted to draw your attention to the saag curry on page 139. In this recipe, the spinach (saag) is simply added and cooked into the curry until it wilts, while the saag curry on page 139 is a traditional Punjabi way of preparing it. It can be eaten as is, or you can add other ingredients such as cooked potatoes, paneer or meat. Two different saag preparations! Which one will you choose for your saag aloo?

PREP TIME: 10 MINS
COOKING TIME: 25 MINS

700g (1lb 9oz) floury potatoes, peeled and cut into bite-sized pieces
3 tbsp rapeseed (canola) oil or ghee
1 tsp black mustard seeds
2 tsp cumin seeds
2 medium red onions, finely chopped
2 tbsp garlic and ginger paste
2 green finger chillies, finely chopped
1 red spur chilli, thinly sliced
1 tbsp tomato purée (paste)
1 tsp garam masala, shop-bought or homemade (see page 259)
1 tsp ground turmeric
125ml (½ cup) unsalted chicken stock
150g (5½oz) baby spinach leaves
1 generous tsp kasoori methi (dried fenugreek leaves)
Salt, to taste
Ground black pepper, to taste (optional)
4 tbsp fresh coriander (cilantro), finely chopped

Place the bite-sized pieces of potato in a large frying pan (skillet) and cover with hot water. Bring to a boil over a high heat and then reduce to medium–high and simmer to par-cook the potatoes until fork-tender – in other words, you should easily be able to stick a fork in, but the potatoes should still be a bit too hard for eating. Drain through a colander and set aside.

Place your pan back over a medium–high heat and add the ghee or oil. (I use ghee). Stir in the mustard seeds. When they begin to crackle and pop, add the cumin seeds and fry for a further 30 seconds.

Now add the chopped red onions and fry for about 7 minutes, or until the onions are soft and lightly browned. Add the garlic and ginger paste and stir it in for about 30 seconds. Then add the green and red chillies, tomato purée (paste) and ground spices. Stir well to combine, so that the onions are coated with the spices.

Return the par-cooked potatoes to the pan and mix well with the other ingredients. Then add the stock and spinach leaves. Stir the spinach into the potatoes. As the spinach cooks, it will wilt and coat the potatoes nicely. Add the kasoori methi (dried fenugreek leaves) by rubbing the leaves between your fingers. Continue simmering until the potatoes are completely cooked through.

Season with salt and pepper to taste and garnish with coriander (cilantro) and more thinly sliced red chillies, if you want more heat.

INDIAN

RAJMA MASALA

SERVES 4

This is a recipe from my friend Reena Arora, who runs a takeaway called Reena's Indian Kitchen in Stanley, Leeds. Caroline and I were visiting our son and his girlfriend in Stanley and ended up at their local pub, The Wheatsheaf, where we met Inder, Reena's husband. We got chatting and he told us about Reena's business. Curious, we ordered a few of her takeaway dishes and they were incredible. So I asked her for a recipe or two and this is one of them. You might also like to try her Punjabi saag, which is on page 139. Reena's recipe called for prepared dried kidney beans, which she cooked before starting the recipe. This recipe uses tinned (canned) kidney beans for ease, but you could use dried beans if you prefer (see note below).

PREP TIME: 15 MINS, PLUS OPTIONAL SOAKING TIME
COOKING TIME: 30 MINS

3 tbsp rapeseed (canola) oil or ghee
1 tsp cumin seeds
3 white onions, roughly chopped
1 tbsp garlic and ginger paste
2 green finger chillies, finely chopped
½ tsp Kashmiri chilli powder (more or less to taste)
½ tsp ground turmeric
1½ tsp ground cumin
1½ tsp ground coriander
2 tsp tomato purée (paste)
125ml (½ cup) unseasoned passata
300g (1½ cups) dried red kidney beans, precooked, or 3 tins (cans)*
Couple pinches of kasoori methi (dried fenugreek leaves)
Salt, to taste
¼ tsp garam masala, shop-bought or homemade (see page 259)
3 tbsp fresh coriander (cilantro), to garnish

Heat the oil in a large saucepan over a medium heat. When visibly hot, add the cumin seeds and stir them into the oil for about 30 seconds. Add the chopped onions and fry for about 8 minutes, or until golden brown. Stir in the garlic and ginger paste along with the chopped chillies. Cover the pan and cook over medium heat for about 5 minutes, lifting the lid every minute to give it all a good stir.

Now add the chilli powder, turmeric, cumin and coriander and stir these spices into the onion mixture. Simmer for another 5 minutes, adding a drop of water if needed so that you don't burn the spices.

Add the tomato purée (paste) and passata and continue simmering until oil bubbles separate and rise to the top. Allow to cool a little and then blend to a smooth and medium-thick sauce using a stick or countertop blender.

Bring this thick sauce to a simmer in the pan and then add the pre-cooked or tinned (canned) kidney beans. Simmer over a low heat for 20–25 minutes, adding a little water to achieve the sauce consistency you prefer.

To finish, add the kasoori methi (dried fenugreek leaves) to the sauce by rubbing it between your fingers. Stir it in and season with salt to taste. Continue simmering over a low heat for another 5 minutes. Sprinkle the garam masala over the top and garnish with the chopped coriander (cilantro) to serve.

NOTE
*Using tinned (canned) beans works well and is less work. However, you could use dried kidney beans for this recipe, prepared as per the instructions on the packet. This is not only cheaper, but you can also use the cooking stock instead of adding plain water for more flavour. Personally, I prefer to use dried kidney beans unless I'm in a real hurry.

THAI RED CURRY WITH GRAPES AND LYCHEE NUTS

SERVES 4

This recipe was inspired by a visit to Têt restaurant in Wakefield. We ordered a red curry that fitted this exact description and I decided to go home and give it a try with my own homemade curry paste and Thai stock. Needless to say I loved the result, because I included it in this book. This is a delicious and unique vegetarian curry, but if you like meat, you might like to add bite-sized duck or chicken pieces when you fry the curry paste. If you don't want to prepare the curry paste, you could substitute 2–3 tablespoons of shop-bought red curry paste, or just add it to taste.

PREP TIME: 10 MINS
COOKING TIME: 10 MINS

FOR THE CURRY PASTE
1 generous tbsp cumin seeds
1 generous tbsp coriander seeds
1½ tsp white pepper
12 dried red finger chillies, soaked in water for 30 minutes and then cut into small pieces
12 garlic cloves, roughly chopped
2 medium shallots, finely chopped
1 thumb-sized piece of galangal, thinly sliced
2 red spur chillies, thinly sliced
1 lemongrass stalk, tough outer part removed and thinly sliced
10 thick coriander (cilantro) stalks (about 1 generous tbsp)
Zest of ½ lime
1 tsp shrimp paste (optional if you are vegetarian)

FOR THE CURRY
2 tbsp coconut oil or rapeseed (canola) oil
About 115g (4oz) red or green seedless grapes
About 115g (4oz) plain lychee nuts
250ml (1 cup) Asian vegetable stock or water
400ml (1¾ cups) thick coconut milk
About 115g (4oz) mix of vegetables such as baby aubergine (eggplant), sliced red (bell) pepper, green (string) beans
3 tbsp Thai fish sauce (gluten-free brands are available)
1 tbsp light soy sauce (gluten-free brands are available)
1 tsp tamarind paste (see page 256 or shop-bought)
1 tbsp palm sugar
Coriander (cilantro) leaves, to garnish
1 tsp roasted Thai chilli oil (optional)

Prepare the curry paste by placing all of the paste ingredients in a food processor or blender and blending to a paste. You can add a drop of water if needed to assist blending. There will be a lot of paste, and yes, you do use it all in this recipe.

Heat the oil over a medium–high heat in a large frying pan (skillet) or wok. When visibly hot, add the red curry paste and fry for about 30 seconds in the oil. Stir in the grapes and lychee nuts and fry for a couple more minutes. Stir in the stock and coconut milk and simmer for 5 minutes to thicken the sauce a little.

Now add your other veggies of choice, the fish sauce, soy sauce, tamarind paste and palm sugar and simmer for about 3 minutes to cook the vegetables through. Taste and adjust the flavours as necessary, then cook the sauce down until you are happy with the consistency. It should be quite thin. Be careful not to overcook the vegetables. Garnish with coriander (cilantro) and drizzle with chilli oil to serve, if you like.

ROASTED AND BAKED

Sometimes it's good to just throw something into a roasting pan or baking tray and let the oven do all the work. For me, that's especially so when I've worked a full day, even if a big part of my job is cooking.

What follows is a collection of recipes that you can prepare ahead of time. It's easy stuff, like marinating chicken or blending a few sambal ingredients or a marinade. Shove it all in the fridge until about 30 minutes before you're ready to cook. Then just heat up your oven, put it in and enjoy delicious food.

CHICKEN FAJITA TRAY BAKE

SERVES 6

Although many people consider fajitas to have originated in Mexico, they were actually first made in Austin, Texas, by Mexican ranch workers in the 1930s. The workers were often paid in meat, and that meat was usually the less desirable, cheaper cuts. They would season it well, fry it up with some veggies and wrap it up in tortillas for a nutritious and delicious meal. Nowadays, fajitas can be found on most Tex-Mex and Mexican menus, and chicken, beef skirt and prawns (shrimp) are usually on offer as a filling. This recipe can be made vegetarian by leaving out the meat and adding more vegetables. Fajitas can be served with a salsa such as pico de gallo (see page 255). You might also like to add guacamole (see page 254), sour cream, cheese and coriander (cilantro).

PREP TIME: 10 MINS, PLUS OPTIONAL MARINATING TIME
COOKING TIME: 15–20 MINS

FOR THE FAJITA SEASONING
1 tsp cayenne chilli powder
1 tbsp smoked paprika
1 tbsp onion powder
1 tbsp garlic powder
1 tbsp ground cumin
1 tbsp dried oregano
1 tbsp salt
2 tsp sugar
1 tbsp black pepper

FOR THE FAJITAS
3 tbsp light olive oil
Juice of 1 lime
1kg (2lb 2oz) chicken breast or thighs, cut into thin slices (I prefer thigh meat)
1 red (bell) pepper, thinly sliced
1 green (bell) pepper, thinly sliced
1 yellow (bell) pepper, thinly sliced
20 baby plum tomatoes
10–12 shop-bought flour tortillas

Mix the fajita seasoning ingredients together in a large mixing bowl and stir in the olive oil and lime juice. Add the chicken and vegetables and mix well so that everything is nicely coated. Allow to marinate for 30 minutes or up to 4 hours, or just carry on with the recipe. Any longer and the meat will turn a bit mushy because of the lime juice.

When ready to cook, preheat the oven to 200°C (400°F/Gas 6). Pour the marinated meat and veggies onto a large baking tray and spread them out, so everything is in one layer. Place the tray in the oven and cook for 15–20 minutes, or until the meat is cooked through. The cooked temperature of chicken is 75°C (165°F). If you want a charred appearance, place the tray under a high grill (broiler) for a couple of minutes.

To warm the flour tortillas, you can heat them in a microwave or wrap tightly in foil and place in the oven with the chicken for about 10 minutes. Add the filling to the tortillas and enjoy.

AYAM PERCIK
(SPICY ROAST CHICKEN)
SERVES 4–6

If more convenient, you could make the spicy sauce for this hugely popular Indonesian chicken dish in another pan up to two days before serving. Just keep it covered in the fridge until required. Ayam percik is normally cooked over fire, but you can get excellent results in the oven, too. I add a little smoked paprika, an ingredient not usually used in ayam percik, to give this indoor version a smokier flavour. You could also leave the paprika out and try the coal-smoking method used in my tandoori chicken on page 203. If you have trouble sourcing candlenuts, use cashews or macadamia nuts instead. I usually serve this with steamed white rice.

PREP TIME: 20 MINS, PLUS
  OPTIONAL MARINATING TIME
COOKING TIME: 45 MINS

6 chicken legs with thigh attached, scored across the skin in 3 places
4 tbsp rapeseed (canola) or coconut oil
400ml (14oz) tinned (canned) coconut milk
3 red spur chillies, thinly sliced at an angle, to garnish
Flaky sea salt, to taste
2 limes, quartered, to garnish

FOR THE MARINADE
6 garlic cloves, roughly chopped
2.5cm (1in) piece of ginger, roughly chopped
1 tsp ground turmeric
½ tsp salt

FOR THE SAUCE
6 garlic cloves
5cm (2in) piece of galangal or ginger
6 banana shallots
1 tbsp red chilli powder (more or less to taste)
8 dried red finger chillies, soaked for 10 minutes in hot water
2 tsp smoked sweet or picante paprika (optional)
4 red jalapeño chillies, roughly chopped (more or less to taste)
4 lemongrass stalks, white parts only, finely chopped
1 tbsp palm sugar or white refined sugar
1 tbsp tamarind paste (see page 256 or shop-bought)
½ tsp shrimp paste (optional)
5 candlenuts
125ml (½ cup) water

Place all the marinade ingredients in a blender or food processor and blend with just enough water to make a smooth paste. Put the chicken legs in a large bowl and rub the marinade all over, ensuring that you get it right into the slits. Cover and put in the fridge to marinate while you prepare the rest of the dish, or overnight – the longer, the better.

Now put all the sauce ingredients in the blender and blend until smooth.

Place your roasting pan over a medium–high heat and add the oil. You could use a different pan if you prefer, but if you're aiming to do this in one pan, your roasting pan will do the job just fine. When the oil is bubbling hot, pour in the blended sauce and fry for a couple of minutes to cook out the rawness. As you do this, the oil will separate from the other ingredients. When it does, this is your cue to pour in the coconut milk. Whisk it in to combine and simmer for about 5 minutes to thicken a little. Scrape it all into a bowl to cool and don't miss a drop – this is too good!

When ready to start cooking, preheat the oven to 200°C (400°F/Gas 6). Place the chicken legs in your roasting pan, skin-side up, and top generously with some of the sauce. It is important not to touch the raw chicken and then dip a spoon back into the sauce, as you will be serving the remaining sauce with the cooked ayam percik. Put the chicken in the oven and roast for 20 minutes. Baste it liberally with more sauce and then roast for another 20 minutes, or until completely cooked through. If you have a meat thermometer, the chicken is cooked when the internal temperature reaches 75°C (165°F).

Serve garnished with the sliced red spur chillies, some flaky sea salt and the quartered limes, with any remaining sauce as a dip.

CHICKEN TIKKA AND VEGETABLE DINNER
SERVES 4–6

This is a really easy way to prepare chicken tikka for dinner. The chicken is delicious as suggested here, but it can also be used in one of the curry house-style curries in this book. The chapattis are wrapped in foil and heated through for the last 10 minutes of cooking, making this a complete meal.

PREP TIME: 15 MINS, PLUS
  MARINATING TIME
COOKING TIME: 30 MINS

1kg (2lb 2oz) chicken breasts or
  thighs, cut into bite-sized pieces
Juice of 2 lemons
Salt, to taste
2 tbsp garlic and ginger paste
1 tbsp mustard oil or rapeseed
  (canola) oil (I use mustard oil)
1 tbsp Kashmiri chilli powder (more
  or less to taste)
1 tbsp ground cumin
2 tsp ground coriander
1 tsp garam masala, shop-bought or
  homemade (see page 259)
2 generous tbsp thick, full-fat yoghurt
Vegetables of choice such as (bell)
  peppers, tomatoes, red onion, etc.
2tbsp melted ghee or butter
8 chapattis
Flaky sea salt, to serve

OPTIONAL ACCOMPANIMENTS
Podina (see page 255)
Spring onion raita (see page 255)
Lime wedges
Hot sauce

Soak about 20 wooden skewers in water for at least 30 minutes.

Place the chicken pieces in a large mixing bowl and add the lemon juice, salt, garlic and ginger paste and oil. Mix well with your hands or a spoon and set aside for about 5 minutes. Add the remaining ingredients up to and including the yoghurt and mix well to coat the chicken pieces equally. Add the vegetables to the marinade and ensure they are all nicely coated, too. Allow to marinate for at least 30 minutes or overnight.

When ready to cook, preheat the oven to 240°C (460°F/Gas 9). Thread the chicken and vegetables onto the wooden skewers and place them on a lightly greased baking tray. Place in the oven and cook for 20–30 minutes, depending on how charred you want the chicken and vegetables to be. Baste with the melted ghee or butter a couple of times as the chicken cooks.

For the last 10 minutes of cooking, wrap the chapattis tightly in a large piece of foil and place in the oven with the chicken skewers. Serve, sprinkled with a bit of flaky sea salt with the optional podina and raita or simply with lime wedges and hot sauce.

JERK CHICKEN WITH RICE AND PEAS

SERVES 4–6

This is an easy one, and it makes a really good weekday meal with very little fuss. The marinade can be made ahead of time – in fact, the chicken is better if it has time to marinate for a day or two, so you really can work ahead. Then all you need to do is give the chicken a quick fry and put it all together to bake for about half an hour.

PREP TIME: 15 MINS, PLUS
OPTIONAL MARINATING TIME
COOKING TIME: 45 MINS

8 bone-in chicken thighs
4 tbsp rapeseed (canola) or coconut oil
400g (2 cups) basmati rice, washed in several changes of water and then soaked for at least 30 minutes in fresh water
600ml (2¼ cups) chicken stock or water
400ml (14oz) tinned (canned) coconut milk
400g (14oz) tinned (canned) kidney beans, drained and rinsed
1 red habanero chilli, left whole
Salt and pepper, to taste
3 spring onions (scallions), thinly sliced, to garnish

FOR THE MARINADE
1 large onion
2 jalapeño chillies or green finger chillies, roughly chopped
1 habanero chilli, roughly chopped
5 garlic cloves, smashed
4 spring onions (scallions), roughly chopped
2 tsp dried thyme
1 tsp allspice
¼ tsp nutmeg
½ tsp ground cinnamon
2 tsp salt
2 tsp black pepper
1 tbsp paprika
1 tbsp light brown sugar
70ml (¼ cup) light soy sauce (gluten-free brands are available)
Juice of 1 lime
2 tbsp olive oil

Place all of the jerk marinade ingredients in a food processor and blend to a paste. Cover the chicken with the marinade and place, covered, in the fridge for 30 minutes or overnight. If in a real hurry, you can forget the marinating and just get cooking, but the longer the chicken marinates, the better.

When ready to cook, preheat the oven to 180°C (350°F/Gas 4). Scrape as much of the marinade off the chicken as you can and retain the marinade. Heat an ovenproof frying pan (skillet) over a medium–high heat and add 2 tablespoons of the oil. Place the chicken thighs in the pan skin-side down and brown the skin for about 3 minutes. Then flip the chicken over to cook the other side for about 3 minutes. Transfer the chicken to a plate and set aside.

Add the remaining oil to the pan and pour in the marinade. Fry this over a medium–high heat for 2 minutes and then add the rice and stir it into the marinade to coat. Now add the chicken stock or water, the coconut milk, kidney beans and habanero chilli and bring to a rolling simmer. Place the browned chicken thighs on top, skin-side up, and put in the oven to bake for 30–35 minutes, uncovered, until the chicken and rice are cooked. Depending on your pan some of the chicken might sink into the liquid, but as the rice soaks up the liquid the chicken will rise to the top and crisp up.

Remove the pan from the oven. Taste and season with salt and pepper if needed, and then garnish with the spring onions (scallions) to serve.

CHICKEN AND CORIANDER CURRY
SERVES 4–6

If you like chicken and coriander, you're going to love this no-fuss curry. Traditionally, it is cooked in a clay pot in a tandoor. If you have a clay pot, use it for this but if not, a heavy saucepan will suffice. This really couldn't be easier! Just make a quick marinade for the chicken and let it marinate, then place everything in the oven to cook. You could even place all of the ingredients in a slow cooker on low and let it cook for 8 hours while you're at work. Serve over white rice.

PREP TIME: 20 MINS, PLUS
   OPTIONAL MARINATING TIME
COOKING TIME: 1½ HOURS

Juice of 2 limes
1.5kg (3lb 5oz) skinned chicken
   thighs, with three shallow slits in
   each thigh
1 tsp salt, plus more to taste
Water or chicken stock, as required

FOR THE MARINADE
500ml (2 cups) natural yoghurt
2 tbsp garlic and ginger paste
1 tsp Mr Naga chilli paste or
   2 chopped green chillies (more
   or less to taste)
1 onion, sliced
3 tbsp garam masala, shop-bought
   or homemade (see page 259)
1 tbsp ground cumin
1 large bunch chopped fresh
   coriander (cilantro), stems and
   leaves

Squeeze the lime juice all over the chicken pieces and sprinkle with about a teaspoon of salt.

Set aside while you make your marinade. Place all the marinade ingredients in a blender and blend until very smooth. Pour the marinade over the chicken and rub it into the flesh.

Allow to marinate for 2 hours or up to 48 hours – the longer, the better. If you're in a hurry, you could skip marinating and just get cooking.

When ready to cook, preheat the oven to 230°C (455°F/Gas 8). If using a clay pot, it is advised to fill it with water to soak for 30 minutes before you start cooking. Pour the chicken and marinade into a lidded clay pot or saucepan. Add a little water or chicken stock if needed to cover the chicken.

Place the pot/pan in the oven, covered, and cook for 1 hour and 15 minutes. Remove from the oven and give it all a good stir and then cook for a further 20 minutes, uncovered, to thicken the sauce. Season with salt to taste.

ROAST BEEF WITH NIHARI-STYLE SAUCE
SERVES 6

One day I visited my butcher to purchase beef shins for a beef nihari I was planning to make. He just happened to have a beautiful 'Thor's hammer' bone-in cut of beef prepared and I wanted it. I took it home and used it for my nihari, and the flavour was out of this world! The beef was fall-apart tender, but it didn't warrant the purchase of a Thor's hammer cut of beef as all of the meat fell off the bone into that amazing-tasting sauce. Not one to give up easily, I decided to make it again but this time roasting the Thor's hammer like you would a lamb raan. The meat stayed intact and was delicious, thinly sliced, served with the nihari sauce. I cooked mine for about 3 hours, which was perfect for slicing, but if you leave the Thor's hammer in an hour or so longer, the meat will come off the bone without needing to slice it. I should mention here that Thor's hammer cuts aren't easy to source and they can be expensive. So I have given an alternative and more authentic cooking method using smaller pieces of beef shin below, too.

PREP TIME: 15 MINS
COOKING TIME: 2–3 HOURS

1 x 3kg (6½lb) in total 'Thor's hammer' cut of beef or 2kg (4½lb) beef shins cut ossobuco style (i.e. cross-cut shanks)*
1 tsp salt
1 whole nutmeg, crushed into smaller pieces
1 tbsp mace blades
2 tbsp fennel seeds
3 Indian bay leaves
2.5cm (1in) cinnamon stick or cassia bark, broken into small pieces
1 tsp black peppercorns
1 tsp nigella seeds (black onion seeds)
1 tsp cloves
2 tsp cumin seeds
1 tsp paprika
1 tsp hot chilli powder
1 tsp ground ginger
40g (1½oz) unsalted butter
1 onion, sliced into rings
125ml (½ cup) rapeseed oil
2 generous tsp chapatti flour
Salt, to taste
4 tbsp (or more) ginger, julienned, to serve
2–3 hot fresh green chillies, finely sliced, to serve
Handful of coriander (cilantro) leaves, to serve
Lemon wedges, to serve

Preheat the oven to 180°C (350°F/Gas 4). Place the beef on a clean surface and sprinkle evenly with 1 teaspoon of salt. Set aside while you prepare the spice masala.

Put the nutmeg, mace, fennel seeds, bay leaves, cinnamon, peppercorns, nigella seeds, cloves and cumin seeds in a spice grinder and grind to a fine powder. Stir in the paprika, chilli powder and ground ginger. Set aside.

Now melt the butter in a roasting pan over a medium heat. Add the onion rings and fry for about 5 minutes until soft, translucent and lightly browned. Stir in the ground spices and mix well to combine. Transfer to a plate with a slotted spoon and set aside.

Pour the oil into the same roasting pan and brown the beef for about 2 minutes over a medium–high heat. Add the browned onions coated with the spices and pour in 1.2 litres (5 cups) of warm water. Cover the roasting pan tightly with foil and place in the oven for 3–3½ hours, turning the meat every hour and basting it with the sauce. After 3–3½ hours, remove the meat from the oven and transfer it to a cutting board to rest while you finish the sauce.

Skim off as much excess oil from the cooking liquid as possible and discard. Take 4 tablespoons of the sauce and place it in a bowl. Allow to cool slightly and then whisk in the chapatti flour. Whisk this slurry into the sauce over a medium–high heat and simmer for 5–6 minutes to thicken. Check for seasoning and add salt to taste. Thinly slice the meat and serve with the sauce either drizzled over it or as a dipping sauce, as photographed. Serve the garnishes (julienned ginger, chillies, coriander/cilantro and lemon wedges) in little bowls on the table, to add to the nihari as you like.

FOR A MORE AUTHENTIC NIHARI
*If you're using beef shins, follow the instructions above but use a large pot instead of a roasting pan. Bring the curry to a simmer and then cover. Reduce the heat to low and simmer for about 3 hours, or until the meat is tender. Stir in the chapatti flour slurry and season with salt to taste. Then serve with the chillies, lemon wedges, coriander (cilantro) and julienned ginger at the table.

COCHINITA PIBIL
(PORK PIBIL)
SERVES 6–8

Originally, pork pibil was cooked in a hole in the ground. A large hole was dug and then hot coals were placed in it. The banana leaf-wrapped meat was then buried in the hole with the hot coals and dug up after a few hours. I have actually done this with pork pibil and other similar recipes. It worked really well, but ovens are certainly a lot more convenient!

PREP TIME: 25 MINS, PLUS
    OPTIONAL MARINATING TIME
COOKING TIME: 4 HOURS

1kg (2lb 2oz) pork shoulder joint
2 tsp sea salt
2–3 large, whole banana leaves and
    string for tying

FOR THE MARINADE
1 tbsp black peppercorns
6 cloves
1 tsp allspice berries
2cm (½in) cinnamon stick
1 tsp light olive oil
10 garlic cloves
1 onion, quartered
1 tsp chilli powder
1 tbsp ground cumin
1 tbsp dried oregano
250ml (1 cup) orange juice
125ml (½ cup) lime juice
50g (2oz) achiote paste, available
    from Mexican grocers online

TO SERVE
20 corn or flour tortillas* (or as many
    as you like), warmed
Pickled onions (optional; see page
    262)
Salsa (optional; see pico de gallo on
    page 255 or shop-bought)

Rub the pork joint all over with the salt. This can be done a day or two before cooking.

To make the marinade, heat a frying pan (skillet) over a medium–high heat and add the black peppercorns, cloves, allspice berries and cinnamon. Move these whole spices around in the pan until warm to the touch and fragrant but not yet smoking. Transfer to a plate to cool a little, and then grind to a fine powder in a pestle and mortar or spice grinder. Set aside.

Now grease the surface of the pan with the olive oil and toast the garlic and onion until lightly charred on the exterior. This should only take a couple of minutes. Transfer to a blender and add the roasted ground spices. Top this up with the remaining ingredients and blend to a paste.

Pour the marinade over the pork and rub it deep into the flesh. You could marinate the meat for a couple of days in this marinade, or just go straight to cooking.

When ready to cook, preheat the oven to 150°C (300°F/Gas 2). Criss-cross two long pieces of string, long enough to tie the banana leaves around the pork, across the roasting pan. Place a piece of foil over the string to catch any marinade that escapes and then place two or three large banana leaves on top of the foil.

Put the pork and all the marinade in the centre of the banana leaves and then fold them around the meat. Fold the foil into a neat parcel around the meat and tie it tightly with the string. Place the tied pork pibil in the oven and cook for 4 hours. When you unwrap the pork after this time it will be fall-apart tender.

Pull the pork into shreds. It is easiest to do this with heatproof gloves, as the meat will still be quite hot. Wrap this saucy, pulled pork in warmed corn or flour tortillas and top with pickled onions and/or salsa.

NOTE
*Most corn tortillas are gluten-free, but make sure you check the packet if you are avoiding gluten.

BALINESE PORK SHOULDER ROAST
SERVES 8

This is my take on the famous babi guling from Bali, which is a slowly roasted suckling pig. I got to have a go at cooking them while in Ubud on long wooden spits over a hot fire. Every day they slaughter and then begin cooking the pigs at 4am. I got there at 9am and turned the spit by hand for about an hour. That was enough! The suckling pigs take 6 hours to cook, and the crackling was perfectly browned and crisp as glass. So this is really nothing like babi guling, but it still brings back great memories and makes a perfect Sunday roast. Serve it with the sides of your choice, as you would any Sunday dinner. I always top mine with a few spoonfuls of sambal oelek (see page 252).

PREP TIME: 15 MINS
COOKING TIME: 2½ HOURS

2.5kg (5lb) rolled pork shoulder, scored
1 tsp ground turmeric
1 tsp fine sea salt

FOR THE STUFFING
2.5cm (1in) piece of ginger, roughly chopped
2.5cm (1in) piece of galangal, roughly chopped
8 garlic cloves, roughly chopped
4 banana shallots, roughly chopped
1 lemongrass stalk, white part only with woody outer removed, thinly sliced
12 green finger chillies, roughly chopped
1 tsp flaky salt
½ tsp ground turmeric
1 tbsp black peppercorns
1 tsp cumin seeds
1 tsp coriander seeds
Juice of 2 limes
1 tbsp oil

Dry the pork skin with paper towels and rub the ground turmeric and salt into the meat and skin. Set aside. Now take the stuffing ingredients and place them all in a food processor and blend to a semi-fine paste – it's okay to have a few small chunks. Stuff the stuffing right into the pork shoulder. As it is rolled with the bone removed, you should be able to find room for the stuffing. If you are finding it difficult, use a sharp knife to open up the centre a little.

When ready to cook, preheat the oven to 220°C (425°F/Gas 7). Place the pork in a roasting pan in the oven and roast for about 30 minutes. After this time, the crackling should be bubbling and getting harder. Reduce the heat to 180°C (350°F/Gas 4) and roast for another 2 hours, or 30 minutes per 500g (1lb 2oz), or until the juices run clear.

Allow it to rest for 30 minutes before carving. The crackling will get harder on sitting. I often remove it completely with a sharp knife so that it doesn't steam and stays crisp.

KOREAN

KOREAN SALMON AND BROCCOLI TRAY BAKE

SERVES 4

This easy Korean-style salmon, pictured opposite, makes a delicious mid-week meal.

PREP TIME: 5 MINS, PLUS OPTIONAL
 MARINATING TIME
COOKING TIME: 25 MINS

2 heads of broccoli, cut into bite-sized florets
4 x 225g (8oz) salmon fillets with skin
3 spring onions (scallions), green parts only, thinly sliced
1 tbsp sesame seeds
1 tsp gochugaru (Korean hot pepper flakes)

FOR THE MARINADE
3 tbsp gochujang (Korean hot pepper paste; gluten-free brands are available)
2 tbsp light soy sauce (gluten-free brands are available)
2 garlic cloves, finely chopped
2 tbsp sesame oil
1 tbsp lime juice

Preheat the oven to 200°C (400°F/Gas 6). Whisk all of the marinade ingredients in a bowl until smooth. Take 2 tablespoons of the marinade and coat the broccoli with it. Then cover the salmon fillets with the remaining marinade. You can allow them to marinate for up to 30 minutes, or start cooking immediately.

Place the broccoli on a lightly greased baking tray and put in the oven to bake for about 10 minutes. Take the baking tray out of the oven and add the marinated salmon. Place it all back in the oven and cook until the marinade on the salmon is sizzling hot and the salmon is opaque in the centre. This should only take about 15 more minutes. I prefer salmon a little pink inside, but you could cook it longer if you like. If the broccoli is ready before you are happy with the doneness of the salmon, transfer it to a serving bowl and keep warm. To check for your preferred doneness, make a small incision into one of the fillets.

Sprinkle with the spring onions (scallions), sesame seeds and gochugaru to serve.

SOUTH EAST ASIAN

ASIAN HONEY-GLAZED BAKED SALMON

SERVES 4–6

This is a recipe I usually prepare on my barbecue in the summer, but it's also delicious simply baked and grilled (broiled) in the oven. The honey sauce is sweet, sour, spicy and savoury, flavours that all go well with a side of salmon. The salmon is great served simply with a green salad, rice or new potatoes.

PREP TIME: 5 MINS
COOKING TIME: 15–20 MINS

2 tbsp soy sauce (gluten-free brands are available)
70ml (¼ cup) honey
4 garlic cloves, finely chopped
1 thumb-sized piece of ginger, finely chopped
2 tsp red chilli flakes
3 green finger chillies, finely chopped
2 tbsp rice wine vinegar
1½ tbsp sesame oil
2 tsp sriracha sauce
1kg (2lb 2oz) side of salmon
3 spring onions (scallions) thinly sliced
1 tsp sesame seeds

Preheat the oven to 200°C (400°F/Gas 6).

Whisk the soy sauce, honey, garlic, ginger, chilli flakes, green chillies, rice wine vinegar, sesame oil and sriracha in a mixing bowl to combine. Place the salmon on a piece of foil that is large enough to wrap around it. Pour the sauce mixture over the top and rub it into the flesh. Then wrap it all up tightly into a packet.

Place the salmon in the oven for 10 minutes. Then unwrap the package so that the salmon is exposed and grill (broil) for 5 minutes, or until the honey has caramelized and charred in places. Garnish with the chopped spring onions (scallions) and sesame seeds to serve.

MEXICAN CHORIZO IN BUTTERNUT SQUASH

SERVES 4—6

This delicious way of preparing Mexican chorizo and butternut squash looks fantastic. It's colourful and the flavours are to die for! I use butternut squash for this recipe as it's the easiest squash to source where I live. You could also use baby pumpkins or a different squash with a larger cavity, if you like. For speed you might want to use two pans for this recipe, but one pan will do the job just fine. The chorizo is best left to marinate overnight, but you could just prepare it and carry on with the recipe as I did below. The achiote paste can be purchased online or at specialist shops. It is an important ingredient for this Mexican chorizo, but you could leave it out if you don't have it.

PREP TIME: 15 MINS
COOKING TIME: 60 MINS

1 large butternut squash, sliced down the middle and seeds removed.
2 tbsp olive oil
1 tsp salt
2 tbsp rapeseed (canola) oil or light olive oil
400g (14oz) tinned (canned) black beans, drained of excess water
2 handfuls of grated cheddar or Wensleydale cheese
2 tomatoes, diced, to serve
10 pickled, sliced jalapeños, to serve

FOR THE CHORIZO

35ml (⅛ cup) cider vinegar
½ onion, roughly chopped
3 garlic cloves, finely chopped
½ medium red (bell) pepper, roughly chopped
1½ tsp ground cumin
1 tsp red cheyenne chilli powder, or paprika
2 tsp freshly cracked black pepper
1½ tsp dried oregano
Pinch of ground cinnamon
Pinch of ground cloves
1 tsp salt
2 tbsp achiote paste
450g (1lb) minced (ground) pork (preferably shoulder meat)

Preheat the oven to 200°C (400°F/Gas 6). Place the butternut squash halves cut-side up in an ovenproof frying pan (skillet). Make diagonal shallow slits every 2.5cm (1in) down the squash and then do it again criss-crossing the first slits. Rub each half with olive oil and season with salt. Place in the oven and roast for 30–35 minutes, or until cooked through.

Meanwhile, prepare the chorizo. Put all of the ingredients except the minced (ground) pork in a food processor and blend to a smooth paste. Transfer to a mixing bowl and add the meat. Using your hands, mix it all together until evenly coated. Allow to marinate while the squash is cooking, or overnight for best results.

Once the squash has cooked, take it out of the oven and transfer it to a plate. Heat the oil in the frying pan over a medium–high heat and add the marinated pork. Fry for about 8 minutes, or until cooked through and a bit crumbly in texture. Stir in the black beans. Look at the hollows in your squash halves and how much meat needs to go in them – you might want to dig out a bit of the squash at this point so that none of the chorizo goes to waste. Pack the chorizo into the recesses and top each with a handful of cheese. Place back in the pan and put it back in the oven to cook for 10 minutes, or until the cheese has melted. Top with the diced tomato and pickled jalapeño to serve.

FRIED AND DEEP-FRIED

Some of my favourite dishes are either deep-fried
or stir-fried. In this section you'll find recipes
that you can whip up in under an hour.

KOREAN FRIED CHICKEN
SERVES 4

I once made this Korean fried chicken with baked, shop-bought chicken nuggets. It worked well, but if you prepare the recipe just as written you will, of course, get better results. You need to fry the chicken first. Then all you need to do is combine the sauce ingredients, heat it up and stir the fried chicken in. This sweet, sour and spicy chicken dish is worth the effort! I recommend serving this with white rice.

PREP TIME: 20 MINS, PLUS MARINATING TIME
COOKING TIME: 20 MINS

900g (2lb) chicken breast, cut into bite-sized pieces
Rapeseed (canola) or peanut oil, for frying

FOR THE MARINADE
2 tsp fine sea salt
2 tsp ground black pepper
1 tbsp garlic powder
2 tbsp rice wine or dry sherry

FOR THE DRY COATING
240g (2 cups) cornflour (cornstarch)
2 tsp fine sea salt
2 tsp ground black pepper
1 tbsp garlic powder

FOR THE SAUCE
2½ tbsp gochujang (Korean hot pepper paste)
1 tbsp dried red chilli flakes (optional)
2 tbsp cider vinegar
2 tbsp brown sugar
2 tbsp honey
3 tbsp soy sauce or tamari (gluten-free brands are available)
4 tbsp rice wine or sherry
3 tbsp garlic, finely chopped
2 tbsp sesame oil

TO SERVE
2 tbsp toasted sesame seeds
4 spring onions (scallions), thinly sliced

Whisk the salt, pepper and garlic powder together with the Chinese rice wine to make the marinade. Add the chicken and mix well with your hands, ensuring the chicken pieces are evenly coated with the marinade. Allow to marinate for a few hours or overnight. The longer the chicken rests in the marinade, the better. That said, if you're in a rush, you could just stir the chicken into the marinade and carry on cooking.

When ready to fry, mix all of the dry coating ingredients together on a large plate, then dust each piece of chicken with the flour mixture and set aside.

Heat a large wok about one-third full with rapeseed (canola) or peanut oil and bring to 175°C (350°F) over a medium–high heat. If you don't have a thermometer, you can check that the oil is hot enough by placing a wooden chopstick in the oil. If lots of little bubbles form around the chopstick instantly, your oil is hot enough.

Be sure to shake off any excess cornflour from the chicken. Cooking in small batches, place a few pieces of the chicken in the hot oil and fry for about 4–5 minutes. Transfer each batch of fried chicken to a rack to drip off any excess oil. Repeat with the remaining chicken.

With all the chicken fried, it's time to make the sauce. Discard or strain the cooking oil into a container for future frying and wipe the wok clean. Add all the sauce ingredients. It is easier to mix the sauce ingredients in a mixing bowl beforehand, but they can be added directly to the wok if it's more convenient for you.

Bring the sauce to a simmer and then add the fried chicken. I usually add the chicken to the sauce in batches, as it makes it easier to ensure that it is all equally coated. Heat the chicken through in the sauce and then add the toasted sesame seeds and chopped spring onions (scallions) to serve.

INDIAN FRIED CHICKEN
SERVES 6

If you like fried chicken, you're going to love this spicy Indian version. If you are on a gluten-free diet, you could use a mixture of cornflour (cornstarch) and rice flour. I like my fried chicken really spicy so I add a bit of naga chilli paste, which is optional, as is the amount of chilli powder used. If you don't want your fried chicken spicy, substitute paprika which will get you the same delicious-looking red colouring. I like to serve this chicken with the podina and spring onion (scallion) raita on page 255.

PREP TIME: 10 MINS, PLUS
   OPTIONAL MARINATING TIME
COOKING TIME: 25 MINS

2kg (4½lb) chicken pieces on the
   bone

FOR THE FIRST MARINADE
3 tbsp distilled white vinegar
3 tbsp garlic and ginger paste
1 tsp salt
3½ tbsp Kashmiri chilli powder

FOR THE SECOND MARINADE
125g (½ cup) full-fat Greek yoghurt
½ tsp ground turmeric
2 tsp garam masala, shop-bought or
   homemade (see page 259)
1 tbsp naga chilli paste (optional)

FOR FRYING
Oil, for deep-frying
120g (1 cup) plain (all-purpose) flour
120g (1 cup) cornflour (cornstarch) or
   150g (1 cup) rice flour
2 tbsp salt
1 tbsp freshly ground black pepper
1 tsp chaat masala, shop-bought or
   homemade (see page 260)
5 tbsp (¼ cup) melted butter or ghee
   (microwaved will do fine)
½ red onion, sliced, to serve
Lemon wedges, to serve

Place the chicken pieces in a bowl and pour the vinegar over them. Then add the garlic and ginger paste, salt and half the Kashmiri chilli powder. Allow to marinate while you prepare the yoghurt marinade, or leave for up to 2 hours.

Whisk the yoghurt, turmeric, garam masala and naga chilli paste, if using, together in a mixing bowl until smooth. Pour this over the chicken and rub it right into the flesh and skin. Allow to marinate for up to 48 hours or continue with the recipe immediately. The longer your marination time, the better the flavour will be.

When ready to start frying, heat your oil to 165°C (325°F) in a large, high-sided saucepan, wok or deep-fat fryer. If you don't have a thermometer, you can check that the oil is hot enough by placing a wooden chopstick in the oil. If lots of little bubbles form around the chopstick instantly, your oil is ready. While the oil is heating up, pour the flours onto a plate and mix with the salt, pepper and remaining Kashmiri chilli powder.

Remove any excess marinade from the chicken and dredge each piece in the flour so it is completely coated. Shake any excess flour off each piece. When your oil is up to heat, fry in small batches for about 10 minutes until lightly golden brown. Transfer the chicken to a wire rack to drip off any excess oil. Once all of the chicken has been cooked, turn up the heat to 200°C (400°F) and fry the chicken in batches for a second time, for about 2 minutes, or until cooked through, golden brown and crispy. It's cooked when the juices run clear when pricked with a fork or knife. If you have a thermometer, the cooked temperature of chicken is 75°C (165°F). Transfer it all to the wire rack.

Stir the chaat masala into the melted butter or ghee and baste each piece of chicken generously. Serve immediately with the sliced red onion and lemon wedges along with your choice of sides.

KUNG PAO CHICKEN
SERVES 4–6

I do love a good, spicy kung pao chicken. This recipe is quite spicy but you can, of course, adjust the amount of chillies. The dried chillies are added to flavour the chicken, and although they are of course edible, they aren't meant to be consumed.

PREP TIME: 15 MINS, PLUS
   OPTIONAL MARINATING TIME
COOKING TIME: 15 MINS

750g (1lb 10oz) chicken breasts or thighs, skinned and cut into 2.5cm (1in) pieces
3 tbsp rapeseed (canola) oil
2 tbsp finely chopped garlic
2 tbsp finely chopped ginger
3 spring onions (scallions) finely chopped
2 tsp Szechuan peppercorns, lightly crushed
12–15 Chinese or dried red finger chillies, cut in half and seeds removed
½ red (bell) pepper, diced
½ green (bell) pepper, diced
1 large handful of roasted peanuts, lightly crushed
1 tbsp sesame oil
2 spring onions (scallions), thinly sliced, to garnish
Dried chilli flakes, to garnish (optional)

FOR THE MARINADE
2 tbsp light soy sauce
1 tbsp Chinese rice wine (Shaoxing) or dry sherry
1½ tsp cornflour (cornstarch)

FOR THE SAUCE
70ml (¼ cup) unsalted chicken stock or water
70ml (¼ cup) light soy sauce
1 tbsp dark soy sauce
1 tbsp hoisin sauce
2 tbsp Chinese black vinegar
1 tsp cornflour (cornstarch)

See the optional note below if you want extra-tender chicken.

In a mixing bowl, whisk the marinade ingredients together until creamy smooth and then stir in the chicken pieces, ensuring that the chicken is nicely coated with the marinade. Set aside while you prepare the sauce or leave for up to 12 hours if more convenient.

Whisk the sauce ingredients together in a jug or bowl and set aside. When ready to cook, heat a large wok or frying pan (skillet) over a medium-high–high heat. Your wok is hot enough when a drop of water evaporates immediately on contact. Swirl in the oil and, when visibly hot, add the marinated chicken and fry, stirring regularly until the exterior is white and the chicken is about 80% cooked through. Transfer the par-cooked chicken to a plate and set aside.

If your chicken released a lot of water, pour it out and wipe your wok clean. Add a little more oil if you need to. When the oil is visibly hot, stir in the chopped garlic, ginger and spring onions (scallions) and fry, stirring continuously for about a minute.

Add the Szechuan peppercorns and dried chillies and give it all a good stir, and then add the diced (bell) peppers and the par-cooked chicken. Fry for another couple of minutes, or until the chicken is cooked through and the peppers are cooked but still fresh looking.

Stir in the lightly crushed, roasted peanuts and drizzle with the sesame oil. To serve, divide between four bowls and garnish with the sliced spring onions and dried chilli flakes, if using. This is good on its own or served over white rice.

VELVETING THE CHICKEN (OPTIONAL)
This is a technique that gets the chicken super tender and delicious. To do it, add one large egg to the marinade and whisk it in. Coat the chicken and let it marinate for about 30 minutes. Bring about 2 litres (8 cups) of water to a boil and when boiling rapidly, add the chicken and boil it for 1 minute or until white on the exterior but still quite raw. This can be done in the same wok you are cooking the rest of the recipe in. Strain and allow to cool and then carry on with the recipe.

FIRECRACKER CHICKEN
SERVES 4

Traditionally, this dish should be fried first in a pan and then baked in a baking tray. You could of course do that too, but I like to cook it and bake it all in the same pan. Take the crispy fried chicken to the table in that flaming hot pan and watch how quickly it gets devoured. There are many different versions of firecracker chicken. Some restaurants add about a tablespoon of soy sauce, but I prefer it sprinkled with flaky salt just before serving, instead.

PREP TIME: 10 MINS
COOKING TIME: 40 MINS

60g (½ cup) cornflour (cornstarch)
1 tsp fine sea salt
½ tsp ground black pepper
3 eggs, beaten
500g (1lb 2oz) chicken breast or
    thighs, skinned and cut into 2.5cm
    (1in) pieces
5 tbsp rapeseed (canola) or peanut oil
90ml (⅓ cup) buffalo hot sauce (any,
    but I use Frank's)
70g (¼ cup) brown sugar
2 tsp rice vinegar

TO SERVE
4 spring onions (scallions), thinly
    sliced into rings
½ tsp red chilli flakes (more or less
    to taste)
Flaky sea salt

Preheat the oven to 200°C (400°F/Gas 6). Mix the cornflour (cornstarch), salt and pepper on a plate. Then whisk the eggs in a large mixing bowl. Dip the chicken pieces in the egg and then dip them in the flour mixture to coat.

In a large, ovenproof pan, heat the oil over a high heat. When a piece of spring onion (scallion) sizzles immediately on contact with the oil, it is hot enough to start cooking. Working in small batches, dip the flour-coated chicken back into the egg wash and then add to the pan. Fry on both sides for about 4 minutes, or until nicely browned and crispy-looking. Transfer the cooked chicken to a paper towel or metal rack to drip away any excess oil.

Once all the chicken is cooked, discard any remaining oil from the pan and wipe it clean. You want to leave a film of oil in the pan, though, so that the chicken doesn't stick. Place the cooked chicken in one layer in the pan. Then whisk the buffalo hot sauce, sugar and rice vinegar together until smooth and pour it all over the chicken.

Place the pan in the oven to bake for 20–30 minutes, or until the chicken is cooked through and it looks suitably crispy. If you have a meat thermometer, the cooked temperature of chicken is 75°C (165°F). Sprinkle with the spring onions (scallions), chilli flakes and some flaky sea salt to serve.

SALT AND PEPPER CHICKEN
SERVES 4

This recipe goes way back for me – I learned it while I was in grade school. One of my friends' parents owned the only Chinese restaurant in town. I used to go to his place after school and always enjoyed tasting the food that was being cooked. He showed me one afternoon how to make salt and pepper chicken, and this recipe is probably pretty close to what I learned, although I've been making it for so long, I'm sure it has changed some over the years. This is good served with white rice.

PREP TIME: 15 MINS, PLUS
    OPTIONAL MARINATING TIME
COOKING TIME: 20 MINS

500g (1lb 2oz) skinless chicken thighs
    or breasts, cut into 2.5cm (1in)
    pieces
Oil, for deep-frying
2 tbsp rapeseed (canola) or peanut oil
2 garlic cloves, thinly sliced
2 red chillies, thinly sliced
4 dried red chillies, cut into thirds
    and seeds removed
1 onion, thinly sliced
4 spring onions (scallions), thinly
    sliced
1 green (bell) pepper, thinly sliced

FOR THE MARINADE
1 large egg white
1 tbsp Chinese rice wine or dry sherry
2 garlic cloves, finely chopped
1 tbsp soy sauce
2 tbsp cornflour (cornstarch)

FOR THE DRY COATING
120g (1 cup) cornflour (cornstarch)
½ tsp baking powder
½ tsp salt
1 tsp ground black pepper
½ tsp Chinese five spice
½ tsp Chinese chicken powder
    (optional)

In a large mixing bowl, whisk all of the marinade ingredients together until thick and smooth. Add the chicken and mix well to coat. Allow to marinate while you prepare the rest of the ingredients, or overnight. The longer the chicken marinates, the better.

Mix all of the dry coating ingredients together on a large plate and set aside until you are ready to fry the chicken.

To fry the chicken, fill your wok about a third full with oil and bring to 175°C (350°F) over a medium–high heat. If you don't have an oil thermometer, place a wooden chopstick or spatula in the oil. If lots of little bubbles form on contact, your oil is ready.

Dredge the marinated chicken in the flour mixture and be sure to shake off any excess. Fry the chicken pieces in batches for about 3–4 minutes, or until light and crispy on the exterior.

Transfer to a wire rack to drip off any excess oil and continue until all the chicken is cooked. Discard or sieve the oil into a container to use again and wipe your wok dry. Heat the wok over a high heat. You can start cooking when a bead of water evaporates on contact with the hot wok.

Heat about 2 tablespoons of rapeseed (canola) or peanut oil in the wok and add the sliced garlic and all of the chillies. Stir into the oil to coat and then add the sliced onion and spring onions (scallions). Stir to combine.

Now add the fried chicken and sliced (bell) pepper and continue cooking until the chicken is heated through and the pepper is cooked but still has a bit of crunch to it. Taste and season with more salt and pepper if you like. Serve immediately.

CRISPY CHILLI CHICKEN AND BROCCOLI

SERVES 4

Although you could deep-fry the chicken, this is another way to get great results using far less oil. Just ensure that the oil is hot enough, as described below.

PREP TIME: 15 MINS
COOKING TIME: 20 MINS

FOR THE SAUCE

1 tbsp oyster sauce
1 tbsp hoisin sauce or more oyster
   sauce
4 tbsp light soy sauce
4 tbsp honey
2 tbsp unsalted chicken stock or
   water
Juice of 2 limes

FOR THE CHICKEN

4 tbsp cornflour (cornstarch)
½ tsp salt
½ tsp black pepper
2 large chicken breasts, cut into bite-
   sized pieces
4 tbsp rapeseed (canola) or peanut oil

TO FINISH

300g (10½oz) tender-stemmed
   broccoli, cut into 2.5cm (1in)
   pieces
2 red finger chillies, seeded and cut
   into rings
1 tbsp rapeseed (canola) oil
4 garlic cloves, finely chopped
2.5cm (1in) piece of ginger, finely
   chopped
3 spring onions (scallions), sliced
   into thin rings

Start by preparing the sauce. Place all of the sauce ingredients in a mixing bowl and whisk until smooth. Set aside.

For the chicken, mix the cornflour (cornstarch), salt and pepper together. Dust the chicken in the mixture so that it is evenly coated, and shake off any excess. Now pour the oil into a wok over a high heat. The oil needs to be about 175°C (350°F). If you don't have an oil thermometer, stick a wooden chopstick or spatula in it. If bubbles instantly form around the wood, the oil is ready for cooking.

Cook the chicken in small batches so that you don't lower the temperature of the oil, and cook until lightly browned and crispy. It should only take about 5 minutes to cook all the chicken. Transfer the cooked chicken to a rack to drain off any excess oil.

To finish, add the broccoli and chillies to the wok and fry for a couple of minutes until just cooked through. Transfer to a plate. Add a little more oil to the wok if required – you need about a tablespoon. Fry the garlic, ginger and spring onions (scallions) for about 30 seconds, or until fragrant. Pour the prepared sauce into the wok and bring to a simmer. Return the chicken and broccoli to the wok, stir well to combine and serve.

THAI CHILLI CHICKEN AND CASHEWS

SERVES 4

This is a really easy stir fry. The cooking oil for the chillies and cashews can be retained and used many times, so don't throw it away, as I explain in more detail on page 11. The retained oil is perfect for any spicy stir fry. Frying the dried chillies gives the dish a nice touch of spiciness without making it really hot. The chillies can be eaten if you like, but they're really only there to give the curry a bit of heat and for presentation.

PREP TIME: 20 MINS
COOKING TIME: 10 MINS

FOR THE SAUCE

2 tbsp light soy sauce
1 tbsp dark soy sauce
1 tbsp oyster sauce
1 tsp Thai seasoning sauce (optional)
70ml (¼ cup) water or chicken stock (see page 250)
1 tsp palm sugar, grated and finely chopped

FOR THE STIR FRY

250ml (1 cup) rapeseed (canola) oil
30 cashews
20 dried red finger chillies
450g (1lb) skinless chicken thigh fillets, cut into small cashew-sized pieces
3 tbsp cornflour (cornstarch)
6 garlic cloves, roughly chopped
1 large onion, thinly sliced
3 red spur chillies, thinly sliced
2 green finger chillies, cut into thin rings
4 spring onions (scallions), sliced, to garnish

Whisk all of the sauce ingredients together and taste it. Add more sugar if you like a sweeter flavour, and then set aside.

Heat the rapeseed (canola) oil in a wok until shimmering hot. Add one cashew. It should sizzle on contact, but not brown too quickly. If that cashew looks like it is happy in the oil, add the rest and cook for about a minute, or until light golden brown in colour. Transfer to a paper towel to soak up any excess oil. Do the same with the chillies, checking the oil temperature first. You want them to become shiny but still retain a deep red colour. If the oil is too hot, they will quickly burn and turn brown. Transfer the fried chillies to the plate with the cashews.

Now dust the small, cashew-sized chicken pieces with the cornflour (cornstarch). Shake any excess flour off and add the flour-coated chicken in small batches to the hot oil. Fry for 3–5 minutes until golden brown and crispy. Transfer to a paper towel to soak up the excess oil.

Pour all but about 3 tablespoons of the oil from the wok out. This oil can be retained for future use (see page 11) or discarded. If flour has accumulated at the bottom of your wok, pour it all out, wipe it clean and add 3 tablespoons of fresh oil. Heat the oil over a medium–high heat. Stir in the garlic, onion, spur chillies and green finger chillies. Fry until the garlic is turning soft and a very light brown colour, but be very careful not to burn it. Stir in the sauce mixture and simmer for about 30–60 seconds to thicken. Then add the chicken, cashews and fried chillies, stirring well to combine.

Continue cooking for a minute or two until the sauce is sticking to the meat and cashews and then taste it, adjusting the seasoning if necessary. Serve immediately, sprinkled with the chopped spring onions (scallions) to garnish.

VIETNAMESE FISH SAUCE CHICKEN WINGS

SERVES 4

Chicken wings with crispy chicken skin and spicy, sweet, sour and savoury coating. Can things really get any better? This is quick and easy to make and I really doubt you will have any leftovers.

PREP TIME: 10 MINS, PLUS
   OPTIONAL MARINATING TIME
COOKING TIME: 15 MINS

900g (2lb) chicken wings
150g (1 cup) rice flour or 120g (1 cup)
   cornflour (cornstarch)
Rapeseed (canola) oil, for deep-frying

FOR THE MARINADE
2 tbsp Chinese cooking wine or dry
   sherry
2 tsp freshly cracked black pepper
1 tsp finely chopped ginger
1 tbsp fish sauce
1 tsp Chinese chicken seasoning or
   MSG (optional)

FOR THE SAUCE
4 garlic cloves, finely chopped
2 green finger chillies, finely chopped
1 red finger chilli, finely chopped
3 tbsp lime juice
2 tbsp fish sauce (gluten-free brands
   are available)
3 tbsp sugar
2 tbsp coriander (cilantro), finely
   chopped, to garnish

Whisk the marinade ingredients together in a large mixing bowl. Add the chicken wings and mix it all up to combine. Set aside while you prepare the rest of the dish, or cover and place in the fridge to marinate for up to 24 hours – the longer, the better.

Remove the chicken from the marinade and retain whatever marinade is left over. Dust the chicken with the flour and shake off any excess. Now heat about 5cm (2in) of oil in a wok and bring it up to about 175°C (350°F). If you don't have an oil thermometer, stick a wooden chopstick or spatula in the oil. If lots of bubbles instantly form around the wood, your oil is ready for frying.

Fry the chicken in small batches for about 10 minutes, or until the chicken is crispy and golden brown. Transfer the cooked chicken to a plate and discard all but about a tablespoon of the oil from the wok. If the oil looks dirty from the flour, pour it all out, wipe your wok clean and start again with a tablespoon of fresh oil.

To make the sauce, fry the garlic over a medium heat until lightly browned and crispy. Be very careful not to burn it. Transfer the fried garlic to a plate with a slotted spoon and set aside.

Now add the chillies to the wok and fry for about a minute. Stir in the retained marinade along with the lime juice, fish sauce and sugar and bring to a simmer for a few minutes to thicken.

Return the fried chicken wings and garlic to the wok and stir it to coat the chicken. Serve immediately, garnished with the chopped coriander (cilantro).

CHICKEN WITH SAMBAL MATAH

SERVES 4

One of the most delicious and easy light meals I tried in Ubud, Bali, was at a place called Biah Biah. The restaurant was recommended by a friend, and every dish was amazing. Chicken with sambal matah was one of many dishes we ordered. It's really just a light chicken salad that's packed with the delicious flavours of a raw sambal. If you can't be bothered to cook one evening and want a healthy dinner, purchase a cooked rotisserie chicken and peel off all the meat to use in this recipe.

PREP TIME: 15 MINS
COOKING TIME: 15 MINS

FOR THE SAMBAL MATAH
8 green finger chillies, finely chopped
2 red jalapeños or finger chillies
8 shallots, thinly sliced
5 garlic cloves, finely chopped
3 lime leaves, stems removed and
   thinly sliced
1 tbsp lime juice
¼ tsp salt
¼ tsp sugar
3 tbsp coconut oil
2 lemongrass stalks, peeled, white
   part only, chopped
½ tsp terasi or Chinese shrimp paste
   (optional)

FOR THE CHICKEN
8 boneless chicken thighs, skinned
Salt and freshly cracked black pepper,
   to taste
2 tbsp rapeseed (canola) oil

To make the sambal matah, place the chillies, shallots, garlic, lime leaves, lime juice, salt and sugar in a mixing bowl. Set aside. Heat the coconut oil in a pan over a medium–high heat and fry the lemongrass for a couple of minutes to soften it. Then add the shrimp paste, if using, and fry, stirring continuously, for another 30 seconds. Pour this over the chopped veggies and mix it in. Taste it and add salt and/or sugar to taste. Set aside.

Season the chicken thighs with salt and pepper to taste. Then heat the oil for the chicken in the same pan over a medium–high heat. When visibly hot, add the chicken thighs and cook for about 4 minutes per side, or until cooked through. The juices should run clear when pricked with a knife. The cooked temperature for chicken is 75°C (165°F).

Cut the cooked chicken into bite-sized pieces and mix it into the sambal matah. Serve immediately.

CAJUN JAMBALAYA

SERVES 4–6

Jambalaya is like a dry version of gumbo (see page 199) and it is also a lot easier and faster to make. This is a no-nonsense jambalaya recipe that is perfect for any day of the week.

PREP TIME: 15 MINS
COOKING TIME: 30 MINS

500g (1lb 2oz) boneless and skinless chicken thighs, cut into bite-sized pieces
3 tbsp Cajun seasoning, shop-bought or homemade (see page 262)
2 tbsp light olive oil
400g (14oz) andouille sausage, cut into bite-sized pieces
100g (3½oz) celery, chopped
1 red onion, finely chopped
100g (3½oz) red (bell) pepper, diced
1–2 jalapeño chillies, finely chopped
10 garlic cloves, finely chopped
185g (1 cup) jasmine rice
400g (14 oz) tinned (canned) chopped tomatoes
500ml (2 cups) chicken stock
100g (1 cup) okra, chopped, or 1 tsp filé powder
500g (1lb 2oz) raw prawns (shrimp), peeled and tails removed
2 tbsp spring onions (scallions), chopped
Hot sauce, to serve

Dust the chicken pieces with 2 tablespoons of the Cajun seasoning and set aside. Heat the oil in a large saucepan over a medium–high heat. When visibly hot and shimmering, add the andouille sausage and cook in one layer until browned on the underside. Then flip the sausage pieces over to brown the other side. Transfer the cooked sausage to a plate and then cook the chicken in the same pan until lightly browned. Transfer the chicken to the plate with the sausages.

Add a drop more oil if needed and fry the vegetables, chillies and garlic with the remaining Cajun seasoning until the onion is soft and translucent. About 5 minutes should do. Pour in the rice and fry it with the vegetables for another 3 minutes.

Add the chopped tomatoes, chicken stock and okra and bring to a simmer over a medium heat. Then return the cooked chicken and sausage to the pan and cover to simmer for about 15 minutes, or until the rice is cooked through.

Push the raw prawns (shrimp) into the hot rice and continue cooking until they are cooked through and pink in colour. Check for seasoning and add more salt if necessary.

Serve immediately, garnished with spring onions (scallions) and your favourite hot sauce.

NOTE
You could leave out the okra and just add filé powder, or use both.

CHICKEN NASI GORENG
SERVES 4

If you travel to Malaysia or Indonesia, it would be difficult to miss nasi goreng. It's everywhere, and comes in many different varieties. This is a great dish for using leftover white rice, as the rice needs to be cooked and cold before starting. Although the most popular version of nasi goreng is made with chicken, there are many other versions such as prawn (shrimp) and vegetarian. In fact, you can make this one completely vegetarian by adding a few more veggies and some tofu for protein. The finished dish is often topped with a scrambled or fried egg, but this is optional. In my opinion, sambal oelek (see page 252), a simple red chilli sauce, is a must.

PREP TIME: 10 MINS
COOKING TIME: 15 MINS

FOR THE CHICKEN

450g (1lb) chicken thighs, cut into
    small, bite-sized pieces
1 tbsp kecap manis (see page 258 or
    shop-bought)
1 tsp soy sauce (gluten-free brands
    are available)

FOR THE RICE

2 tbsp kecap manis (see page 258 or
    shop-bought)
2 tbsp soy sauce (gluten-free brands
    are available)
2 tbsp rapeseed (canola) or peanut oil
    (plus more if required)
4 shallots (or ½ red onion), finely
    chopped
4 garlic cloves, finely chopped
2 green finger chillies, finely chopped
    (more or less to taste)
½ tsp shrimp paste
800g (4 cups) cooked, chilled basmati
    or jasmine rice
½ tsp white pepper or to taste

TO SERVE

4 fried eggs (optional)
1 English cucumber, sliced
4 medium tomatoes, quartered
Sambal oelek (see page 252)
Crispy fried shallots or onions (see
    page 262 or shop-bought)

Place the chicken in a mixing bowl and top with the kecap manis and soy sauce. Mix with your hands so that the chicken is equally coated with the sauces. Set aside.

For the rice, combine the kecap manis and soy sauce in a bowl and stir to combine. Set aside. Heat the oil over a medium–high heat in a wok and, when visibly hot, add the chopped shallots and fry for a minute or so before stirring in the garlic, chillies and shrimp paste. Give this all a good stir and the push it all to the sides of your wok, leaving room in the centre for the chicken. Pour the chicken in and cook it all for 5 minutes, or until lightly browned, and then stir the vegetables and meat together. If your wok is looking dry, add another tablespoon of oil but, if not, leave it as is and add the cold, cooked rice. Give it a couple of good but delicate stirs to combine. Add the kecap manis and soy sauce mixture and continue stirring and frying until the rice is equally coated with the sauces and a beautiful golden brown colour. Sprinkle with the white pepper.

Divide the fried rice between four shallow bowls. Top each with a fried egg, if liked, and serve with the cucumber, tomatoes, sambal oelek and fried shallots or onions.

PAD THAI WITH PEANUT BUTTER SAUCE

SERVES 6

This is an increasingly popular take on the more authentic pad thai recipe featured in my book, *The Curry Guy Thai*. I really like the addition of peanut butter and soy sauce. If you like your noodles really saucy, squirt some sriracha over it or double the sauce recipe and drizzle it over the noodles at the table.

PREP TIME: 20 MINS, PLUS
    SOAKING TIME
COOKING TIME: 15 MINS

FOR THE SAUCE

3 tbsp soy sauce (gluten-free brands
    are available)
6 tbsp Thai fish sauce (gluten-free
    brands are available)
2 tbsp sugar
70ml (¼ cup) tamarind paste (see
    page 256 or shop-bought)
1½ tbsp fresh lime juice (more or less
    to taste)
1½ tbsp white distilled vinegar
2 tbsp sriracha sauce
10 tbsp (½ cup) peanut butter,
    microwaved for 45 seconds

FOR THE NOODLES

2 tbsp rapeseed (canola) oil
¼ cup dried baby shrimp
6 garlic cloves, roughly chopped
100g (½ cup) tofu puffs
2 skinless chicken thigh fillets, cut
    into small pieces
2 eggs
6 jumbo prawns (shrimp), peeled and
    deveined
2 tsp salted turnip (optional)
200g (7oz) dried rice noodles soaked
    in hot water for 5–10 minutes
5 spring onions (scallions), cut into
    5cm (2in) pieces
150g (5½oz) bean sprouts, plus extra
    to garnish
50g (¼ cup) dry-roasted, unsalted
    peanuts, crushed
1 tsp chilli flakes, to garnish
Lime wedges, to serve

Start by mixing all the sauce ingredients except for the peanut butter in a bowl, adjusting to taste as necessary. Transfer 4 tablespoons of this sauce to another bowl for later, and then whisk the warmed peanut butter into the remaining sauce until smooth.

Heat the oil in a wok over a high heat. When the oil begins to shimmer, add the dried shrimp and garlic and sauté for about 30 seconds. Add the tofu and chicken and brown in the oil for about a minute.

Push all of these ingredients to the side of the wok and crack the eggs into the empty side, stirring to scramble. Allow them to cook for about a minute and then stir the par-cooked egg into the other ingredients.

Add the prawns (shrimp) and let them cook with the other ingredients until about half cooked through. This should only take a minute or two. Then add the peanut butter sauce.

Stir in the salted turnip, if using, and the soaked rice noodles until the noodles are nicely coated in the sauce mixture. Fold in the spring onions (scallions) and bean sprouts. The hot noodles will cook the sprouts and onions, but you are only really steaming them.

Stir in half of the crushed peanuts and continue cooking until the noodles look wet but there isn't a lot of sauce left. You don't want the noodles dripping with sauce; they should just be moist from having cooked in it.

Transfer to four heated plates and garnish with the remaining peanuts, the chilli flakes and remaining bean sprouts. You can also drizzle some of the reserved soy sauce mixture over it. Serve with lime wedges.

CURRY RAMEN
SERVES 4–6

This is a ramen dish that Caroline and I tried for the first time in Bangkok. Ramen is, of course, Japanese but the chef at the restaurant served us his signature Thai-inspired version. It was so good! He explained the recipe to me and this was one of the first dishes we tested when we got home. There is a lot of liquid going into this recipe, so you will need to use a large wok or high-sided frying pan (skillet).

PREP TIME: 10 MINS
COOKING TIME: 20 MINS

1kg (2lb 2oz) chicken breasts and/or thighs, cut into thin strips
Salt and pepper, to taste
2 tbsp rapeseed (canola) or coconut oil
3 garlic cloves, finely chopped
2.5cm (1in) piece of galangal or ginger, finely chopped (preferably galangal)
6 spring onions (scallions), cut into 2.5cm (1in) pieces
½ tsp ground turmeric
1 generous tbsp S&B Oriental curry powder, homemade curry powder (see page 259) or another good-quality curry powder
3 tbsp Thai green curry paste (shop-bought is fine for this one)
2 litres (8 cups) Asian-style chicken stock (see page 250 or shop-bought)
6 packs of instant ramen noodles
2 x 400ml (14oz) tins (cans) thick coconut milk
1–2 tbsp fish sauce (gluten-free brands are available)

OPTIONAL GARNISHES
Coriander (cilantro)
Crispy fried onions
Julienned carrots
Chinese chilli oil
Sriracha

Season the chicken strips with salt and pepper and then heat the oil in a large wok or high-sided frying pan (skillet). Place the chicken in the hot oil and fry for about 10 minutes, turning often until it is cooked through and lightly browned on the exterior – you might need to do this in a couple of batches. The chicken needs to be cooked to 75°C (165°F). Transfer the cooked chicken to a plate and keep warm.

Add a little more oil to the wok, if necessary, and fry the garlic, galangal or ginger and spring onions (scallions) for about 30 seconds, or until fragrant. Then stir in the ground turmeric, curry powder and the Thai curry paste. Let this all sizzle for about a minute, stirring continuously.

Stir in the chicken stock. Bring to a rolling simmer for about 5 minutes to reduce a little. While the stock is simmering, cover the instant ramen noodles with hot water. They usually only need to soak for about 5 minutes, but follow the packet instructions.

Once the stock has simmered for 5 minutes, add the coconut milk and again bring to a simmer. Stir in the fish sauce and then taste it. You can spice it up by adding more green paste, or add a bit more salt or some sugar. Make it taste perfect for your preference.

To serve, divide the cooked ramen noodles between four to six bowls. Top with some of the cooked chicken and pour the sauce over them. Garnish each as you wish with the suggested options, or whatever sounds good to you.

CAJUN GUMBO

SERVES 4–6

You should find this recipe quite easy, but to make a Cajun gumbo properly takes time. In fact, you will need to stand over your pan for up to an hour while cooking the roux, so you've been warned – although the rest is a breeze. You want that roux to get as dark as you can get it without burning. It should be a deep, chocolatey brown but don't let it go black! If you do, it's burnt and you will need to start over. I recommend using a saucepan that has a light-coloured base, if you have one, so that you can watch the roux darken until it's perfectly cooked. The okra is used as a sauce thickener and is the original gumbo thickener. The use of filé powder came much later and it can be substituted, or you could use both. This gumbo is often served with white rice, which is what I do.

PREP TIME: 15 MINS
COOKING TIME: 2 HOURS

250ml (1 cup) rapeseed (canola) oil
8 boned chicken thighs, skin removed
24 medium sized prawns (shrimp), peeled and cleaned
500g (1lb 2oz) andouille sausage or another European-style smoked sausage, cut into 1.25cm (½in) slices
120g (1 cup) plain (all-purpose) flour
2 large red onions, diced
1 green (bell) pepper, diced
1 yellow or orange (bell) pepper, diced
3 celery sticks, diced
10 garlic cloves, finely chopped
1 tsp cayenne chilli powder
1 tbsp dried thyme
1 tsp dried oregano
3 bay leaves
1.5 litres (6 cups) chicken stock (fresh stock or use stock cubes)
Salt and freshly grated black pepper, to taste
450g (1lb) fresh okra, cut into thin rounds and/or 1 tsp filé powder

Heat about 2 tablespoons of the oil in a large saucepan and add the chicken thighs. Cook over a medium–high heat, turning from time to time for about 5 minutes, or until they are cooked through. Transfer to a plate. Now add the prawns (shrimp). Cook until they are turning pink and then transfer them to the plate with the chicken. Fry the sliced sausage in the same way, until it has turned crispy. Transfer to the plate with the chicken and prawns. This can all be done earlier in the day. When the chicken has cooled a little, tear it into bite-sized pieces.

To begin the roux, pour the remaining oil into the pan. When hot, lower the cooking temperature to low and add the flour. Stir this into the oil until smooth. It should look quite soupy at this point. If it doesn't, add a little more oil until it does. Now your work begins! Simmer the oil and flour mixture continuously until it turns a dark brown, which over a low heat could take up to an hour. A low heat is best, as there is a very fine line between perfectly brown and black, but to speed things up, you could cook over a higher heat. Just bear in mind that this is riskier, so be sure to turn it back down to low when it's looking like it's almost ready.

Once you have a deep brown roux, add the diced onions, (bell) peppers, celery and garlic and stir well to coat the vegetables with the roux. Add the chilli powder, thyme, oregano and bay leaves and then add the chicken stock. Bring to a simmer over a medium–high heat, and then reduce the heat to medium to simmer for 45 minutes to 1 hour to thicken a little. Try it and season with a little salt and freshly ground black pepper to taste and then add the shredded chicken and the sliced sausages along with the okra, if using. Simmer for another 30 minutes. The sauce should be looking deliciously thick now, so add the prawns and stir them in. If you like, you could add a little filé powder at this point to thicken it some more. The gumbo is ready when you are happy with the consistency and flavour.

MEE GORENG
SERVES 4

It's believed that mee goreng originated in Indonesia, but it is equally popular in Malaysia, Singapore and Brunei. At times I thought it was a bit too popular, because it seemed to be served for almost every hotel breakfast we had, and they weren't always worth writing home about. What you have here, however, is mee goreng the way it should be. There are many versions of this dish, and though I have used chicken and baby shrimp in my recipe, you could use the protein of your choice. A popular vegetarian version is made with firm tofu or tofu puffs. In the Malay language, mee means 'noodles' and goreng means 'fried'. That's what you're getting here in this easy, one-wok, fried noodle recipe.

PREP TIME: 10 MINS
COOKING TIME: 15 MINS

4 packs of instant ramen noodles

FOR THE SAUCE
2 tbsp sambal oelek (see page 252) or sriracha sauce
1 tbsp sesame oil
1 tbsp light soy sauce (gluten-free brands are available)
1 tbsp dark soy sauce (gluten-free brands are available)
3 tbsp kecap manis (see page 258 or shop-bought)
1 tbsp ketchup

FOR FRYING
1 tbsp rapeseed (canola) oil
1 tbsp sesame oil
4 garlic cloves, finely chopped
1 tbsp dried baby shrimp (optional)
250g (9oz) chicken thighs, cut into small, bite-sized pieces
2 eggs, beaten
½ small savoy cabbage, finely shredded
1 large handful of bean sprouts
4 spring onions (scallions), roughly chopped
2 red spur chillies, thinly sliced, to garnish

Soak the noodles in hot water for about 10 minutes, or until soft. Strain and put to one side. Whisk all of the sauce ingredients together and set aside.

Now heat a wok over a medium–high heat* and add the oils. Stir in the garlic and fry for about 30 seconds, or until fragrant. Then add the dried baby shrimp and fry for another minute, giving it all a good stir from time to time.

Add the chicken and fry for a couple of minutes, until the meat has turned white all over. Push this all to one side of the wok and then add the beaten eggs to the empty side. Stir the egg to scramble and when cooked, stir it into the chicken. Add the cabbage, bean sprouts and half the spring onions (scallions) and fry for about 30 seconds. Then add the noodles and prepared sauce. Stir this all together until the noodles are nicely coated in the sauce, and then continue frying until the sauce thickens and begins to caramelize on the noodles.

Divide between four serving bowls and garnish with the remaining spring onions and sliced spur chillies.

NOTE

*I have suggested cooking this over a medium–high heat, which is the right temperature if you are new to cooking in woks. If you have been cooking in woks for a while and are comfortable with tossing the ingredients, you might want to turn the heat up to high. This will get you a smokier flavour that tastes fantastic.

SPICY CHICKEN CHOW MEIN
SERVES 4

Chow mein is usually quite mild, but this is a spicier version like the one I enjoyed at a Chinese hakka stall in Kuala Lumpur. If you prefer a milder chow mein, just leave out some or all of the spicy ingredients and you'll get just that. You can make this dish vegetarian by adding more veggies and/or substituting firm tofu or pre-fried tofu for the chicken.

PREP TIME: 15 MINS, PLUS OPTIONAL MARINATING TIME
COOKING TIME: 15 MINS

225g (8oz) chicken thigh or breast, cut into 2.5cm (1in) pieces
200g (7oz) dried Chinese egg noodles
2 tbsp rapeseed (canola) or peanut oil
2 tbsp toasted sesame oil
1 generous tbsp finely chopped garlic
1 tbsp finely chopped ginger
3 spring onions (scallions), white parts only, finely chopped
1–2 green finger chillies, finely chopped
1 red onion, thinly sliced and cut into 5cm (2in) pieces
1 small green (bell) pepper, thinly sliced and cut into 5cm (2in) pieces
1 small red (bell) pepper, thinly sliced and cut into 5cm (2in) pieces
1 carrot, grated
2 large handfuls of bean sprouts
1 tsp red chilli flakes
Chopped coriander (cilantro), to garnish

FOR THE MARINADE
½ tsp white pepper
1 tbsp soy sauce (gluten-free brands are available)
1 tbsp Chinese cooking wine or dry sherry
1 tsp cornflour (cornstarch)

FOR THE SAUCE
2 tbsp soy sauce (gluten-free brands are available)
1 tbsp rice wine vinegar
1 tbsp mirin (optional)
1 tsp brown sugar (optional)
1½ tbsp oyster sauce
1–2 tbsp Chinese chilli garlic sauce
1 tsp Chinese chicken powder (contains MSG, optional)

Start by mixing all the ingredients for the marinade in a large bowl. Add the chicken pieces, mix well to coat and allow to marinate while you prepare the rest of the dish (or overnight). In another bowl, whisk all the sauce ingredients together until smooth. Set aside. This can be done a day or two ahead of cooking if more convenient.

When ready to cook, pour boiling water over the dried egg noodles. Break them apart a bit and let them soak for about 10 minutes, or until al dente. Strain and set aside.

Heat the rapeseed (canola) or peanut oil along with 1 tablespoon of the sesame oil in a wok over a medium–high heat.★ When visibly hot, stir in the garlic, ginger, spring onions (scallions) and chillies. Fry for about a minute and then stir in the onion, (bell) peppers and grated carrot. Continue frying, tossing and stirring so that everything cooks evenly, for a couple of minutes. Stir in the chicken pieces and fry until about 80% cooked through. Keep stirring and shaking that wok so that nothing burns.

Add the bean sprouts followed by the cooked noodles and the sauce, and continue stirring rapidly until the noodles are completely coated with the other ingredients and cooked to your liking. Add the chilli flakes and serve, garnished with the chopped coriander (cilantro).

NOTE
★I have suggested cooking this over a medium–high heat, which is the right temperature if you are new to cooking in woks. If you have been cooking in woks for a while and are comfortable with tossing the ingredients, you might want to turn the heat up to high. This will get you a smokier flavour that tastes fantastic.

STOVETOP TANDOORI CHICKEN TIKKA
SERVES 6

I have included two recipes for chicken tikka in this book – see also the baking tray chicken tikka on page 158. The marinades in these two recipes are different but the recipes are interchangeable, so you could use the baking tray chicken tikka marinade for this recipe, too. This stovetop chicken tikka is delicious served as is, but it will also work well added to any of the curry house-style recipes in this book, or used as a meaty butter chicken-style substitute for the paneer in my paneer makhani (see page 140). In this recipe I've included a technique using a piece of burning charcoal to give the chicken a tasty, smoky flavour (see note below), but that is optional.

PREP TIME: 15 MINS, PLUS
  MARINATING TIME
COOKING TIME: 20 MINS

900g (2lb) chicken thighs or breasts,
  cut into bite-sized pieces

FOR THE FIRST MARINADE
1 tsp red food colouring powder
  (optional)
2 tbsp garlic and ginger paste
Juice of 1 lemon
¾ tsp salt

FOR THE SECOND MARINADE
2 tbsp ginger and garlic paste
200g (7oz) Greek yoghurt
1 tbsp cream cheese
1 tbsp rapeseed (canola) oil
1 tsp ground turmeric
1 tbsp ground cumin
1 tsp ground coriander
1 tbsp smoked paprika (optional)
1 tbsp Kashmiri chilli powder
1 tbsp tandoori masala, shop-bought
  or homemade (see page 260)
Salt, to taste

TO FINISH
3 tbsp ghee or rapeseed (canola) oil
Coriander (cilantro) leaves
2 limes, quartered

Place the chicken in a bowl and mix well with the red food colouring (if using), garlic and ginger paste, lemon juice and salt. Set aside while you make the second marinade. In another bowl, whisk all the second marinade ingredients together until you have a smooth emulsion. Pour the marinade over the chicken and rub it into the flesh. Cover with cling film (plastic wrap) and marinate for at least 30 minutes or overnight – the longer, the better.

When ready to cook, add the ghee or oil to a frying pan (skillet) over a medium–high heat. When visibly hot, place the chicken pieces in the pan, removing as much marinade as you can from each piece as you do. Don't overcrowd your pan as the chicken will release water and it won't char correctly, so do this in batches if necessary.

Fry on the first side for about 2 minutes, or until nicely charred. Turn the chicken over and fry on the opposite side for another 2 minutes to char.

You should now have a nice crust on both sides. Reduce the heat to medium and continue frying for about 8 more minutes, turning from time to time until the chicken is cooked through. The cooking time will of course vary depending on the size of the chicken pieces you are cooking. If testing with a thermometer, the chicken needs to be cooked until the internal temperature reaches 75°C (165°F). Transfer to a serving plate and serve hot garnished with the coriander (cilantro) leaves and lime wedges, or store in the fridge or freezer for use in a curry.

THE DHUNGAR SMOKING METHOD

If you would like to add a lovely, smoky flavour to your chicken, you could use this method before frying, while the chicken is marinating. Light two pieces of lumpwood charcoal that is natural and not treated with lighter fuel and let them turn white hot. When the charcoal is ready, place it on top of a folded-over piece of foil. Make a small well in the centre of the marinating chicken, and place the burning charcoal on the foil in it. Drizzle with about ½ teaspoon of rapeseed (canola) oil. When you do this, the charcoal will begin smoking like crazy. Quickly cover the bowl tightly with a glass lid and allow to smoke until almost all of the smoke has disappeared. This should only take about 10 minutes and can all be done a day or so ahead of cooking, if more convenient.

BALINESE CRISPY FRIED DUCK

SERVES 3–4

Being a big fan of crispy fried duck, I've probably tried hundreds of different recipes and this is one of my favourites. The cooking liquid can be used as a dipping sauce, or you could save it and stir in some instant ramen for a quick weekday meal. I recommend serving crispy fried duck and the cooking liquid as a special meal, as simmering the duck in the sauce and then drying and frying it takes some time and effort. Serve the crispy fried duck with sambal matah and/or sambal oelek (see page 252) if you like. This is traditionally served with the Balinese green bean recipe on page 250, though a simple green salad and some shop-bought hot sauce will do nicely.

PREP TIME: 15 MINS, PLUS
   OPTIONAL SITTING TIME
COOKING TIME: 60 MINS

FOR THE SPICE BLEND
2.5cm (1in) piece of ginger
5cm (2in) piece of galangal
2 lemongrass stalks, white parts only,
   peeled and thinly sliced
15 green finger chillies, roughly
   chopped
8 garlic cloves, peeled and smashed
2 tbsp black peppercorns
2 tbsp coriander seeds

FOR THE DUCK
4 duck legs
1 tbsp rapeseed (canola) oil
2 makrut lime leaves
2 lemongrass stalks, lightly smashed
10 curry leaves
250ml (1 cup) coconut milk (optional)
Oil, for deep-frying
Salt, to taste

Blend all of the spice blend ingredients in a food processor or pestle and mortar until you have a smooth paste and set aside.

Prick each duck leg about 20 times with a knife. Now heat the oil in a large frying pan (skillet) or wok over a medium–high heat. When visibly hot, add the duck legs skin-side down and fry for about 5 minutes, turning once. As the duck fries, the fat in the skin will render into the pan. Transfer the duck legs to a plate and set aside. Add the lime leaves, lemongrass and curry leaves to the rendered duck fat and allow these flavours to infuse into the oil for about 30 seconds. Then add the prepared spice paste and fry it for a couple of minutes. Return the duck legs to the pan and stir them into the sambal, and then add the coconut milk and enough water to cover. Simmer the duck over a medium heat, covered, for 1 hour. Transfer the duck legs to a plate and save the sauce for dipping or later use.

For best results, allow the duck legs to dry, uncovered, in the fridge overnight or as long as you can. This will produce a crispier exterior. That said, you could just dry the skin with paper towels and carry on with the recipe. If using the cooking liquid as a dipping sauce, be sure to season it with salt to taste.

Heat sufficient oil for deep-frying in your pan to 170°C (340°F). If you don't have an oil thermometer, the oil is ready when you add one of the duck legs and it begins to sizzle, with lots of little bubbles around it. Fry the duck for 10 minutes, or until the skin looks golden brown and crispy. Transfer the fried duck to a wire rack to drain off any excess oil, season the skin with a little salt and serve.

AIR FRYER INSTRUCTIONS
If you'd prefer to air-fry this dish, dry the duck skin after simmering and place the legs in an air fryer at 200°C (400°F). Cook for about 15 minutes, or until the duck skin is crispy brown and to your liking.

Top left: Balinese green beans (page 250)
Centre: Balinese crispy fried duck

CHINESE CRISPY CHILLI BEEF

SERVES 4

I love Chinese crispy beef and always order it when I want to treat myself to a Chinese takeaway. It's always amazing, but doesn't really compare to what you can make at home. Taking the crispy fried beef out of the oil and then stir-frying right back in the wok creates the crispiest and most tender Chinese crispy beef you'll ever try.

PREP TIME: 10 MINS, PLUS
    MARINATING TIME
COOKING TIME: 20 MINS

400g (14oz) sirloin steak
60g (½ cup) cornflour (cornstarch)
75g (½ cup) rice flour
Rapeseed (canola) or peanut oil, for
    frying
1 small onion, thinly sliced
½ red (bell) pepper, thinly sliced
½ yellow (bell) pepper, thinly sliced
4 spring onions (scallions), cut into
    2.5cm (1in) pieces
4 garlic cloves, finely chopped
2.5cm (1in) piece of ginger, finely
    chopped
2 red finger chillies, thinly sliced
¾ tsp salt
¾ tsp ground black pepper
3 tbsp coriander (cilantro), very finely
    chopped, to garnish

FOR THE MARINADE
1 egg, beaten
1 tbsp sesame oil
2 generous tbsp cornflour
    (cornstarch)
2 tbsp light soy sauce
1 tbsp dark soy sauce
½ tsp ground white pepper
1 tsp sugar

FOR THE SAUCE
3 tbsp light soy sauce
1 tsp dark soy sauce
3 tbsp ketchup
4 tbsp sugar
2 tbsp black rice vinegar
1 tsp dried chilli flakes (optional)
3 tbsp sweet Chinese chilli sauce, or
    another of your choice

Place the marinade ingredients in a large mixing bowl and whisk until smooth. Add the thinly sliced beef and stir until the meat is completely coated with the marinade. Allow to marinate for at least 30 minutes, or up to 24 hours for the best results.

Now make the sauce by whisking the sauce ingredients together in a bowl and setting aside. This can be done a day or two ahead of cooking if more convenient.

When ready to cook, pour the flours onto a large plate and mix well. Remove the beef from the marinade and dust it with the flour mixture. Be sure to shake the meat a little to remove any excess flour. Set aside.

Heat about 7.5cm (3in) of oil in a wok. The oil is ready when a piece of the spring onion (scallion) sizzles and rises to the top immediately when you drop it in. Fry the meat in small batches until cooked through and crispy. Transfer the cooked beef to a wire rack so that any excess oil can drip off. Repeat until all of the beef is cooked.

Discard all but about 3 tablespoons of the cooking oil and place your wok back over a medium–high heat. If there is a lot of flour in the oil, discard it and use fresh oil. Stir in the sliced onion, (bell) peppers and half the chopped spring onions and fry for about 5 minutes, or until just cooked through but still a bit crispy.

Stir in the finely chopped garlic and ginger along with the thinly sliced chillies and fry for a further 30 seconds. Add the fried beef and stir it all up to combine. To finish, slowly pour in the prepared sauce. You need to decide how saucy you want this, so you might not need to add all of it. Stir well until the meat is coated completely with the sauce to your liking. Season with salt and pepper to taste and serve garnished with the remaining chopped spring onions and the coriander (cilantro).

BEEF BULGOGI
SERVES 4–6

Beef bulgogi is a recipe with a history of about 2,000 years, and when you try it, you'll understand why. This is so simple to make. My Korean language skills are pretty much non-existent, but I've been told that bulgogi translates as 'fire meat'. It isn't really spicy, so the name probably refers to the fact that it is traditionally cooked over a live fire on skewers. Nowadays, it's more likely that your beef bulgogi will be cooked in a hot wok. The meat and the accompanying sauce are delicious over rice or wrapped into crisp lettuce leaves to eat by hand.

PREP TIME: 20 MINS, PLUS
    FREEZING AND MARINATING
    TIME
COOKING TIME: 15 MINS

900g (2lb) sirloin or ribeye steaks, cut thinly across the grain
2 tbsp rapeseed (canola) oil (optional)
Lettuce leaves, to serve

FOR THE MARINADE
6 tbsp soy sauce (gluten-free brands are available)
2 tbsp light brown (or white) sugar
1 tbsp honey (or 2 tsp sugar)
4 tbsp rice wine or dry sherry
2 tbsp sesame oil
12 garlic cloves, finely chopped
1½ tsp ground black pepper
2 tsp toasted sesame seeds
1 tbsp chopped green onion
4 tbsp grated onion

FOR THE SAUCE
7 garlic cloves, finely chopped
3 spring onions (scallions), thinly sliced
2 tbsp toasted sesame seeds
2 tbsp sugar (more or less to taste)
2 tbsp honey (more or less to taste)
5 tbsp rice wine or dry sherry
2 tbsp apple cider vinegar
3 tbsp gochujang (Korean hot pepper paste; gluten-free brands are available))
2 tsp dried red chilli flakes
2½ tbsp sesame oil
4 tbsp soy sauce (gluten-free brands are available)

Put the beef steaks in the freezer for about 60 minutes – this will make them easier to slice. Slice the meat as thinly as you can with a sharp knife, against the grain. Then place the marinade ingredients in a mixing bowl and add the sliced beef. Marinate for at least 30 minutes or overnight – the longer, the better.

Before cooking, prepare the sauce. Place all of the sauce ingredients in a bowl and whisk to combine. Set aside.

When ready to cook, heat a lightly greased pan over a medium–high heat. If using a non-stick pan, oil is not required.

When smoking hot, add a few pieces of the beef. This will get you a nicely charred and caramelized appearance. Transfer the cooked beef to a serving plate and keep hot while you fry the remaining batches.

Serve immediately, wrapped in lettuce leaves, which you can dip into the prepared bulgogi sauce.

BUN BO NAM BO
(BEEF VERMICELLI SALAD)
SERVES 4

I absolutely love this warm salad of beef, rice vermicelli and loads of veggies and herbs. The delicious dressing brings it all together, and it is on the dressing that you really need to focus your attention. It offers a tasty combination of sweet, sour, savoury and spicy flavours. My version below is a good place to start, but be sure to taste it and adjust, adding more sugar for sweetness, lime juice for sourness, fish sauce if you want it to be more salty and more or fewer chillies depending on your heat preference. The rest of the recipe is simply a matter of following the instructions and enjoying what has to be one of my all-time favourite salads. I think I must have watched this dish being prepared for about an hour while in Hoian at a restaurant called Bun bo nam bo (it's common in Vietnam for restaurants to be named after their specialty dish). The chef tossed the beef in a fiery hot wok and the smokiness really added to the flavour.

PREP TIME: 20 MINS, PLUS
    OPTIONAL MARINATING TIME
COOKING TIME: 10 MINS

450g (1lb) lean beef such as fillet, thinly sliced against the grain
200g (7oz) rice vermicelli

FOR THE MARINADE

2 tbsp light soy sauce (gluten-free brands are available)
1 tsp sugar
1 tbsp sesame oil
4 garlic cloves, smashed and finely chopped
½ onion, thinly sliced and cut into 2.5cm (1in) pieces
10cm (4in) piece of lemongrass, white part only, finely chopped

FOR THE DRESSING

3 tbsp fish sauce (gluten-free brands are available)
3 tbsp sugar
3 tbsp lime juice
2 red finger chillies, cut into thin rings (more or less to taste)
4 garlic cloves, finely chopped

TO FINISH

Crispy fried shallots or onions, shop-bought or homemade (see page 262)
1–2 carrots, skinned and julienned
½ English cucumber, sliced lengthwise in half, seeds removed and then sliced into long thin strips
Cos (romaine) lettuce, mint leaves and coriander (cilantro) leaves, as needed
110g (4oz) roasted peanuts, lightly crushed

Start by making the marinade. Mix all the ingredients for the marinade together and pour over the beef. This can be done a day or two in advance of serving if more convenient, and the longer marinating time will also deepen the flavour. However, if you're short on time it's fine to do it just before cooking.

Next, make the dressing. As with any recipe you want this to be prepared exactly to your personal taste, so whisk all the dressing ingredients together, taste it and then adjust as instructed in the intro to this recipe. Set aside.

Boil some water and pour it over the dried rice vermicelli in a bowl to soak for about 10 minutes, or until you are happy with the doneness. Strain and set aside.

When you're ready to fry the meat, heat a wok over a high heat. When smoking hot,* add the beef mixture and stir continuously until the meat is cooked through.

To finish, divide the noodles, beef, fried onions and salad ingredients between four plates. Serve the dressing in a small jug, so that each person can add as much or as little as they like. Then stir it all together and eat!

NOTE

*If you aren't sure about cooking over such a high heat, that's fine. Cook the meat over a medium–high heat or at a temperature that you are comfortable with.

BEEF KHAO SOI
SERVES 4

This beef khao soi is quite a lot different to the chicken version I featured in *The Curry Guy Thai*, but just as popular. In that recipe, a yellow curry paste was used. In this recipe you will be making a red curry paste. It's a bit spicier, but it shouldn't blow your head off. Although fried crispy noodles are often served on top of the curry, that part is optional so only do it if you feel like it. I always feel like it.

PREP TIME: 15 MINS
COOKING TIME: 40 MINS

225g (8oz) flat egg noodles

FOR THE PASTE
8 dried chillies, soaked in water for 20 minutes
3 fresh red finger chillies
4 shallots
8 garlic cloves
1 thumb-sized piece of galangal, finely chopped
2 lemongrass stalks, white parts only, thinly sliced
1 tsp lime zest
1 tsp ground turmeric
2 tsp ground coriander
1 tsp shrimp paste
1 tbsp Madras curry powder (see page 259) or good-quality shop-bought

FOR THE CURRY
2 tbsp rapeseed (canola) or coconut oil
1kg (2lb 2oz) beef shank, cut into 2.5cm (1in) pieces
3 cups homemade unsalted beef stock (see page 251) or water
400ml (1¾ cups) thick coconut milk
2 tbsp fish sauce (gluten-free brands are available)
2 tbsp soy sauce (gluten-free brands are available)
2 tsp sugar or grated palm sugar

TO GARNISH
Finely chopped shallots
Red chilli flakes or pickled chillies
Chopped coriander (cilantro)
Lime wedges

Place the egg noodles in a large bowl and pour boiling water over them. They should be soft in about 10 minutes. When soft, strain and rinse with water. Set aside.

While the noodles are soaking, prepare the spice paste by blending all the ingredients with just enough water to make a thick paste. Set aside.

For the curry, heat the oil in the wok over a medium–high heat and brown the meat for about 5 minutes. Once the beef is looking cooked on the exterior, add the prepared paste and stir well to combine. Cover with the water or beef stock and simmer for about 20 minutes or longer. The meat needs to be tender, and the longer simmering will also flavour the stock.

When the meat is nice and tender, stir in the coconut milk until there are no lumps. Then add the fish sauce, soy sauce and sugar. Try the broth and adjust the flavours to taste.

Divide the soaked noodles between four bowls and cover with the meat and broth. Garnish with the crispy noodle nests (optional – see below), chopped shallots, chilli flakes or pickled chillies, coriander (cilantro) and lime wedges.

NOTE
To make the optional crispy noodle nests, soak egg noodles in boiling water for about 10 minutes. Heat enough oil for shallow-frying in a wok. The oil is hot enough for frying when bubbles form instantly around a wooden chopstick or spatula when lowered into the oil. When ready to fry, take a small handful of noodles and pat them dry. Slowly lower your noodle nest into the oil and fry, turning from time to time until crispy. This should take about 3 minutes per nest. Use a slotted spoon to transfer to a paper towel to soak up any excess oil, and use to garnish your dish.

★ **MAKE IT EASIER** ★
If you don't have time to make the red curry paste in this recipe, you could substitute 2–3 tablespoons of shop-bought paste, or add it to taste.

BALINESE BEEF SKEWERS WITH DIPPING SAUCE
SERVES 2–4

In Bali, beef skewers are hugely popular, especially those cooked with Wagyu ribeye beef. Wagyu beef isn't cheap, though, so I often make these at home with nicely marbled and aged ribeye. Wagyu is saved for special occasions so if you can get it, do! The fat in the well-marbled meat renders over the heat and makes the beef skewers deliciously tender and flavourful. If time permits, I recommend rubbing the salt and pepper into the meat a day ahead of cooking, but it isn't essential. The beef is served with a delicious and easy sambal matah and kecap manis sauce that's not to be missed. If you're really hungry, just cook more beef. There will be plenty of sauce to dip it in.

PREP TIME: 10 MINS, PLUS
SOAKING AND OPTIONAL
MARINATING TIME
COOKING TIME: 10 MINS

700g (1lb 9oz) or about 2 wagyu ribeye steaks (or well-aged beef ribeye steaks)
Salt and pepper, to taste
10–12 wooden skewers
2 tbsp rapeseed (canola) or melted coconut oil
85ml (⅓ cup) kecap manis (see page 258), or shop-bought is fine, to serve
1 lime, quartered, to serve

FOR THE SAMBAL
4 banana shallots, thinly sliced
4 red finger chillies, thinly sliced at an angle
½ lemongrass stalk, peeled, white part only, finely chopped
1 medium tomato, diced
½ tsp salt or to taste
½ tsp sugar
1 tbsp lime juice
Zest of 1 lime

Rub the steaks all over with the salt and pepper. If working ahead, you can do this a day before cooking and store uncovered in the fridge.

When ready to cook, place your wooden skewers in water to soak for about 30 minutes. Then cut the steaks into bite-sized pieces and mix with the oil to coat. Set aside.

While the skewers are soaking, prepare the sambal. Mix the shallots, chillies, lemongrass and tomato in a bowl and mix well. Season with a little salt and sugar to taste. Remember that the meat and kecap manis will be salty, so don't add too much. Mix in the lime juice and zest and set aside. Skewer the meat onto the wooden skewers.

Now heat a griddle pan or large frying pan (skillet) over a high heat. You want that pan to be smoking hot! Place the skewered meat in the pan and fry until nicely charred on the exterior. Turn often to ensure that the meat cooks evenly. I like mine medium-rare, which only takes a few minutes, but I've seen these nuked over hot coals so if you like your meat well done, you need to cook for a few more minutes before serving.

While the meat is cooking, pour the kecap manis onto a small, shallow plate. Spoon the prepared sambal over half the plate and garnish with a couple of quartered limes, if you like.

To serve, I usually just place the whole pan on the table next to the sauce with a few spoons, so people can dip in, spooning the sambal over each bite of kecap manis-dipped meat as they see fit.

BUN CHA
SERVES 4

Bun cha is a hugely popular minced (ground) pork patty dish from Hanoi. It's also really easy to make, though I have taken the liberty of simplifying the recipe even more in this case. Traditionally, these pork patties are prepared with homemade Vietnamese caramel. I learned to make it while there, but it isn't an easy task and takes some time to get right. You could use shop-bought caramel or maple syrup, as I do in the recipe below.

PREP TIME: 15 MINS, PLUS OPTIONAL MARINATING TIME
COOKING TIME: 15 MINS

700g (1lb 9oz) minced (ground) pork shoulder
200g (7oz) dried rice vermicelli noodles

FOR THE MARINADE

1 generous tbsp maple syrup or Vietnamese caramel
2 tbsp finely chopped garlic
3 lemongrass stalks, white part only, finely chopped
2 banana shallots, finely chopped
1½ tbsp fish sauce (gluten-free brands are available)
2 tbsp oyster sauce
½ tsp black pepper

FOR THE SAUCE

70ml (¼ cup) lime juice
1 tbsp sugar (more or less to taste)
1 cup water
3 tbsp fish sauce (gluten-free brands are available)
1½ tbsp finely chopped garlic
½ carrot, grated
½ green papaya, grated

TO SERVE

Herbs such as coriander (cilantro) and mint
Green or red chillies, thinly sliced (optional)
Soft lettuce

Place all of the marinade ingredients in a bowl with the minced (ground) pork and mix well with your hands. Set aside to marinate while you prepare the rest of the dish (or overnight).

In another bowl, whisk all of the sauce ingredients together and set aside.

When ready to cook, place the rice vermicelli in a bowl and cover with boiling water. They should become soft in about 10 minutes, but please refer to the instructions on the side of the packet.

Heat a non-stick frying pan (skillet) over a medium–high heat and divide the pork into large or small patties – the choice is yours, as both are served in Vietnam. Fry the patties until cooked through. Divide the rice noodles between four bowls and serve topped with the pork patties, some of the dipping sauce, herbs, chillies (if using) and lettuce. Serve at the table with more dipping sauce and dig in.

GARLICKY AND SPICY SPARE RIBS
SERVES 4

If you love Chinese-style spare ribs as much as I do, you are going to want to make this simple recipe. It does take a good hour and a half to prepare and cook, but it's worth the wait. I recommend using a non-stick pan for this, so that the ribs and sauce don't stick to the pan. Cleaning up will also be much easier.

PREP TIME: 10 MINS
COOKING TIME: 80 MINS

4 tbsp rapeseed (canola) or peanut oil
10 garlic cloves, finely chopped
1kg (2lb 2oz) pork spare ribs, 7.5cm
    (3in) in length
500ml (2 cups) water
3 tbsp light soy sauce (gluten-free
    brands are available)
5 tbsp Chinese rice wine or dry sherry
2 tbsp oyster sauce
2.5cm (1in) piece of ginger, cut into
    thin discs
1 tsp sugar
2 tbsp red chilli powder of your choice

Heat the oil over a medium heat in a saucepan that is large enough to contain the pork ribs. Add the chopped garlic and fry until light golden brown in colour. Be careful not to burn it. Take off the heat, transfer the garlic to a plate with a slotted spoon and retain the oil, setting aside for later.

Now, using the same pan, add the pork ribs and cover with water. Bring to a boil and simmer for about 8 minutes. Strain and wash off any scum that has accumulated on the spare ribs. Place the washed ribs back in the pan and cover with 500ml (2 cups) of water, plus the soy sauce, rice wine, oyster sauce, ginger and sugar. Cover the pan, bring to a simmer and cook over a medium heat for 1 hour.

After one hour, take the lid off and turn the heat up to high. Continue simmering until almost all the liquid has evaporated and you are left with a thick, sticky layer of sauce on the ribs. Pour in the retained garlic oil and continue cooking for about 5 minutes, or until the ribs and sauce are sizzling and delicious looking.

Sprinkle the ribs with chilli powder to taste and cover with the browned garlic. Serve immediately with your sides of choice.

KOREAN PORK CHOPS

SERVES 4

This is my pork chop recipe for special occasions. Although they are marinated in a Korean-style marinade, they can be served with any side dishes you like. Garlicky mashed potatoes or simple white buttered rice come to mind. You could also just serve them with a simple green salad. Cooking the thick pork chops on the bone makes them extra juicy when done.

PREP TIME: 15 MINS, PLUS
  OPTIONAL MARINATING TIME
COOKING TIME: 15 MINS

2 x 2.5cm- (1in-) thick pork chops on
  the bone
1 tbsp rapeseed (canola) oil

FOR THE MARINADE
2 tbsp gochujang (Korean hot pepper
  paste; gluten-free brands are
  available)
1 tbsp soy sauce (gluten-free brands
  are available)
1 tbsp light brown sugar
3 garlic cloves, finely chopped
1.25cm (½in) piece of ginger, finely
  chopped
1 tbsp rice wine vinegar
1 tsp sesame oil
¼ tsp black pepper
Sesame seeds, to garnish

Mix the marinade ingredients together in a bowl and add the pork chops. Ensure they are thoroughly covered with the marinade and allow to marinate for about 30 minutes or overnight – the longer, the better. If you're short of time, you could just get cooking right away, as the flavour of the marinade will still taste amazing on the pork chops.

Preheat the oven to 200°C (400°F/Gas 6). Heat a cast iron or stainless-steel pan over a medium–high heat. Add the oil to the pan and either brush it all over the surface or tilt the pan until the whole surface is lightly coated with oil. When sizzling hot, rub as much marinade off the pork chops as you can and carefully add them to the pan. Cook on one side for about 4 minutes without turning, then flip them over and baste generously with the leftover marinade. Place in the oven to roast for 8–10 minutes, or until the internal temperature has reached 63°C (145°F).

Remove from the oven and allow to rest for a few minutes before serving.

VIETNAMESE PORK STIR FRY
SERVES 4–6

This is a quick stir fry that we tried with wild boar in Vietnam. When I can get it, I use that at home, too, but pork belly is a good substitute so I have used that for this recipe. The stir-fried pork is often served with rice paper that is dampened with wet lettuce and then rolled up into a delicious spring roll, with lots of herbs and a dipping sauce such as soy sauce, sriracha or sambal oelek. These sauces aren't necessarily Vietnamese in origin but are popular additions. You could just serve this over rice, though, and you won't be disappointed.

PREP TIME: 15 MINS
COOKING TIME: 15 MINS

2 tbsp rapeseed (canola) oil
500g (1lb 2oz) pork belly strip, sliced into small 1.75cm (½in) pieces
5 garlic cloves, finely chopped
2.5cm (1in) piece of ginger, finely chopped
1 lemongrass stalk, white part only, thick exterior removed and thinly sliced
3 green finger chillies, thinly sliced
4 spring onions (scallions), thinly sliced
1 small onion, cut into petals
½ tsp sugar (more or less to taste)
1 large handful of bean sprouts
1 red spur chilli, thinly sliced
1 tbsp fish sauce (gluten-free brands are available)
1 tbsp light soy sauce (gluten-free brands are available)
4 tbsp peanuts, lightly crushed
Freshly ground black pepper, to taste

Heat the oil over a medium–high heat in a large wok. When visibly hot, add the pork belly pieces and fry for about 5 minutes, stirring regularly until the meat is beginning to char on the exterior. Stir in the garlic, ginger and lemongrass and let them come to a sizzle. Then stir in the finger chillies, half of the spring onions (scallions) and the onion petals. Fry to soften for about 3 minutes and then add the sugar, bean sprouts, spur chilli, fish sauce and soy sauce.

Give everything a good stir to combine and add the peanuts and black pepper to taste. That's it! Quick and easy and so good!

VIETNAMESE PORK-STUFFED TOFU IN TOMATO SAUCE
SERVES 4–6

Caroline and I tried pork-stuffed tofu for the first time at a little restaurant in Tam Coc, Vietnam, called 'Minh Toàn Restaurant – Father Cooking' and loved it. It was surprisingly good as I'm not usually a huge fan of tofu, but this and many other dishes they served made us want to visit the restaurant three more times during our stay in the area. The first time we had it, the stuffed tofu was served without a sauce, other than a few dipping sauces such as sriracha and a spicy soy sauce. Done that way, it makes a good canapé. We later ordered the pork-stuffed tofu in a tomato sauce, which we liked so much it ended up in this book.

PREP TIME: 25 MINS
COOKING TIME: 15 MINS

800g (1lb 12oz) firm tofu
Rapeseed (canola) oil, for shallow-frying

FOR THE PORK STUFFING
225g (8oz) minced (ground) pork
4 spring onions (scallions), finely chopped
3 green finger chillies, finely chopped (optional)
1 tsp light brown sugar
Salt and pepper, to taste
1 tsp sesame oil

FOR THE SAUCE
2 shallots, finely chopped
3 garlic cloves, finely chopped
400g (14oz) tinned (canned) chopped tomatoes
1 tbsp oyster sauce
2 tsp fish sauce (gluten-free brands are available)
Salt and ground black pepper, to taste
2 red spur chillies, thinly sliced

Take the tofu out of the packaging and drain. Pat it dry and cut into large, bite-sized rectangles. Carefully cut the centre of the tofu out of each piece. This is where you will stuff the pork. You can discard the tofu you dig out, or use it in a soup in another recipe.

Place the minced (ground) pork in a bowl and add the chopped spring onions (scallions), chillies (if using), light brown sugar and salt and pepper to taste. Mix well to combine and then stuff each tofu rectangle generously with this pork stuffing.

Cover the base of a large frying pan (skillet) with a generous amount of rapeseed (canola) oil and place over a medium–high heat. The oil is hot enough when bubbles form immediately when you place one of the stuffed tofu cubes in it. If they don't, heat it up for longer.

Place the tofu meat-side down in the hot oil. As it fries, you will see the tofu cooking up the sides. When nicely browned on the bottom, carefully turn the tofu cubes over and fry the other side. Then move them around a bit so that the tofu is nicely browned all over. You might need to do this in batches, and you can plan on about 10 minutes per batch. Transfer the cooked tofu to a plate and set aside.

To make the tomato sauce, you only need about 2 tablespoons of oil in the pan. If you have more in your pan, discard the excess. Then toss in the finely chopped shallots and garlic and fry for about a minute to soften a little. Then add the chopped tomatoes and bring to a simmer over a medium–high heat. Cook the sauce down for about 5 minutes, pressing down on the chopped tomatoes as you do. You can add a drop of water if your pan is looking too dry. To finish the sauce, stir in the oyster sauce and fish sauce. Try a spoonful and adjust the seasoning to taste.

Once you are happy with the flavour of the sauce, place the fried, stuffed tofu pieces in it meat-side up. Cover the pan and let it simmer for a couple of minutes until the tofu and pork is hot. Serve garnished with the thinly sliced red chillies.

BÁNH XÈO
(CRISPY VIETNAMESE RICE FLOUR PANCAKES)
SERVES 6

On our second evening in Ho Chi Minh City in Vietnam, Caroline and I decided to take a food tour and found 'Back of the Bike Tours' online. They picked us up from our hotel, we got on the back of their mopeds and off we went exploring. We had so many amazing and uniquely Vietnamese meals that night. Cooking and trying bánh xèos was one of the highlights of the evening. We got to make them at a popular street-food stall, and this is how they were done. The finished pancakes are often broken into pieces and served wrapped in rice paper with lettuce leaves and herbs and dipped in nuoc cham dipping sauce (see page 255), sriracha or Vietnamese sate, but they are also regularly served folded over. If serving a group, use a large pan and keep them coming. You could place the finished bánh xèos in a low oven to keep warm, but I usually just fry them up and serve hot out of the pan.

PREP TIME: 15 MINS
COOKING TIME: 15 MINS

FOR THE PANCAKES
300g (2 cups) rice flour
1 tbsp ground turmeric
1 tsp salt
400ml (1¾ cups) water
170ml (¾ cup) coconut milk
4 spring onions (scallions), thinly
    sliced

FOR FRYING
450g (1lb) streaky bacon, cut into 5cm
    (2in) pieces
450g (1lb) prawns (shrimp), peeled
    and deveined
300g (10½oz) bean sprouts
Approx. 300ml (1¼ cups) rapeseed
    (canola) oil

TO SERVE
Nuoc cham and/or Vietnamese
    sate (see page 255 and/or 253), or
    another hot sauce for dipping
Cos (romaine) lettuce
Mint leaves
Coriander (cilantro) leaves
Basil leaves
Rice paper (optional)

Start by making the batter for the pancakes. In a large mixing bowl, whisk all of the ingredients together until you have a creamy batter.

Divide the bacon, prawns (shrimp) and bean sprouts so that you have eight equal portions. Heat up your frying pan (skillet) over a medium–high heat (for pancakes, I recommend using a non-stick pan as it is a lot easier). When hot, add about 2 tablespoons of oil. If you're using a cast-iron pan, which is what is used most often in Vietnam, you will need to be a bit more liberal with how much oil you add. Another 1–2 tablespoons should do. Then add a portion of the bacon and prawns, spreading them out equally in the pan and frying until cooked through, turning once.

Now add about a ladle or a bit more of the batter – enough to fill your pan with a thin layer. Move the pan around while you do this so that the result looks like a nice, thin pancake, or crêpe. Reduce the heat to medium and allow to cook for a further couple of minutes, or until the bottom begins to brown. Top the pancake with some of the bean sprouts and cover the pan to continue cooking for another minute or so. The pancake should lift off the pan easily when it is cooked through, so don't rush this. When your first pancake is cooked through and crispy, remove from the pan and repeat with the remaining batter.

Serve the pancakes as and when they are ready with a dipping sauce, such as nuoc cham, and/or Vietnamese sate, lettuce and herbs. The bánh xèo can be served folded in half or you could also serve them in rice paper, which is delicious.

To do this, take a piece of freshly washed lettuce and rub it on to a piece of rice paper. The rice paper might still be a bit hard but as the moisture from the lettuce soaks in, it will soften. Then fill the rice paper with a few pieces of the bánh xèo and lettuce and herbs. Roll it all up like a spring roll and start dipping.

SPICY DAN DAN NOODLES

SERVES 4

Now hugely popular at Chinese restaurants, dan dan noodles are originally from northern China and are enjoyed at street-food stalls all over South East Asia. Just a quick note here: the required sesame paste is not tahini, which is made from raw sesame seeds and is popular in Mediterranean cooking. Asian recipes often call for sesame paste, which is made with toasted sesame seeds. The flavour difference is similar to the difference between white bread and toast. You can substitute peanut butter, or use tahini with a little toasted sesame oil stirred in for more depth of flavour if you must. Or just purchase some Asian sesame paste, as you are probably going to want to make dan dan noodles quite often once you try this recipe.

PREP TIME: 10 MINS, PLUS
  OPTIONAL MARINATING TIME
COOKING TIME: 15 MINS

400g (14oz) dried Chinese ramen
  noodles, or similar
1 tbsp Szechuan peppercorns
1 tbsp toasted sesame oil
250g (9oz) minced (ground) pork

FOR THE MARINADE
50g (2oz) preserved salted turnip
  (optional)
1 tbsp light soy sauce (gluten-free
  brands are available)
1 tbsp dark soy sauce or 1 extra tbsp
  light soy sauce (gluten-free brands
  are available)
2 tbsp Shaoxing rice wine or dry
  sherry

FOR THE SAUCE
2 tbsp rapeseed (canola) or peanut oil
3 garlic cloves, finely chopped
2.5cm (1in) piece of ginger, finely
  chopped
4 spring onions (scallions), finely
  chopped
1 red finger chilli, finely chopped
  (more or less to taste)
2 tbsp smooth Asian sesame paste
2 tbsp light soy sauce (gluten-free
  brands are available)
175ml (¾ cup) chicken stock
1 tbsp Chinese chilli oil, shop-bought
  or homemade (see page 246)

Put the noodles in a bowl, cover with boiling water and soak until soft. This usually only takes about 5–10 minutes. You might need to adjust this instruction depending on the noodles you are using.

Meanwhile, heat your wok over a medium heat and add the Szechuan peppercorns. Dry-fry, stirring continuously for about 30 seconds, or until warm to the touch and fragrant. Transfer the peppercorns to a pestle and mortar and lightly crush. Set aside.

Place the pork in a mixing bowl and add all of the marinade ingredients. Mix well and allow to marinate until needed. This can be done a day ahead of cooking, but it's not necessary.

When ready to cook, heat your wok over a high heat and stir in 1 tablespoon of oil. Add the marinated meat and cook, stirring continuously, for about 5 minutes, or until the pork is cooked through and crispy. Transfer the cooked pork to a plate and set aside.

Add another tablespoon of oil to the wok and stir in the garlic, ginger, spring onions (scallions) and chilli and fry over a medium–high heat for about a minute. Stir in the sesame paste, soy sauce and stock and simmer for a couple of minutes. Return the cooked crispy pork to the wok and stir it into the sauce to heat through.

To serve, strain the noodles and stir in the sesame oil. Divide the noodles between four bowls, top with the pork, sprinkle with the toasted Szechuan peppercorns and drizzle with chilli oil. Dig in!

TEX MEX LAMB CHOPS WITH CHIMICHURRI

SERVES 4–6

I could seriously eat lamb chops with chimichurri every day. My wife won't let me do that though, so this is a recipe I only make on special occasions. Usually I cook the chops on my barbecue, but you can get really good results in your kitchen, too, by using a little smoked paprika. The chimichurri is used both to top the lamb chops and to marinate them.

PREP TIME: 10 MINS, PLUS
   OPTIONAL MARINATING TIME
COOKING TIME: 10 MINS

8 lamb chops, on the bone, preferably
   of about the same thickness

FOR THE SPICE RUB
1 tsp salt
½ tsp ground black pepper
1 tsp smoked paprika
1 tsp garlic powder

FOR THE CHIMICHURRI
2 big bunches of coriander (cilantro)
1 big bunch of parsley
250ml (1 cup) olive oil
4 green finger chillies
½ tsp ground black pepper
70ml (¼ cup) lime juice
Salt, to taste

Mix all of the spice rub ingredients together in a bowl and then sprinkle evenly all over the lamb chops. For best results, this should be done a day ahead or at least a couple of hours before cooking, but don't let that stop you. You can also do this right before cooking.

Place all of the chimichurri ingredients in a blender and blend until creamy smooth. If you prefer a chunkier chimichurri, that's fine too – just don't blend for as long. Take about one quarter of the chimichurri and rub it all over the spice-rubbed lamb chops and allow to marinate for 20–30 minutes.

When ready to cook, place a heavy-based frying pan (skillet) that is large enough to contain all the chops over a medium–high heat. When smoking hot, add the lamb chops to the pan and cook for 3–4 minutes, or until you are getting a good char on the meat. Turn over and cook the other side for another 2–4 minutes, or until cooked to your liking. The internal temperature for medium-rare is 53°C (127°F), or for medium 60°C (140°F). Transfer to a serving platter and top with the rest of the chimichurri.

SPANISH

GAMBAS PIL PIL
SERVES 4

Spanish food is normally quite mild. Gambas pil pil can be mild or spicy, depending on your preference. I travelled for three weeks around Spain looking for dishes I might be able to include in this book, and gambas pil pil ticked all the boxes. I didn't want to leave the country responsible for introducing chillies to Europe out, after all. Be sure to use light olive oil for this, as extra virgin oil has a lower smoking point and can taste bitter if cooked at too high a heat. Perhaps more than other recipes, you should really use this simple recipe as a guide. Add the garlic, chillies, spicy or sweet paprika, parsley, salt and pepper to taste. I like to serve this with a loaf of hot sourdough, perfect for dipping and soaking up the amazing flavours.

PREP TIME: 5 MINS
COOKING TIME: 10 MINS

8 tbsp light olive oil
6 garlic cloves, finely chopped
1–2 red finger chillies, cut into thin rings
12 (600g/1lb 5oz) prawns (shrimp), peeled
1 tsp smoked sweet or hot paprika
2 tbsp parsley, finely chopped
Salt and black pepper, to taste

Pour the oil into a frying pan (skillet) over a medium–high heat and add the chopped garlic. You can add the garlic when the oil is still cool, as it will infuse its flavour into the oil as it heats up. When bubbles begin to form around the garlic, stir in the chillies and prawns (shrimp) and fry until the prawns are pink on the exterior and just cooked through. This should only take a couple of minutes. Be sure to stir regularly so that you don't burn the garlic.

When the prawns are cooked, stir in the smoked paprika and parsley and season with salt and pepper to taste.

SRI LANKAN

DEVILLED PRAWNS
SERVES 4

Hikkaduwa is a town on the south-west coast of Sri Lanka and as it is right on the sea, there is some amazing seafood to be found there. At one place Caroline and I visited, they cooked up two massive prawns (shrimp) for us and served them in a delicious 'devilled' sauce. Those fresh prawns were the size of lobsters! We loved the dish so much, we simply had to go back and watch the curry being made in their open kitchen so that I could recreate it at home. Here I have used less expensive, smaller prawns but you could change this to the main ingredient of your choice. Cuttlefish, squid, chicken and tofu are all popular options in a devilled sauce.

PREP TIME: 10 MINS
COOKING TIME: 10 MINS

70ml (¼ cup) coconut oil
600g (1lb 5oz) prawns (shrimp), peeled but with tails left intact
2 banana chillies, cut into large slices
1 medium red onion, cut into 6 wedges
10cm (4in) piece of leek, white part only, cut into cubes
3 garlic cloves, thinly sliced
1 tomato, quartered
1 tbsp Chinese chilli paste
1 generous tsp red chilli flakes
2 tbsp ketchup
2 tsp soy sauce (gluten-free brands are available)
Salt, to taste

Heat the oil in a wok until bubbling hot and then stir in the prawns (shrimp). Fry for a couple of minutes, or until almost cooked through. Remove the prawns with a slotted spoon and set aside. Discard all but 2 tablespoons of the oil. Add the banana chillies, red onion, leek and garlic to the remaining oil and sauté for about 2 minutes, or until fragrant but still not completely cooked through. Add the tomato wedges, chilli paste, red chilli flakes, ketchup and soy sauce and heat it all through.

To finish, return the prawns to the wok and toss it all together. Adjust the spicing and add salt to taste.

BUTTER EGG FLOSS PRAWNS

SERVES 4

This is one of those recipes that I never knew existed until travelling to Kuala Lumpur. Since then I have seen it on many Western menus, too. It looks impressive and tastes even better, so you might want to give these egg floss prawns a go. The flaky egg yolk floss , which resembles candy floss, cooked in butter and oil makes this a dish I reserve for the most special of occasions. Who would have thought you could make floss out of eggs? They don't even taste like eggs! This is a buttery and indulgent meal you've simply got to try. It's delicious served with white rice (see page 248), egg fried rice (page 233) or simply on its own.

PREP TIME: 15 MINS
COOKING TIME: 15 MINS

12 jumbo prawns (shrimp), deveined
1½ tsp salt
4 tbsp cornflour (cornstarch)
625ml (2½ cups) rapeseed (canola) oil
7 egg yolks, lightly beaten
150g (5½oz) unsalted butter
5 red finger chillies, thinly sliced
5 garlic cloves, finely chopped
20–30 fresh or frozen curry leaves
½ tsp Chinese chicken stock granules
   (contains MSG, optional)

Place the prawns (shrimp) in a bowl and season with the salt. Pour in the cornflour (cornstarch) and mix to thoroughly coat the prawns. Set aside.

Now heat 500ml (2 cups) of rapeseed (canola) oil in a large wok over a high heat. The oil is ready for cooking when lots of little bubbles form immediately when a wooden chopstick or spatula is dipped in. Shake off any excess cornflour from the prawns and fry half of them in the oil until they just turn pink. This will only take about a minute. Transfer to a wire rack and repeat with the remaining prawns. With all of the prawns par-cooked, ensure the oil is still hot enough by testing it with a wooden chopstick or spatula and then fry the prawns again for another minute or until cooked through. Transfer them all back to the rack and set aside.

Pour your beaten egg yolks through a fine sieve into a jug, preferably one with a small spout, and set aside. Discard the dirty cooking oil from your wok and wipe it clean. Then add the remaining oil and the butter. Melt the butter into the oil over a low–medium heat. Once the butter has melted, start stirring in one direction. When the butter and oil begin to bubble slightly and you have a steady current going in one direction, begin pouring in the egg yolks in a thin stream from a height of about 30cm (1ft) while continuing to stir in one direction. Once you have added all the egg yolk, continue stirring and when the butter and oil turn foamy, add the sliced red chillies, chopped garlic and curry leaves. Fry, while continuing to stir, for about a minute and then add the prawns. Keep stirring!

Add the Chinese chicken stock granules, if using, and keep up the stirring for another 30 seconds. Pour it all through a fine sieve, allowing the excess oil to drip through the sieve for a minute or so. You can discard the oil/butter mixture.

To serve, pick the prawns out and place them on a serving dish. Some of the egg floss will stick to the prawns. Give the remaining ingredients in your sieve another good shake or two. The eggs will look more like floss as they dry and become less saturated with the butter and oil. Pile the prawns high with all the delicious toppings.

THAI DRUNKEN NOODLES WITH JUMBO PRAWNS
SERVES 4

I have used prawns (shrimp) here, but this quick and easy Thai noodle dish can be made with the protein of your choice. Chicken, tofu and pork are all popular options. There are a few explanations about how this dish got its name, but no one will ever know the truth. The version I like best is that a man returned home a bit tipsy from a bar one evening and was feeling peckish, so he grabbed what he had in and whipped up this classic. Drunken noodles are just that... something you can cook up on a whim, with ingredients you might already have on hand or can easily get.

PREP TIME: 15 MINS
COOKING TIME: 10 MINS

FOR THE SAUCE
4 tbsp oyster sauce
2 tbsp light soy sauce (gluten-free brands are available)
1½ tbsp dark soy sauce (gluten-free brands are available)
1 tbsp sugar

FOR THE NOODLES
200g (7oz) wide Thai dried rice noodles
3 tbsp rapeseed (canola) oil
1 banana shallot, thinly sliced
12 garlic cloves, roughly chopped
2–3 green finger chillies, sliced thinly
225g (8oz) medium-sized prawns (shrimp), peeled and deveined
5 spring onions (scallions) cut into 5cm (2in) pieces
1 large handful of Thai sweet basil

Whisk all of the sauce ingredients together in a bowl and set aside.

Fill a large bowl with bath-hot water and submerge the dried rice noodles in it. The noodles only need to soak for about 5–7 minutes, so do this right before you start cooking.

Heat a wok over a high heat and add the oil. When it begins to shimmer, add the sliced shallot and fry for about 2 minutes. Stir in the chopped garlic and chillies and fry for a further minute, stirring regularly. Now add the prawns (shrimp) and fry for about 2 minutes, or until they turn pink.

Pour in the prepared sauce, the spring onions (scallions) and noodles. Don't worry about drying them off, just pick them out of the water. Any water that drips off them will help cook them.

Submerge the noodles in the sauce and stir lightly and continuously. They will cook quickly, but test them before serving. They really need to be covered in the sauce to cook until soft, but there isn't a lot of sauce so keep stirring until cooked.

Stir in some of the basil then serve immediately, garnishing with the remaining basil.

EGG FRIED RICE WITH PRAWNS

SERVES 4

As simple as it may be, this egg fried rice recipe is one of my favourite side dishes when I cook up a Chinese feast. You don't need to be cooking a feast, though, to enjoy this one – it's a quick and easy meal any day of the week. As with all fried rice recipes, it is important to cook the rice and chill it in the fridge or use leftover rice. The rice needs to be cold when it hits the pan.

PREP TIME: 10 MINS
COOKING TIME: 10 MINS

2 tbsp rapeseed (canola) oil
1 onion, finely chopped
3 garlic cloves, finely chopped
225g (8oz) small prawns (shrimp), peeled and cleaned
800g (4 cups) cooked jasmine or long grain rice
2 tbsp sesame oil
2 eggs, beaten
2 tbsp soy sauce (or more to taste; gluten-free brands are available)
1 tbsp lemon juice
½ tsp ground white pepper
4 spring onions (scallions), thinly sliced, to garnish

Add the oil to a hot wok and stir in the chopped onion. Fry to soften for about 3 minutes and then stir in the chopped garlic and fry for a further 30 seconds. Stir in the prawns (shrimp) and fry until they begin to turn pink and are almost cooked through.

Stir in the cooked rice and the sesame oil, and move it all around in your wok to fry until hot and well coated with the oil. Push the rice to one side and add the beaten eggs and soy sauce. Stir the eggs to scramble and then push them into the rice mixture.

Be sure to move the rice around with your spoon or spatula. You are not trying to stir the rice, but instead push it around in the wok. Taste it and add more soy sauce if you prefer a more savoury flavour.

Squeeze in the lemon juice – this, too, should be done to taste. Serve immediately, garnished with the chopped spring onions (scallions).

SRI LANKAN HOT BUTTER CALAMARI
SERVES 4–6

Calamari simply doesn't get any better than this! I learned this recipe at a restaurant called Refresh in Hikkaduwa, on the south-west coast of Sri Lanka. Refresh specializes in fresh seafood, and I got to watch the chefs there prepare many different dishes one afternoon. Having tried their hot butter calamari the day before, I simply had to know how it was done. This recipe, however, is a mix of my own way of preparing calamari for frying and their amazing spicy butter and garlic sauce. If you're in a rush, you can skip soaking the calamari in milk, which is a natural tenderizer, but you will be amazed at how tender your calamari is if you do.

PREP TIME: 15 MINS, PLUS
    OPTIONAL SOAKING TIME
COOKING TIME: 15 MINS

900g (2lb) baby squid tubes, cleaned and cut into small bite-sized rings
500ml (2 cups) full-fat milk
2 eggs
120g (1 cup) cornflour (cornstarch)
150g (1 cup) rice flour or 120g (1 cup) more cornflour (cornstarch)
1 tsp salt
1 tsp black pepper
1 tbsp red chilli powder
Rapeseed (canola) oil, for deep-frying

TO FINISH

5 generous tbsp butter
6 garlic cloves, finely chopped
2 tbsp Chinese chilli paste
2 red spur chillies, thinly sliced at an angle
3 dried finger chillies, roughly cut and soaked in water for 30 minutes
6 spring onions (scallions), cut in half and sliced into thin strips lengthwise
1 green (bell) pepper, thinly sliced into strips to match the spring onions (scallions)
Salt and pepper, to taste
Juice of 1 lime

Place the squid in a bowl and cover with the milk. Milk is a natural tenderizer and this gives the squid a perfect texture when fried, so be sure the squid is completely covered. Cover the bowl with cling film (plastic wrap) and place in the fridge overnight to marinate. The milk will turn pink, which is natural and fine. When ready to cook, remove the squid and discard the milk. Whisk the eggs in a bowl and place the squid in it.

Now mix the two flours on a plate with the salt, pepper and chilli powder. Dust the egg-coated squid thoroughly with the flour mixture and shake off any excess. Set aside. Heat about 500ml (2 cups) of oil in a wok and heat to 190°C (375°F) over a medium–high heat. If you don't have an oil thermometer, place a wooden chopstick or spatula in the oil. If lots of little bubbles form and sizzle on contact, your oil is ready to cook.

Cook the squid in small batches until crispy and lightly browned, which will take about 1 minute per batch. Do not overcook the squid or it will become chewy. Transfer the cooked calamari to a paper towel-lined plate and set aside. Discard the cooking oil.

Wipe your wok clean and add the butter. Melt the butter over a medium–high heat and add the chopped garlic. Swirl the garlic around in the butter for about a minute and then stir in the chilli paste. Let this all sizzle for about 30 seconds and then stir in the chillies, spring onions (scallions) and (bell) pepper. Fry for a further minute or so and then pour in the fried calamari. Toss the calamari in the sauce to coat, and then pour it all onto a serving plate. Season with salt and pepper to taste and squeeze the lime juice all over it.

SAMBAL LALA
(SAMBAL CLAMS)
SERVES 2–4

There are many different versions of this famous dish and while in Kuala Lumpur and Bali, we loved trying many of them. I could probably write a whole book now on sambal lala but probably won't. For now, give this recipe a try. It gets amazing results every time. We saw this dish being made, and they used a special Malaysian curry powder, but it's very close to Madras curry powder so that is fine to use. Although I don't personally mind preparing live clams, it does take some time. Frozen clams work really well here and they come ready to cook.

PREP TIME: 10 MINS
COOKING TIME: 15 MINS

FOR THE SAMBAL
8 large red finger chillies, or similar
10 garlic cloves, smashed
5cm (2in) piece of ginger, roughly chopped
8 shallots, peeled and roughly chopped
1 lemongrass stalk, peeled, white part only, thinly sliced
4 lime leaves, stems removed and roughly chopped

FOR THE SAUCE
2 tbsp ketchup
1 tbsp oyster sauce
1 tbsp kecap manis
3 tbsp rice wine vinegar
1 tsp palm sugar or light brown sugar (optional)
125ml (½ cup) water
70ml (¼ cup) fish sauce (more or less to taste; gluten-free brands are available))

TO FINISH
3 tbsp rapeseed (canola) oil
1 tbsp Madras curry powder
1kg (2lb 2oz) frozen clams or cleaned fresh clams
2 limes, quartered, to serve

For the sambal, place all the ingredients in a food processor and blend with just enough water to make a thick paste. This is your quick and easy sambal! Set aside.

Now whisk all the sauce ingredients together. The fish sauce adds a salty flavour, so you might want to add a little less at first and then top it up at the end of cooking to your own taste preference.

To finish, heat the oil over a medium–high heat in a wok or similar. When visibly hot, stir in the Madras curry powder and fry for 15 seconds, then add the prepared sambal. Fry for about 3 minutes and then stir in the prepared sauce.

Turn the heat up to high and add the clams. Simmer until all of the shells have opened, discarding any that don't. Check for seasoning, adding more fish sauce for a savoury flavour and oyster sauce or kecap manis for a sweeter flavour. Serve hot with lime wedges at the table, squeezed over the clams to taste.

CHA CA
(FISH WITH TURMERIC AND DILL)
SERVES 4

A must-try dish in Hanoi! And a must-try dish at home, too, for that matter. I was blown away by how much I loved this simple fish dish and ended up ordering it on numerous occasions while in Hanoi. I'm not normally a big fan of dill, but it just works and I think you'll find it's one of the ingredients that make this dish special. In Hanoi they use local catfish; I use tilapia or lemon sole. I love it with rice vermicelli noodles.

PREP TIME: 15 MINS
COOKING TIME: 10 MINS

200g (7oz) rice vermicelli noodles
700g (1lb 9oz) tilapia or lemon sole, cut into 5cm (2in) chunks
Approx. 4 tbsp rapeseed (canola) oil
4 garlic cloves, finely chopped
1–2 red spur chillies, thinly sliced
4 spring onions (scallions), thinly sliced
1 huge bundle of dill
3 spring onions (scallions), slit once down the centre
4 tbsp roasted peanuts, to garnish

FOR THE MARINADE
1 tsp ground turmeric
½ tsp chilli powder
½ tsp ground coriander
½ tsp sugar
2 tbsp rapeseed oil

FOR THE DRESSING
3 tbsp fish sauce (gluten-free brands are available)
3 tbsp sugar
3 tbsp lime juice
2 red finger chillies, cut into thin rings (more or less to taste)
4 garlic cloves, finely chopped

Place the vermicelli rice noodles in a bowl and cover with boiling water. Allow to soak for about 10 minutes, or until cooked through to your liking. Drain and keep warm.

Now whisk the marinade ingredients together in a mixing bowl and add the fish. Mix well to coat and set aside while you prepare the rest of the recipe.

Whisk the dressing ingredients together in another bowl. This should be prepared to taste, so adjust the sweet, sour, savoury and spicy flavours as you wish, adding the ingredients and adjusting the quantities to your preference. Set aside.

Heat the oil in a large frying pan (skillet) over a medium–high heat. If frying fish in a pan is new to you, you might like to use a non-stick pan. If you do, you can use less oil. When the oil is really hot, place the fish in the pan in one layer. Fry on one side until crispy brown and the fish easily comes free from the pan. Turn over each piece and continue frying until almost cooked through and a light golden brown all over. Add the chopped garlic, chillies and sliced spring onions (scallions) and fry to cook through. Drain away any excess oil. You want about a tablespoon and a half left in the pan. Top with a good healthy handful of fresh dill and the remaining spring onions, pushing them right into the oil in the pan to cook slightly.

Take off the heat and serve over the vermicelli rice noodles, drizzled with some of the dressing and garnished with peanuts.

IKAN BAKAR
SERVES 2–4

Ikan bakar is a delicious fried fish that is first smothered with a spicy sambal and then wrapped in a banana leaf to cook. Cooking ikan bakar in this way makes the fish deliciously moist, and also flavours it with the subtle flavour of the banana leaf. The flavour and aroma are to die for. This recipe is often cooked over a hot fire, giving the dish a mild smoky flavour. You could try it on your barbecue, but it is really good cooked indoors, too. Different food stalls cook ikan bakar with different fish, and the best we had was meaty chunks of sting ray, which was out-of-this-world amazing. You could wrap any meaty fish in those banana leaves though and not be disappointed.

PREP TIME: 10 MINS
COOKING TIME: 20 MINS

2 fish such as bass, snapper, mackerel
   or tilapia
5 tbsp rapeseed (canola) oil
1 large banana leaf, cut into strips as
   shown opposite

FOR THE SAMBAL
5 garlic cloves
5cm (2in) piece of ginger
5cm (2in) piece of galangal
3 red chillies
5 shallots
1 tbsp ground coriander
½ tsp ground turmeric
½ tsp ground cumin
2 tbsp unsalted butter
80ml (⅓ cup) kecap manis (see page
   258) or shop-bought

With a sharp knife, make three shallow incisions on both sides of each fish and set aside.

For the sambal, use a spice grinder, food processor or pestle and mortar to grind the garlic, ginger, galangal, chillies and shallots to a paste. Heat a frying pan (skillet) over a medium–high heat and add half of the oil. When the oil is visibly hot, stir in the blended sambal paste and fry it for a couple of minutes. Add the ground spices and stir to combine. Then add the butter, stirring regularly until the butter melts into the sambal.

Transfer the sambal to a mixing bowl and add the kecap manis. Stir until smooth and quite dark in colour.

When you're ready to cook the fish, rub the sambal mixture all over the surface, in the cavity and in the slits, and wrap tightly in a strip of banana leaf. Any leftover marinade can be used for basting while you cook.

Heat your pan over a medium–high heat and add the remaining oil. When visibly hot, place the fish in the pan, fry on one side until cooked through and then flip it over to cook the other side. Baste the fish from time to time with the remaining marinade. Cooking times will vary depending on the size of your fish, but it's ready when the exterior is nicely charred and the meat easily flakes away from the bones with a fork. Serve as is or with the optional sambal matah (see page 252), which I highly recommend doing.

PAKISTANI FISH FRY
SERVES 6

I must have made this fish fry recipe hundreds of times. It's that good, and so simple to make. I like to serve it with heated parathas or rotis topped with salad vegetables, hot sauce and coriander (cilantro) chutney (see page 254). The ajwain (carom) seeds have a strong flavour and are optional.

PREP TIME: 10 MINS, PLUS
   OPTIONAL MARINATING TIME
COOKING TIME: 15 MINS

900g (2lb) white fish such as cod or
   halibut, cut into bite-sized pieces
Rapeseed (canola) oil, for shallow-
   frying

FOR THE MARINADE
1 tbsp kasoori methi (dried fenugreek
   leaves)
2 tbsp tamarind sauce (see page 256
   or shop-bought)
2 tbsp garlic and ginger paste
2 tsp ground cumin
2 tsp ground coriander
2 tsp salt
½ tsp ajwain (carom) seeds (optional)
½ tsp ground turmeric
1 tsp garam masala, shop-bought or
   homemade (see page 259)
1 tbsp Kashmiri chilli powder
1 tbsp dried red chilli flakes
2 tbsp rice flour or cornflour
   (cornstarch)
3 tbsp gram flour

Rub the kasoori methi (dried fenugreek leaves) between your fingers into a bowl. Then add the remaining marinade ingredients and whisk until smooth. Add the fish to the marinade and coat completely. You can fry the fish immediately, or allow it to marinate for up to 1 hour.

When ready to cook, heat about 7.5cm (3in) of oil in a large frying pan (skillet) or wok. When lots of bubbles form instantly around a wooden chopstick or spatula dipped into the oil, it is hot enough to start cooking.

Carefully and slowly lower a piece of fish into the oil. If there aren't thousands of little bubbles around it when you do, take it out and allow the oil to get a bit hotter. Lower each piece of fish into the oil this way. You might need to cook in batches to maintain the heat of the oil. Cook the fish until crispy brown and cooked through. Transfer the cooked fish to a wire rack to drip off any excess oil and repeat with any remaining fish.

STIR-FRIED MORNING GLORY
SERVES 2–4

Stir-fried morning glory, or water spinach, is popular all over South Asia. I have ordered it a lot as a side dish, but you could also eat this as a light vegetarian main over some rice. Recipes vary, but the end results are usually quite similar. In Vietnam I noticed that chillies were never added, or at least not that I found, but this Thai version offers a spicier combo that I really like. Fresh morning glory is available at large Asian grocers and online, but you could substitute young broccoli or even shredded savoy cabbage in this recipe. You will find a photo of this stir-fried morning glory on page 240, served next to the ikan bakar.

PREP TIME: 10 MINS
COOKING TIME: 10 MINS

500g (1lb 2oz) fresh morning glory
(water spinach) or young broccoli
2 tbsp rapeseed (canola) oil
5 garlic cloves, thinly sliced
5 red finger chillies, sliced into thirds
1 tbsp oyster sauce
1 tbsp soy sauce (gluten-free brands
are available)
1 tsp sugar (more or less to taste)

Slice the water spinach in half so that you have stem ends and leafy ends. Then slice the thicker stems of the morning glory into 2.5cm (1in) pieces and cut the leafy ends in half.

Heat the oil over a medium heat in a wok or large frying pan (skillet). Stir in the sliced garlic and fry for about 30 seconds to a minute. You just want to crisp the garlic a bit, but be careful not to overcook and burn it. Stir in the sliced chillies (remove the seeds if you don't want it too spicy) and fry for a further 15 seconds before adding the morning glory stems. Cook for 15 seconds and then add the leaves.

Toss this around in the wok/pan until the morning glory is nicely coated with the garlicky oil. Stir in the oyster sauce, soy sauce and sugar and serve immediately.

PAKISTANI CHICKPEA BIRYANI

SERVES 6

If you want to cook a delicious and satisfying vegetarian meal, you can't really go wrong with this Pakistani chickpea biryani. I love Pakistani food, which normally includes lots of meat that is cooked to perfection! This, however, is a popular street-food vegetarian biryani that has people lining up to get some. I must have made it ten times in the past year, and that wasn't just because I was testing the recipe for this book. It is amazing! If you're vegetarian, you are going to be in food heaven. If you're not, you are still going to be in food heaven. If you prefer, you can purchase fried onions instead of frying them yourself. When cooked, this is good served with a raita (see page 255), some shop-bought hot sauce of your choice and/or some more lemon wedges.

PREP TIME: 15 MINS, PLUS
    SOAKING TIME
COOKING TIME: 60 MINS

400g (2 cups) long grain basmati rice
250ml (1 cup) rapeseed (canola) oil
2 medium red onions, thinly sliced
1 tbsp cumin seeds
1 tbsp coriander seeds, crushed
1 stick cinnamon
4 green cardamom pods, bruised
2 black cardamom pods, bruised,
    or 4 more green cardamom pods
1 tsp black peppercorns
5 cloves
1 tbsp Kashmiri chilli powder (more
    or less to taste)
½ tsp ground turmeric
3 medium tomatoes, diced
2–3 green chillies, finely chopped
    (more or less to taste)
4 garlic cloves, finely chopped
2.5cm (1in) piece of ginger, finely
    chopped
3 tbsp natural yoghurt
2 x 400g (14oz) tins (cans) chickpeas
4 small Pakistani lemons or 2 larger
    lemons, cut in half
750ml (3 cups) water or chicken or
    vegetable stock
1 tsp salt
4 tbsp coriander (cilantro), finely
    chopped

Pour the basmati rice into a large bowl and cover with water, swirling the water around with your hand. The water will become milky from the starch. Pour the water out and repeat at least three times, or until the water is almost clear. Cover the rice again with fresh water and allow to soak for at least an hour.

Heat the oil in a large saucepan over a medium–high heat and, when visibly hot, add the sliced onions. Fry for about 10–15 minutes, or until they are golden brown. I fry the onions until they are a deep brown but be careful if doing this, as there is only a couple of seconds between deliciously browned and burnt! Transfer to a paper towel to soak up any excess oil. Then discard all but 2 tablespoons of the oil or filter and save it for another use (see page 11). I highly recommend saving it, as that seasoned oil is great used in a curry instead of plain oil.

Over a medium–high heat, add the whole spices to the remaining oil in the pan and infuse their flavours into the oil for about 40 seconds. Now add the chilli powder, turmeric, tomatoes, green chillies, garlic and ginger and fry for about 2 minutes, stirring well to make a thick sauce. Stir in the yoghurt one tablespoon at a time. Then stir in all but a couple of tablespoons of the reserved fried onions, followed by the chickpeas, and continue stirring to coat the chickpeas in the sauce.

Squeeze the juice from the lemons into the mixture and then throw them in, too. Add the soaked rice and stir again to combine before adding the water or stock. Bring this all to a rolling boil and then turn off the heat and cover tightly with a lid. No steam should escape, so if your lid is not tight enough, cover the pot tightly first with foil and then cover with the lid.

Allow the rice to steam for 40 minutes. Do not be tempted to lift the lid, just walk away and do something else! After 40 minutes, lift the lid and check the rice. It should be cooked to perfection. Carefully stir the biryani with a fork. Don't stir too hard or the delicate rice grains will split.

Taste it and season with more salt if desired. Garnish with the chopped coriander (cilantro) and serve.

CHILLI GARLIC RAMEN
SERVES 2–4

The chilli garlic oil used in this ramen recipe is perfect as a garnish for many South East Asian curries. You will make much more than you need here, so use the rest to garnish any of the curries in this book. Store the oil you don't use in the recipe in an air-tight jar in the fridge and use as needed. You can, of course, purchase good-quality chilli garlic oil at Asian shops, but it only takes minutes to prepare and you will get a lot more for your money. Whenever you make flavoured oils, it's a good idea to use an oil thermometer so that you don't burn the ingredients, but I have given instructions below so that you can make this without a thermometer.

PREP TIME: 15 MINS
COOKING TIME: 15 MINS

FOR THE OIL
100g (3½oz) dried red chilli flakes
6 garlic cloves, roughly chopped
3 shallots, finely chopped
½ tsp salt
2 tbsp roughly chopped ginger
625ml (2½ cups) rapeseed (canola) or
    peanut oil
125ml (½ cup) roasted sesame oil

FOR THE NOODLES
4 packs of instant ramen noodles
3 spring onions (scallions), thinly
    sliced, to garnish

To make the chilli garlic oil, add all of the ingredients to a saucepan over a low–medium heat. If you have an oil thermometer, you are aiming for a cooking temperature between 110°C (225°F) and 120°C (250°F). It is important not to allow the temperature of the oil to rise above 120°C (250°F) or the ingredients will burn. If you don't have a thermometer, the oil should just lightly bubble. Watch it carefully, and if it looks like the ingredients in the oil are darkening, take it off the heat.

Simmer for 15 minutes and then turn off the heat and allow to cool. You can use this oil immediately while still hot, or you could allow it to cool to room temperature overnight. Pour any unused oil and the solids into a sterilized jar and use the oil and solids as needed. It keeps indefinitely, and the flavour intensifies after being stored for a few days.

To make the ramen, soak the noodles in boiling hot water for about 10 minutes, or according to the package instructions. Then toss the hot noodles with some of the oil and a couple of tablespoons of the goop from the bottom. This can be done to taste. Season with more salt if you like.

Serve hot, garnished with spring onions (scallions).

SIDES, ACCOMPANIMENTS AND BASICS

Those of you who have read my other books and/or blog know that I love to cook. My goal with this book was to feature recipes that can be made in one pot, pan or baking tray and I did exactly that. The thing is, I really want you to be able to try the recipes as I did while researching, as well as experience them the way I serve them at home. This often means making extra, complementary dishes and basic recipes to get the most out of each dish.

Please don't let that scare you off, though. Most of the accompaniments and basic recipes featured in this chapter, such as the sauces, spice blends and cooked rice, can be purchased ready-made. There's nothing wrong with that, but if you would like to try making these recipes yourself, I'm sure you will be very happy with the results, and hopefully enjoy making them, too.

STEAMED BASMATI RICE
SERVES 4

Perfectly steamed basmati rice makes a delicious meal served simply with a few chutneys, and this recipe has never failed me. It works best if you are cooking rice for eight people or fewer, so as this recipe serves four, you can double it if you're cooking for more. I often cook the rice and freeze the leftovers, if there are any, in freezer bags. Cooked basmati rice freezes really well. All you need to do is stick the frozen bag of rice in your microwave for about 3 minutes and it will be as good as the day you cooked it. As cold, cooked rice is needed for fried-rice recipes, it is good to have on hand. The rice can also be steamed with additional spices such as cardamom pods and a cinnamon stick, or whatever flavours you would like steamed into the rice.

PREP TIME: 5 MINS
COOKING TIME: 45 MINS

370g (2 cups) basmati rice
1 tbsp butter (optional)
½ tsp salt (optional)

Put the rice in a bowl and run water over it. Swirl the rice around in the water and carefully pour the water out. The water will be white from the starch. Continue rinsing in the same way until the water runs almost clear. Cover the rice with fresh water and allow to soak for about 30 minutes, then strain.

When ready to cook, put the soaked rice, butter and salt, if using, in a saucepan that has a tight-fitting lid. Pour 750ml (3 cups) of water over it and cover with the lid. Bring to a boil, then turn off the heat. Don't be tempted to lift the lid – just let it sit there undisturbed for 40 minutes.

After 40 minutes, take the lid off and, using a fork or a chopstick, gently stir to separate the grains. Do not stir too vigorously as basmati rice has a tendency to turn to mush if stirred too hard. Serve immediately or run water over the rice to cool it and place, covered, in the fridge to heat up later in the microwave or serve fried. Please note that rice should not be eaten if it has been at room temperature for more than 1 hour.

JASMINE RICE
SERVES 4

Jasmine rice goes so well with South East Asian food. The grains are thicker and naturally softer than basmati and the cooked rice is also slightly sticky, making it perfect for moulding into shapes, as is so often done at restaurants. Also, unlike basmati and other rice varieties, it should never be soaked before cooking.

PREP TIME: 5 MINS
COOKING TIME: 30 MINS

370g (2 cups) jasmine rice

Put the rice into a bowl and cover with cold water. Swirl the water around a few times with your hand until the water turns milky white. That's the starch on the rice, and most of it should be rinsed off so that the cooked rice isn't too sticky. Pour this water away and repeat one or two more times until the water is almost clear. Drain and then tip the rice into a saucepan that has a tight-fitting lid. Add 750ml (3 cups) of cold water.

Cover with the lid and bring to a boil over a high heat. Once boiling, reduce the heat to low and simmer, covered, for about 15 minutes. Remove from the heat and allow to steam for an additional 10 minutes without lifting the lid.

Check the rice. If there is any water left in the pan, cover again until all the water has been absorbed. Stir lightly with a fork to loosen the grains and serve.

INDIAN

MATTA (RED) RICE

SERVES 4–6

This rice is popular in south India and Sri Lanka. The red tone of the rice is the outer pericarp, which is removed from processed white rice, leaving it with little nutritional value. The earthy flavoured matta rice is full of vitamins and fibre. So if you're looking for a good, healthy rice that is filling and tasty too, give this a try.

PREP TIME: 5 MINS, PLUS SOAKING TIME
COOKING TIME: 30 MINS

370g (2 cups) matta rice (available online and from Asian grocers)
1.5 litres (6 cups) water
½ tsp salt
1 cinnamon stick
5 black peppercorns
5 cloves

Rinse the rice in a large bowl in several changes of water until the water runs clear. Soak the rinsed rice for 30 minutes to 1 hour.

When ready, put the water in a large saucepan, add the spices and bring to a boil. Drain the rice, add it to the pan and cook for about 20 minutes, or until tender. Some brands take longer to cook, so read the packet instructions. The rice is ready when you can squish a grain of rice between your fingers, but it should not be at all mushy. If in doubt, try it. The rice should be enjoyable to eat and still have a bit of bite to it.

INDONESIAN, MALAYSIAN AND SINGAPOREAN

MALAY CUCUMBER AND CARROT SALAD

SERVES 2–4

A simple salad is all that's needed with so many Malay dishes. This cucumber and carrot salad can be served on its own as a snack, or as an accompaniment for rice or grilled and fried meat and seafood. It is very popular served like this but you might prefer to cut the veggies in another way, such as larger chunks or julienned. This salad is photographed on page 231 with the butter egg floss prawns.

PREP TIME: 10 MINS

1 tbsp lime juice
1 tbsp white distilled vinegar
1 tbsp toasted sesame oil
½ tsp sugar
Salt and pepper, to taste
1 English cucumber, cut into small dice
1 large carrot, cut into small dice
3 banana shallots, thinly sliced
1 red finger chilli, seeds removed and thinly sliced or left whole

Whisk the lime juice, vinegar, sesame oil and sugar together until the sugar dissolves. Season with salt and pepper to taste. Add the cucumber, carrot, shallots and chilli and toss to combine. This salad can be served immediately or stored in the fridge for up to three days.

BALINESE GREEN BEANS

SERVES 2–4

Although this popular side dish is often served cold, I like to heat it before serving. I learned the recipe in Ubud, Bali. It is pictured on page 205.

PREP TIME: 15 MINS
COOKING TIME: 15 MINS

300g (10½oz) fresh green beans, slit down the middle and cut into 1.75cm (½in) pieces
2½ tbsp rapeseed (canola) oil
3 tbsp shallots, finely chopped
3 tbsp garlic, roughly chopped
50g (2oz) fresh or frozen coconut, grated
½ tsp shrimp paste
100g (3½oz) cooked jackfruit, finely chopped (optional)
Salt, to taste

FOR THE SAMBAL
1.25cm (½in) piece of ginger
2.5cm (1in) piece of galangal
2 makrut lime leaves, stems removed and finely julienned
½ lemongrass stalk, white part only, peeled and thinly sliced
5 green finger chillies, roughly chopped
3 garlic cloves, peeled and smashed
2 candlenuts
1 tsp black peppercorns
1–2 tbsp lime juice

Bring some water to a boil in a frying pan (skillet) and add the beans. Simmer for about 5 minutes, or until tender. Transfer to a plate and set aside. Dry your pan, then add the oil and place over a medium heat. Fry the shallots and garlic for a couple of minutes, until they are a light, crispy brown. Be careful not to burn the garlic. Transfer to the plate with the beans. Add the grated coconut to the oil and fry for a few minutes until it is turning a light brown. Transfer to the plate with the other cooked ingredients.

Place all of the sambal ingredients in a blender or food processor and blend to a semi-smooth or smooth paste. In your pan, heat the oil still in it over a medium–high heat, adding a drop more if needed, and fry the sambal for about 2 minutes. Stir in the shrimp paste then cook for about 30 seconds. Add the cooked jackfruit, if using, and stir it all together. Then return the cooked ingredients to the pan to heat through. Taste it and add more lime juice if you want a tarter flavour, then season with salt to taste.

ASIAN-STYLE CHICKEN STOCK

MAKES APPROX. 4 LITRES (16 CUPS)

This basic stock works well with any of the recipes in this book. You can also adapt it as you wish to suit the dish you are making. For example, if you are preparing a Thai soup, you might want to omit the ginger and use galangal instead. Or if you are making a Mexican recipe, perhaps leave out the ginger and add a bit of Mexican oregano.

PREP TIME: 15 MINS
COOKING TIME: 4 HOURS

1.5kg (3lb 5oz) chicken bones
2.5kg (5lb) whole chicken
5cm (2in) piece of ginger, thinly sliced and lightly crushed
8 garlic cloves, smashed
8 spring onions (scallions)
1 onion, peeled and quartered
2 carrots, roughly chopped
½ bunch of coriander (cilantro)
20 black peppercorns
5 litres (4½ quarts) cold water

This step is optional but will give a clearer stock. Place the chicken bones and chicken in a large stockpot and cover with water. Bring to a boil and simmer for 5 minutes. Strain the stock and discard the liquid.

Wash the stockpot and put the bones and chicken back in it. Add all the remaining ingredients, including the water, and bring to a boil over a medium–high heat. Once boiling, reduce the heat to medium and simmer for 4 hours, skimming off any foam that rises to the top.

Strain the stock into a bowl. Discard the bones and aromatic ingredients. The chicken will be overcooked but the meat is great in sandwiches, soups or sauces so don't throw it away. Allow the stock to cool a little, then place it, covered, in the fridge for up to three days. It can be frozen for up to six months.

NOTE

Most good chicken stock recipes call for chicken bones. So if you are roasting a chicken, use the leftover carcass to make a stock or freeze it for another day. Don't go looking in countless butcher shops for chicken bones though; just use the equivalent amount of chicken wings, legs or other cheap cuts.

ASIAN-STYLE MEAT STOCK
MAKES APPROX. 4 LITRES (16 CUPS)

The beef pho recipe on page 25 is delicious when made with this stock instead of a shop-bought alternative. I have used beef bones and beef brisket in this recipe but other meat bones such as pork and lamb could also be used, or a combination, in the same way. Whenever I make a beef stock, I always throw in a bit of brisket. After it is used to make the stock, it can be thinly sliced for sandwiches or cubed and used in a stew with the stock. Using the meat as well as the bones makes a richer stock and, as you are simmering the stock for 4 hours, you might as well have something besides stock at the end of it all.

PREP TIME: 15 MINS
COOKING TIME: 4 HOURS

3kg (6lb) beef marrow bones – ask your butcher to cut them into small pieces that will fit into your pan
1.5kg (3lb 5oz) beef brisket (optional)
6 green onions, roughly chopped
5cm (2in) piece of ginger, sliced and lightly smashed
8 garlic cloves, smashed
4 cloves
1 tbsp black peppercorns
1 tsp coriander seeds
1 star anise

Place the bones in a large stockpot and cover with water. Cover and bring to a boil and then simmer for about 10 minutes, skimming off any foam and other impurities that rise to the top. Pour the bones through a colander, discarding the cooking water, and wash them, removing any remaining blood and impurities.

Wash your stockpot thoroughly with water and return the bones to the pot. Add the beef brisket and all of the remaining ingredients and then cover with at least 5cm (2in) of water. Cover and bring to a simmer over a medium–high heat and then reduce the heat to medium to simmer for 4 hours. Be sure to skim off any foam for a clearer stock.

Strain. This stock will keep in the fridge for at least three days and can be frozen for up to six months.

SRI LANKAN POL SAMBOL
SERVES 4–6

I visited Sri Lanka for the first time back in 2013, and it was then that I got the chance to make my first authentic pol sambol. Although it is spelt and pronounced 'sambol' in Sri Lanka, it is similar and has the same meaning to 'sambal', which is found in other South East Asian recipes. This is pretty much what I made that day, grinding the ingredients on a wet stone grinder. You can make this and other sambols in a food processor, but grinding by hand does take it all up a notch. This easy sambol is the perfect accompaniment to Sri Lankan curries, grilled seafood and meat or can be enjoyed simply with rice. It is pictured on page 120 with the Sri Lankan black pork curry.

PREP TIME: 20 MINS

150g (5½oz) coconut, grated
15 dried red chillies
8 small shallots, roughly chopped
½ tsp sugar
Salt, to taste
Juice of 1 lime

Place the coconut and chillies in a pestle and mortar and begin pounding. Adding a little water makes this easier. Add the shallots and continue pounding until you have a coarse paste. Add sugar and salt to taste and then squeeze in the lime juice. Mix well to combine and adjust the ingredients to taste.

★ MAKE IT EASIER ★
Although traditionally pounded to a paste, you could use a small food processor or blender for this recipe. You might need to add a drop of water to assist blending.

INDONESIAN, MALAYSIAN, SINGAPOREAN

SAMBAL OELEK
MAKES APPROX. 250ML (1 CUP)

Sambal oelek is a really easy and delicious spicy hot chilli sauce that is served as an accompaniment with meat, fish, vegetable and noodle dishes all over Indonesia, Malaysia and Singapore. Try it with ikan bakar (see page 241) or mee goreng (see page 200), and if you like your food spicy, you won't be disappointed. For that matter, this spicy chilli sauce can be used to spice up pretty much anything, regardless of the cuisine. It's traditionally made with just three ingredients: chillies, vinegar and salt, although I have tried other versions with more ingredients such as garlic, lime juice and shallots. This sauce is pictured on page 205.

PREP TIME: 10 MINS

225g (8oz) red finger chillies or similar
1 tbsp white rice wine vinegar
1 tbsp lime juice or more rice wine vinegar
1 clove garlic (optional)
1½ tsp salt or to taste

Place all of the ingredients in a pestle and mortar or food processor and grind to a paste. If using a food processor or blender, you might need to add a drop of water or vinegar to make blending easier. If the paste is looking watery on the top, just give it a stir. Pour the thick paste into a clean jar that has a tight-fitting lid and bring it out whenever you want a good, spicy kick.

INDONESIAN, MALAYSIAN, SINGAPOREAN

SAMBAL MATAH
MAKES APPROX. 500ML (2 CUPS)

Sambal matah is a delicious raw sambal that goes with just about everything. If you just want a simple but tasty meal, make up some of this and even the most boring steamed trout can be lifted up to excellence. Sambal matah is amazing served over fried, steamed or baked fish, meats or vegetables.

PREP TIME: 5 MINS
COOKING TIME: 1 MIN

8 green finger chillies, finely chopped
2 red jalapeños or finger chillies
8 shallots, thinly sliced
5 garlic cloves, finely chopped
3 makrut lime leaves, stems removed and thinly sliced
1 tbsp lime juice
¼ tsp salt
¼ tsp sugar
3 tbsp coconut oil
2 lemongrass stalks, white part only, peeled and very thinly sliced
½ tsp shrimp paste (optional)
Sugar, to taste

Place the chillies, shallots, garlic, lime leaves, lime juice, salt and sugar in a mixing bowl. Stir well and set aside. Add the coconut oil to a frying pan (skillet) over a medium–high heat and fry the lemongrass to soften a little. Then add the shrimp paste and fry for another 30 seconds. Pour this over the chopped veggies. Taste it and add more salt and/or sugar as wished.

VIETNAMESE

VIETNAMESE SATE
(CHILLI SAUCE)
MAKES APPROX. 300ML (1¼ CUPS)

There are many different recipes for this oily Vietnamese condiment, but this is an easy one that you can prepare in less than half an hour. It's delicious served with Vietnamese dishes such as pho and bun bo hue. For that matter, it's good served with many different South East Asian dishes to add a bit of heat. It is pictured on pages 224 and 22 with the bánh xèo and beef congee.

PREP TIME: 5 MINS
COOKING TIME: 25 MINS

250ml (1 cup) rapeseed (canola) oil
2 lemongrass stalks, thinly sliced
6 garlic cloves, finely chopped
2 banana shallots, finely chopped
50g (2oz) dried red finger chillies, finely chopped, or the equivalent red chilli flakes
1 tbsp fish sauce (gluten-free brands are available)
1 tsp salt

When making a flavoured oil like this, the cooking temperature is important. Heat the oil in a saucepan over a medium–high heat and add the sliced lemongrass. You're aiming for a cooking temperature between 110°C (225°F) and 120°C (250°F). Do not allow the temperature of the oil to rise above 120°C (250°F) or the ingredients will burn. If you don't have a thermometer, the oil should just lightly bubble. Watch it carefully, and if it looks like the lemongrass is darkening, take it off the heat. Simmer the lemongrass for 5 minutes and then stir in the garlic and shallots and continue frying for 10 minutes. Watch that cooking temperature! Add the finely chopped red chillies and fry for a further 10 minutes.

Take off the heat and allow to cool a little. Add the fish sauce and season with salt to taste, if needed. This should last indefinitely but it is a good idea to ensure that all the solid ingredients are covered in oil when jarred.

THAI

CHILLI JAM
MAKES APPROX. 400ML (1¾ CUPS)

Chilli jam, or nam prik pao, is a good one to have in your Thai recipe library. Nam prik means 'chilli dip' and pao means 'roast' or 'burn'. That's exactly what you're getting here. Perfectly roasted, fresh ingredients with a delicious spicy bite.

PREP TIME: 15 MINS
COOKING TIME: 5 MINS

2 banana shallots, peeled and roughly chopped
10 large garlic cloves, roughly chopped
10 dried red bird's eye chillies, cut into small pieces
10 red spur chillies, roughly chopped
2 tbsp dried shrimp
1 tsp shrimp paste
2 tbsp palm sugar or caster (superfine) sugar
2 tbsp tamarind paste (see page 256 or shop-bought)
1 thumb-sized piece of galangal, finely chopped
3 tbsp Thai fish sauce (gluten-free brands are available)
125ml (½ cup) rapeseed (canola) oil

Heat a dry frying pan (skillet) or wok over a medium–high heat and add the shallots and garlic. Move the garlic and shallots around in the pan continuously until they begin to smoke and char in places. Be careful not to burn the garlic; we are just toasting it. Transfer to a plate to cool.

Add the chillies to the pan and toast lightly until fragrant. This should only take about 40 seconds. Transfer to the plate with the garlic and shallots.

Put the garlic, shallots and chillies into a food processor along with all the remaining ingredients and 2 tablespoons of water and blend for about a minute until you have a thick paste. Transfer to a wok or frying pan and fry until the colour has darkened by about two shades and the oil is separating from the paste. Taste it and add more sugar for extra sweetness, more fish sauce if you like it saltier or more tamarind for sourness. Whisk the separated oil into the jam.

Blend again if needed and store in a sterilized jar in the fridge. This jam will keep for a good two weeks.

CORIANDER CHUTNEY

SERVES 4

I literally make some of this every week; it goes well with pretty much anything. Try it simply with rice, or use it as a dip for chicken tikka (see pages 158 and 203). Make it, taste it and I bet you can think of many other ways to use it. It is pictured on page 245 with the Pakistani chickpea biryani.

PREP TIME: 10 MINUTES

1 large bunch of coriander (cilantro)
2–3 green chillies
1 tsp roasted cumin seeds
3 garlic cloves
Juice of 1 lime
3 tbsp yoghurt
Salt, to taste
Sugar, to taste (optional)

Place the coriander (cilantro), chillies, cumin seeds, garlic, lime juice and half the yoghurt in a blender and blend to a thick paste. Whisk in the rest of the yoghurt and add salt to taste. You could also add a little sugar if you prefer a sweeter chutney.

EASY GUACAMOLE

SERVES 4–6

There are many recipes for guacamole. Some are more fussy than others, with roasted pablano chillies, tomatoes and garlic, while others are much more straightforward, like this one I make when I can't get the pablano chillies. When purchasing the avocados, be sure to squeeze them. They should be slightly soft and give a little. If rock hard, they aren't ripe enough to use in this recipe. If you are also making the pico de gallo (see opposite), you could just add some of that instead of the red onions, chillies, coriander (cilantro) and tomatoes used in this recipe.

PREP TIME: 10 MINUTES

3 ripe avocados
Juice of 1 lime
4 tbsp red onion, finely chopped
2 green finger chillies or 1 jalapeño, finely chopped
2 tbsp coriander (cilantro), finely chopped
1 medium tomato, diced
Salt and pepper, to taste

Peel and slice the avocados in half. Remove the stones and retain one. Place the avocados in a pestle and mortar and pound until you are happy with the consistency. If you prefer a really smooth guacamole you could blitz them in a food processor or blender, but I prefer the pestle and mortar method.

Squeeze in the lime juice and give it a good stir. Then stir in the remaining ingredients and season with salt and pepper to taste. If not eating immediately, stick the retained stone into the guacamole and cover tightly with cling film (plastic wrap). This will help ensure it doesn't turn brown, which is rather unsightly but does not affect the flavour. If it does discolour a little, just give it a good stir which usually solves the issue. Place in the fridge until ready to serve.

INDIAN/PAKISTANI

SPRING ONION RAITA
SERVES 4

This quick, simple raita tastes amazing. Try it as a dip for chicken tikka (see page 158 or 203) or even go fusion and try it over the fajita traybake (see page 155). You really can't go wrong.

PREP TIME: 10 MINUTES

250ml (1 cup) Greek yoghurt
2 garlic cloves, finely chopped
4 spring onions (scallions), finely chopped
Juice of 1–2 limes
Salt, to taste

Place all of the ingredients except the salt in a mixing bowl and stir until smooth. Season with salt to taste.

INDIAN/PAKISTANI

PODINA
SERVES 4–6

Podina means 'mint' in Urdu. This chutney works as a dip for chicken tikka (see pages 158 and 203), vegetables or papadams.

PREP TIME: 10 MINS

½ bunch of fresh mint leaves
½ bunch of fresh coriander (cilantro)
10–15 green finger chillies
250ml (1 cup) yoghurt
Salt, to taste

Place all of the ingredients except the salt in a blender and blend until smooth. This is a rather runny sauce – if you prefer it thicker, only add about a quarter of the yoghurt to the blender then whisk the resulting paste into the remaining yoghurt. Add salt to taste. Podina is best served chilled, so if possible make it ahead of time and store, covered, in the fridge before serving.

MEXICAN

PICO DE GALLO
SERVES 4–6

This salsa is Mexican in origin but there are duplicate recipes used in other cuisines, so it is also good with or any roasted meat or fish.

PREP TIME: 10 MINS

6 medium tomatoes, cut into small dice
1 small onion, finely chopped
1–2 jalapeño chillies or 3–4 green finger chillies, finely chopped
4 tbsp coriander (cilantro), finely chopped
2 tbsp beer (optional)
3 garlic cloves, finely chopped
Juice of 1 lime
Salt, to taste

Stir all of the ingredients together in a mixing bowl. If time permits, place in the fridge for 30 minutes before serving. Season generously with salt. If you prefer a smoother salsa, blend to your own preference.

VIETNAMESE

NUOC CHAM
SERVES 4

This Vietnamese dipping sauce also makes a delicious marinade. You will need to taste as you go to achieve the best flavour combination.

PREP TIME: 5 MINS

70ml (¼ cup) fish sauce (gluten-free brands are available)
125ml (½ cup) water
3 tbsp sugar (approx. and to taste)
1 tbsp distilled white vinegar
3 tbsp lime juice
2 garlic cloves, finely chopped
2 red finger chillies, finely chopped (more or less to taste)
2 tbsp carrot, finely chopped

Place all of the ingredients up to and including the chillies in a bowl and whisk until the sugar has dissolved. It keeps in the fridge for up to three days. Add the carrot just before serving so it stays crunchy.

INDIAN

TAMARIND PASTE (CONCENTRATE)

MAKES 500ML (2 CUPS)

Tamarind paste is a delicious souring agent. It is readily available at supermarkets and Asian shops, but it is easy to make your own and it tastes much better. Blocks of tamarind come in different sizes but the first time you make this recipe, try making it as written; once you know how it should look, you can use larger or smaller blocks and scale the recipe up or down accordingly

PREP TIME: 20 MINS, PLUS SOAKING TIME

250g (9oz) block tamarind
500ml (2 cups) boiling water

Break up the tamarind into a large bowl and cover with the boiling water to break down the fibres and release the edible pulp. Soak for as long as the manufacturer advises on the packet. Some brands may require an hour or two. When the water cools, break the block up with a wooden spoon and/or your hands. Squeeze the tamarind with your hands until it melts into the water and breaks away from the seeds and fibres.

   Pass the pulp through a fine sieve into another bowl, pressing down to get all the pulp into the bowl. Discard the leftover fibres and seeds. Once you have your smooth paste, stir it. It should be about the same consistency as ketchup and pourable. If you find that your paste is thinner than that, you could simmer it in a large saucepan for a few minutes until it thickens. You need to use a large pan, though, as the paste will splatter as it simmers. Cool and then store the finished paste in a glass jar with a tight-fitting lid. It should keep in the fridge for up to one month.

INDIAN

TAMARIND SAUCE

MAKES APPROX. 200ML (GENEROUS ¾ CUP)

Good-quality tamarind sauce is commercially available. It has a deliciously tart flavour that can be added to taste to different curries. If you fancy having a go at making your own, this recipe gets great results.

PREP TIME: 5 MINS
COOKING TIME: 30 MINS

1 tbsp rapeseed (canola) oil
1 tsp cumin seeds
1 tsp cayenne pepper
1 tsp ground ginger
½ tsp asafoetida* or garlic powder
½ tsp fennel seeds
½ tsp garam masala, shop-bought or homemade
   (see page 259)
200g (7oz) caster (superfine) sugar
3 tbsp tamarind paste

Heat the oil in a saucepan over a medium–high heat. When visibly hot, stir in the cumin seeds, cayenne, ginger, asafoetida or garlic powder, fennel seeds and garam masala. Stir the spices around in the oil to flavour it for about 30 seconds, then pour in the sugar and tamarind paste along with 450ml (scant 2 cups) of water.

   Bring to a rolling simmer and let the sauce reduce until it has a chocolatey colour and is thick enough to coat the back of a spoon. This should take about 20–30 minutes. The sauce will be thin but will thicken once cooled. Store in the fridge in a squeezy bottle, if you have one, and use as required. This sauce will keep for two weeks.

NOTE

*If you are gluten-free, please check the asafoetida packaging as some brands contain wheat flour.

BRITISH INDIAN

PASSATA ALTERNATIVES

Tomato purée is used at many curry houses to add a little tomato colour and flavour to a curry. In this book, I have substituted passata, which works well too, but here are two more ways you can achieve the smooth sauce needed in the recipes.

METHOD 1
MAKES 4 TBSP

PREP TIME: 2 MINS

1 tbsp concentrated tomato purée (paste)
3 tbsp water

Simply mix the ingredients together to form a thinner paste. This recipe can be easily scaled up or down: just use 1 part tomato paste to 3 parts water.

METHOD 2
MAKES 425ML (1¾ CUPS)

PREP TIME: 2 MINS

400g (14oz) tin (can) plum tomatoes
Concentrated tomato purée (paste), to taste (optional)

Blend the plum tomatoes to make a smooth purée. If you want a deeper red colour, add in a little concentrated tomato purée (paste).

INDIAN

GARLIC AND GINGER PASTE
MAKES 15 GENEROUS TBSP

Many of the recipes in this book call for garlic and ginger paste. If you want to purchase it, I recommend purchasing the garlic and ginger paste cubes in the freezer section of Asian grocers. It's easily made though.

PREP TIME: 5 MINS

150g (5½oz) garlic, peeled and chopped
150g (5½oz) ginger, peeled and chopped

Place the garlic and ginger in a food processor or pestle and mortar and blend with just enough water to make a smooth paste. Some chefs finely chop their garlic and ginger instead, which is a good alternative to making a paste. Store in an air-tight container in the fridge for up to three days and use as needed. If you're planning a curry party, go ahead and get this job ticked off early.

I often make larger batches and freeze them in ice-cube trays. Frozen cubes can be transferred to air-tight plastic bags in the freezer, ready for when you get that curry craving. Be sure to let them defrost a little first.

KECAP MANIS
MAKES APPROX. 250ML (1 CUP)

This thick, sweet soy sauce is just as good when shop-bought, however it is quite easy to make. Scale this recipe up or down as required.

PREP TIME: 2 MINS
COOKING TIME: 10 MINS

250ml (1 cup) light soy sauce (gluten-free brands are available)
200g (1 cup) light brown sugar

Pour the soy sauce into a small saucepan. Bring to a simmer over a medium–high heat and stir in the sugar. Continue stirring often while the sugar dissolves into the soy sauce. Then simmer over a medium heat to reduce down by about half, or until the soy sauce is a thick, syrupy consistency. That's it! Done. This will keep for ages in the fridge.

BASIL OIL
MAKES 250ML (1 CUP)

Thai sweet basil oil tastes great and has many uses. I rarely strain the oil, but it is done at some fancy restaurants. It adds a nice green colour to green curry (see page 96).

PREP TIME: 5 MINS
COOKING TIME: 5 MINS

60g (3 packed cups) Thai basil leaves
250ml (1 cup) rapeseed (canola) oil

Bring a saucepan of water to a boil and then add the basil leaves. Simmer for a couple of minutes, or until the leaves are really soft. Strain and place the basil in a bowl of ice-cold water to cool. Once cooled, place in a blender with the oil and blend until very smooth. Pour into a sterilized glass container and keep in the fridge to use as a garnish.

UNROASTED CURRY POWDER
MAKES 2 TBSP

Where dark-roasted curry powder is used a lot in Sri Lankan meat curries because the meat can stand up to its intense flavour, unroasted curry powder is the curry powder of choice for seafood and some vegetable dishes.

PREP TIME: 5 MINS

4 tsp coriander seeds
3 tsp cumin seeds
½ tsp mustard seeds
2 tsp black peppercorns
1 tsp fennel seeds

Finely grind all of the spices and set aside. This recipe can be scaled up according to your requirements.

MIXED POWDER
MAKES 17 GENEROUS TBSP

Feel free to scale this recipe up or down. Simply substitute the word 'tbsp' with 'parts'.

PREP TIME: 5 MINS

3 tbsp ground cumin
3 tbsp ground coriander
4 tbsp curry powder
3 tbsp paprika
3 tbsp ground turmeric
1 tbsp garam masala, shop-bought or homemade (see page 259)

Mix all of the ingredients together and store in an air-tight container in a cool, dark place and use as required.

CURRY POWDER
MAKES APPROX. 250ML (1 CUP)

This is a good all-round curry powder that is great to have on hand. In fact, it is what would be sold as a Madras curry powder because of the chillies, but you could leave them out or reduce the amount for a milder version.

PREP TIME: 10 MINS
COOKING TIME: 10 MINS

3 tbsp coriander seeds
3 tbsp cumin seeds
2 tbsp black peppercorns
1 tbsp fennel seeds
1 tbsp black mustard seeds
5cm (2in) piece of cinnamon stick or cassia bark
1½ tbsp fenugreek seeds
2 star anise
7 cardamom pods, lightly bruised
4–8 Kashmiri dried red chillies (optional)
1 tbsp ground turmeric
1 tbsp hot chilli powder (optional)
1 tsp garlic powder
1 tsp onion powder

Roast all the whole spices, including the dried chillies, if using, in a dry frying pan (skillet) over a medium–high heat until warm to the touch and fragrant. Be sure to move them around in the pan so that they roast evenly. Be careful not to burn the spices. You want them to be quite warm to the touch and fragrant but not yet smoking. If the spices start smoking, get them off the heat!

Tip the warm spices onto a plate and leave to cool, then grind to a fine powder in a spice grinder or pestle and mortar. Add the turmeric, chilli powder, if using, garlic powder and onion powder, and stir to combine. Store in an air-tight container in a cool, dark place and use within two months for optimal flavour.

GARAM MASALA
MAKES 250ML (1 CUP)

There are countless recipes for garam masala. Garam means 'warming' and masala means 'mixture', so garam masala is a mixture of warming spices. The spices used can vary depending on what is being made, but this all-purpose blend will get you much better results than what you will get from your local supermarket. I tend to double or triple this recipe so that I always have some on hand. Garam masala is best prepared on the day you are serving it, however, so if I'm preparing a special dinner I'll scale it down to make the right amount for the recipe/s.

PREP TIME: 10 MINS
COOKING TIME: 10 MINS

3 heaped tbsp coriander seeds
3 heaped tbsp cumin seeds
3 tsp black peppercorns
2 heaped tbsp fennel seeds
1½ tsp cloves
5cm (2in) piece of cinnamon stick
2 dried Indian bay leaves (optional)
10 green cardamom pods, seeds only
1 blade mace

Toast all the spices in a dry frying pan (skillet) over a medium–high heat until fragrant and warm to the touch but not yet smoking, moving them around in the pan and being careful not to burn them. If they begin to smoke, take them off the heat. Tip the warm spices onto a plate and leave to cool.

When cool, grind the spices to a fine powder in a spice grinder or with a pestle and mortar. Store in an air-tight container in a cool, dark place and use within two months for optimal flavour.

INDIAN

TANDOORI MASALA

MAKES 120G (1¼ CUPS)

Most commercial tandoori masalas taste fantastic because they are loaded with salt and tangy citric acid powder. The spices used are usually quite cheap, such as ground coriander and cumin, and they are made more visually appealing with the use of red food colouring. I use a lot more spices and leave the salt and citric acid powder out, substituting the latter for the natural tanginess of amchoor (dried mango powder). You can always add more salt to the finished dish, which gives you a lot more control over the end result. If you would like to omit the red food colouring, remember that your masala will not be the bright red of commercial brands. Food colouring powder becomes redder when it is stirred into a sauce.

PREP TIME: 8 MINS
COOKING TIME: 2 MINS

3 tbsp coriander seeds
3 tbsp cumin seeds
1 tbsp black mustard seeds
5cm (2in) piece of cinnamon stick or cassia bark
Small piece of mace
3 dried Indian bay leaves (cassia leaves)
1 tbsp ground ginger
2 tbsp garlic powder
2 tbsp dried onion powder
2 tbsp amchoor (dried mango powder)
1 tbsp (or more) red food colouring powder (optional)

Roast the whole spices in a dry frying pan (skillet) over a medium–high heat until warm to the touch and fragrant, moving them around in the pan as they roast and being careful not to burn them. If they begin to smoke, take them off the heat. Tip onto a plate to cool.

Grind to a fine powder in a spice grinder or pestle and mortar and tip into a bowl. Stir in the ground ginger, garlic powder, onion powder and amchoor.

Stir in the red food colouring powder, if using. The masala will not look overly red like the commercial brands. Store in an air-tight container in a cool, dark place and use as required, within two months for optimal flavour.

INDIAN

CHAAT MASALA

MAKES 160G (12 GENEROUS TBSP/SCANT 1 CUP)

Chaat masala, which has a quite distinctive flavour, is usually used in small amounts, sprinkled over finished dishes and included in marinades to give them a bit more kick. Citric acid is used in a lot of commercial brands but I've chosen to use the more authentic and healthier amchoor (dried mango powder), which gives the spice blend a nice citric flavour. Another important ingredient is the kala namak (black salt powder). I've only seen this in Asian grocers and a few gourmet spice shops. It has a strong sulphuric aroma that may take some getting used to, but before long you'll probably be hooked.

PREP TIME: 8 MINS
COOKING TIME: 2 MINS

3 tbsp cumin seeds
3 tbsp coriander seeds
1 tsp chilli powder
4 tbsp amchoor (dried mango powder)
3 tbsp kala namak (black salt powder)
1 tbsp freshly ground black pepper
Pinch of asafoetida (gluten-free brands are available)
1 tbsp dried mint (optional)
1 tbsp garlic powder
1 tsp ajwain (carom) seeds

Roast the cumin and coriander seeds in a dry frying pan (skillet) over a medium heat until warm to the touch and fragrant, moving them around in the pan as they roast and being careful not to burn them. If they begin to smoke, take them off the heat. Tip onto a plate to cool.

Grind the roasted seeds to a fine powder in a spice grinder or pestle and mortar. Add the remaining ingredients and grind some more until you have a very fine powder.

Store in an air-tight container in a cool, dark place and use as needed, within two months for optimal flavour.

SRI LANKAN

DARK-ROASTED CURRY POWDER
MAKE APPROX. 250ML (1 CUP)

This special dark-roasted curry powder is used a lot in 'black' Sri Lankan meat curries. It is available online and at specialist Sri Lankan shops, but making your own will give an amazing flavour boost. The spices are roasted until chocolate brown, but be careful not to burn them or they will turn bitter. This is a lengthy process, and you will need to stir and keep a watchful eye on your spices as they roast. The rice is added to thicken the curries you use this in, but can be left out. The chillies can be added to taste or left out.

PREP TIME: 15 MINS
COOKING TIME: 1 HOUR

3 tbsp cumin seeds
4 tbsp coriander seeds
1 tbsp fennel seeds
1 tsp fenugreek seeds
1 tbsp basmati rice (optional)
20 dried red chillies, or to taste (optional)
2 tbsp black peppercorns
1 tsp black mustard seeds
10 cloves
5cm (2in) piece of cinnamon stick
Seeds from 8 green cardamom pods

Over a low heat, roast the cumin seeds until they are beginning to turn chocolate brown. Be careful, as you don't want to burn the spices. Just toast the exterior and be sure to keep stirring and shaking the pan from time to time so that they toast without burning. Transfer to a plate to cool. Repeat by toasting the coriander seeds, fennel seeds and fenugreek seeds separately until they turn a deep brown.

Now toast the rice, if using, until lightly browned and transfer to the plate to cool. If using the red chillies, toast them also until fragrant and darkened but not black. Allow to cool.

Place the remaining ingredients in the pan and toast until fragrant and warm to the touch. Don't let them smoke! Allow to cool with the other spices. Once cooled, grind everything to a fine powder with a pestle and mortar or spice grinder. This dark curry powder can be kept in an air-tight container in a cool place for up to two months.

JAPANESE

JAPANESE CURRY POWDER
MAKES 10 TBSP

Curry was introduced to Japan by the British in 1870. The Japanese took the recipes and developed them to their own taste, but it wasn't until the 1950s that food company S&B started supplying Japanese curry kits and a special curry powder on a massive scale, and curry became a favourite in households all over Japan. This is my attempt at recreating 'S&B oriental curry powder'. This curry powder is also delicious stirred into other curries or soups.

PREP TIME: 5 MINS
COOKING TIME: 2 MINS

1½ tbsp coriander seeds
1 tbsp fenugreek seeds
1 tbsp cumin seeds
1 tbsp black peppercorns
2 tbsp fennel seeds
4 cloves
1 star anise
5cm (2in) piece of cinnamon stick
1–2 tbsp dried orange peel, finely chopped
1 tsp ground ginger
Seeds from 5 green cardamom pods
1 tsp cayenne chilli powder
2 tsp ground turmeric
½ tsp ground nutmeg
1 Indian bay leaf
1 tsp dried sage
1 tsp dried thyme

Place the coriander seeds, fenugreek seeds, cumin seeds, black peppercorns, fennel seeds, cloves, star anise and cinnamon stick in a large frying pan (skillet) over a medium heat. Toast the spices for a minute or two, or until fragrant and warm to the touch but not yet smoking. Transfer to a plate to cool a little.

Put the dried orange peel and toasted spices into a spice grinder and grind until you have a fine powder. This can also be done in a pestle and mortar, but it takes longer.

Stir in the remaining ingredients and use as needed. This curry powder can be kept for up to six months in an air-tight container stored in a cool, dark place, such as a cupboard. It will be at its best, however, the day you make it.

CAJUN SEASONING
MAKES APPROX. 250ML (1 CUP)

You can purchase Cajun seasoning but it is so easy to make. Use it when called for in this book or use it in a marinade.

PREP TIME: 5 MINS

3 tbsp smoked paprika
1½ tbsp cayenne chilli powder (more or less to taste)
2 tbsp salt
2 tbsp garlic powder
2 tbsp ground black pepper
1½ tbsp onion powder
1 tbsp dried oregano
1 tbsp dried thyme

Place all the ingredients in a storage jar with a tight-fitting lid. Mix well with a spoon and screw the lid on until needed. Depending on the freshness of the ingredients, it should last for about six months.

WORLDWIDE

PICKLED ONIONS
SERVES 4–6

Onions, lightly pickled in this way, can be found all over the world. Not only do they taste great, they also make an attractive garnish. You can scale this recipe up or down, as required.

PREP TIME: 35 MINUTES

2 red onions, thinly sliced
½ tsp salt
Juice of 3 limes

Place the onions in a bowl, sprinkle with the salt, then cover with lime juice. Allow to pickle for at least 30 minutes, stirring a couple of times as they marinate. Although the onions will be ready to serve in just over half an hour, they benefit from soaking overnight.

WORLDWIDE

MICROWAVED CRISPY FRIED GARLIC AND SHALLOTS
MAKES ½ CUP

There are dishes that will benefit from being topped with crispy fried garlic and/or shallots in most cuisines. You could simply fry them in oil on the stove until crispy, but you've really got to watch them so they don't burn. This is a foolproof microwave recipe but please do use your eyes, as microwaves do vary. If the garlic or shallots look like they are burning, they are. So get them out. The oil can be kept and used as a flavoured oil instead of using plain oil.

PREP TIME: 5 MINS
COOKING TIME: 11 MINS

65g (2½oz) garlic or shallots, thinly sliced
125ml (½ cup) rapeseed (canola) oil
Salt and sugar, to taste

Place either garlic or shallots in a suitably sized microwave-safe bowl and cover with the oil. The bowl should not be filled to the rim, so find a large enough bowl to do this. Place in the microwave for 5 minutes on high. Open the door and stir well, then place back in the microwave and cook on high for another 2 minutes. Open and stir again. Place it back in the microwave and cook for another 2 minutes, or until the garlic or shallots are turning crispy and golden brown. You may need to cook for another 2 minutes to do this depending on the microwave you have.

Transfer the fried shallots or garlic to a paper towel with a slotted spoon to soak up any excess oil. Season with salt to taste. If the garlic tastes bitter at all you can also dust with a pinch of sugar, which will take away the bitterness. Let them sit for at least 5 minutes before serving – the shallots and garlic will become crispier with sitting.

SUPPLIERS

I have personally used each of the following suppliers and had good service. Unless otherwise stated, I do not have any affiliation with them.

INDIAN INGREDIENTS

SPICE KITCHEN ONLINE LTD
Spice Kitchen supplies excellent quality spices and has also begun producing Curry Guy-branded spice blends from my books, such as mixed powder, garam masala, tandoori masala and chaat masala. You can also order spice tins filled with whole spices or their own spice blends from around the world. If you are interested in making your own spice blends, co-owner Sanjay Aggarwal has an excellent new book out, also with Quadrille called *Spice Kitchen*.
www.spicekitchenuk.com

SPICES OF INDIA
In addition to groceries and spices, you will also find a fantastic range of Indian kitchen and tableware.
www.spicesofindia.co.uk

CEYLON SUPERMART
In addition to many ingredients used in Indian cuisine, Ceylon Supermart supplies a good range of Sri Lankan ingredients such as dark-roasted curry powder and matta (raw red) rice.
www.ceylonsupermart.com

MEXICAN INGREDIENTS

COOL CHILE COMPANY
I have used this company a lot for Mexican ingredients such as homemade corn tortillas and dried ancho and guajillo chillies. In addition to ingredients, they also supply a good range of Mexican cookware.
www.coolchile.co.uk

MEXGROCER
This company supplies a good range of Mexican ingredients as well as corn tortillas imported from Mexico.
www.mexgrocer.co.uk

CHINESE AND SOUTH EAST ASIAN INGREDIENTS

THE ASIAN COOKSHOP
I normally purchase Asian ingredients locally but have used this company and liked their service. You'll find pretty much everything you need for the Asian recipes in this book on this site.
www.theasiancookshop.co.uk

MEAT AND SEAFOOD

SWALEDALE BUTCHERS
I have worked with Swaledale Butchers in the past and recommend their service. They ship excellent quality meat to your door and even supply special cuts such as Korean-style beef ribs and beef, pork, lamb and chicken bones for stock.
www.swaledale.co.uk

THE FISH SOCIETY
This company supplies a massive range of fresh and frozen seafood that can be delivered to your door.
www.thefishsociety.co.uk

RECIPE INDEX BY REGION

The whole idea behind this book was to create one-pot dishes that are authentic to their origin. You might, however, decide you want to make a feast, preparing a few dishes from a region or cuisine. If that is the case, I have listed the main dishes below so you can quickly find what you're looking for. Sides are not included in this list as I suggest accompaniments in each main recipe.

This wasn't an easy list to put together because so many of the cuisines overlap. Chinese and Indian recipes influenced dishes in the Far East. They in turn influenced each other's cuisines. Then recipes from the West influenced or were influenced by the others. This means that you really can mix this list up as you see fit. There is no reason why you can't serve a British chicken tikka masala with a South African bunny chow and Sri Lankan dal. Likewise, you could serve up a Chinese kung pao chicken with Balinese babi kecap and not be disappointed. So many of the ingredients in these recipes are similar or the same and will go nicely together.

INDEX

ACKNOWLEDGEMENTS

It was a pleasure to again work with everyone at Quadrille to create this cookbook. Thank you to Sarah Lavelle for commissioning the project, copy editor Sarah Greaney and to my project editor Louise Francis for all her hard work bringing this book together. Thank you also Alicia House in design.

Thanks to photographer Kris Kirkham, who has worked with me on every cookbook I've written, and food stylist Rosie Reynolds. I'm sure you'll agree that together Kris and Rosie really made the recipes in this book look amazing! Thank you also to Jessica Geddes, who worked with Rosie, testing the recipes and keeping all those dishes coming out of the kitchen during the photoshoot. I would also like to thank Kris' assistant, Phoebe Pearson, for all her hard and excellent work at the photoshoot. Thank you also to recent graduate Toby Woollen in the studio. You're going to go far!

Thank you to prop stylist Faye Wears, who sourced the props and dishes. They were perfect!

I've learned recipes and techniques from so many amazing chefs and home cooks. There are far too many to mention here but thank you! I do want to mention chefs Sanaka Jayasinghe, Pasan Attanayaka and Chaminda Kumara for inviting me to spend hours with them in their kitchens, learning amazing recipes. Thank you!

A special thank you goes out to the moderators of my Facebook group, who kept everything going while I was busy writing. Thank you to Jon Monday, Steven Lumsden, Tim Martin, Karen Bolan, Claire Rees, Anne-Marie Goodfellow, James Vaisey and Derek Turnball. You have been a huge support and I appreciate it a lot!

Thank you to my agent, Clare Hulton, for all her support over the years and for making this book happen.

I could not have written this book without my wife Caroline's support. She helped cook every recipe in this cookbook to ensure that the recipes worked and tasted as they should. Thanks!

One last big thank you and that goes out to you for picking up this book. I appreciate it so much and hope you enjoy the book and recipes as much as I enjoyed putting this collection together.

Publishing Director: Sarah Lavelle
Project Editor: Louise Francis
Designer: Alicia House
Cover Design: Smith & Gilmour
Photographer: Kris Kirkham
Photography Assistant: Phoebe Pearson
Food Stylist: Rosie Reynolds
Food Stylist Assistant: Jess Geddes
Props Stylist: Faye Wears
Head of Production: Stephen Lang
Production Controller: Martina Georgieva

First published in 2023 by Quadrille, an imprint of Hardie Grant Publishing

Quadrille
52–54 Southwark Street,
London SE1 1UN
quadrille.com

Text © 2023 Dan Toombs
Photography © 2023 Kris Kirkham
Design and layout © 2023 Quadrille

Cataloguing-in-Publication Data. A catalogue record for this book is available from the British Library.

ISBN 978-1-78713-920-6

Printed in China

FSC
www.fsc.org
MIX
Paper | Supporting responsible forestry
FSC™ C020056

In five short years, Dan took The Curry Guy from an idea to a reliable brand. The recipes are all developed and tested in Dan's home kitchen. And they work. His bestselling first cookbook – *The Curry Guy* – and the 250,000 curry fans who visit his blog, www.greatcurryrecipes.net, every month can testify to that fact.

If you have any recipe questions you can contact Dan (@thecurryguy) on Twitter, Facebook or Instagram.